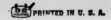

A PICTORIAL HISTORY
OF EMBROIDERY

Marie Schuette
Sigrid Müller-Christensen

A PICTORIAL
HISTORY
OF EMBROIDERY

Frederick A. Praeger, *Publisher*
New York

Contents

Text translated by Donald King

The drawings in the section Materials and Techniques
were made by Hildegard Huber, Munich

Published in the United States of America in 1964
by Frederick A. Praeger, Inc., Publisher
64 University Place, New York 3, N.Y.

Foreword

This book of embroidery is a harvest culled from the fertile field of the greatest creations of European needlework. Many of these are well known, but also included are others which, although perhaps not of the same standard, deserve consideration. It is only a selection, for it was impossible to obtain illustrations of all the characteristic specimens which might have been desirable. But selections are often fortunate in that they have the advantage, unlike exhaustive repertories, of avoiding dullness and monotony and of offering an element of surprise.

It will be clear from this that the book does not pretend to be a history of embroidery. The indispensable regional studies are as yet too incomplete for such a purpose, although research on textiles has made great advances since the war. Interest in old textiles and the study of these has increased everwhere, while the conservation-work, carried out on many extremely important objects, represents a notable achievement.

Worthy of mention in this connection is the foundation of the Centre International d'Étude des Textiles anciens in Lyon, which brings together all those who are interested in ancient textiles, from all parts of the world.

The text aims to guide the reader through the illustrations, which are not always easy to interpret, and to help towards a more intimate appreciation of the embroideries. The catalogue provides the facts about the individual objects; the bibliographical notes, restricted to the essential and the most recent literature, are signposts to further study of the material.

The embroidery of the Near and Far East is only represented by a few fine and characteristic examples, included for purposes of comparison and to illustrate certain historical links which are important in the development of style.

The book is based on the personal observations of the authors, who have themselves examined, with very few exceptions, all the embroideries reproduced here, although local difficulties sometimes made it impossible to study the objects as closely as might have been desired.

We offer our sincere thanks to the ecclesiastical authorities, museums, colleagues and friends who have so generously assisted us and who have provided us with photographs. Unfortunately all the sources cannot be mentioned here, but we express our particular gratitude to the Badische Anilin- und Soda-Fabrik in Ludwigshafen, the Director of the Castle of Rosenborg in Copenhagen, the Director of the Museum für Kunst und Gewerbe in Hamburg and the Director of the Bayerisches Nationalmuseum in Munich, who have so kindly allowed us the use of the blocks for the colour plates. We hope that this book of embroidery will give pleasure to those for whom it was designed, and that it will gain new friends for the art of fine needlework.

Marie Schuette
Sigrid Müller-Christensen

Materials and Techniques

To Agnes Geiger

It is a striking fact that in the development of embroidery, as displayed in this book, there are no changes in materials or techniques which can be felt or interpreted as advances from a primitive to a later, more refined stage. On the contrary, we often find in early works a technical accomplishment, and high standard of craftsmanship rarely attained in later times. On the other hand, many late works show a notable lack of technical and artistic distinction. It is certainly a mistake, therefore, to measure these phenomena by the standards of hypothetical "progress". Some periods have been naturally conservative in both technique and style, while others have been impelled, by their livelier imagination, to adopt technical as well as stylistic innovations.

It seems likely that embroidery has always been an organised activity of courts, convents and cities, as well as a simple domestic pursuit, and until the nineteenth century it was by no means an exclusively feminine occupation. We find that identifiable groups of embroideries appear in places where social organisation has advanced to the point of forming craft-guilds, and this was certainly true of Egypt, Byzantium and the Islamic world as well as of medieval Europe. The stylistic links between embroidery and the other artistic activities of a particular period resulted partly from natural observation and borrowing and partly from the use of specially prepared designs. Yet at the same time the constant factors of embroidery technique tended to impose their own laws upon the artistic effect of the work.

The materials on which the embroideries here illustrated were executed, are all – apart from a leather bag of 1604 – woven cloths, which, according to the period, place, and purpose, are of wool, linen, silk or cotton. Many of these works have suffered severely from wear, damage, or neglect. In some important examples the embroidery itself has disappeared, so that the original design can be traced only from the holes left by the needle; in other cases the ground material has been destroyed and only a thin web of silk and gold threads remains (2, 11–13). Such fragments show to how great an extent the preservation of fragile objects through many centuries depends on chance. Often the intrinsic value of an object was its own worst enemy for in times of want the most costly and beautiful relics were burned to recover the pure gold which they contained.

Since the ground material serves merely as a support, it is irrelevant to the designation of the actual embroidery, which is invariably classified according to the nature of the thread or technique employed. Thus we speak of linen embroidery, wool embroidery, silk embroidery, or gold embroidery, and also of flat embroidery, raised work, cross-stitch embroidery, applied work, and so on.

For many centuries woollen stuffs were used as a ground material for embroidery. In Scandinavia simply embroidered woollen garments have been preserved from the Bronze Age. Wool likewise formed the basis of Greek embroideries of the fourth century B.C. found in the Crimea, and of those recovered from Mongolia and Siberia dating from the 4th – 1st centuries B.C. (3–5). In later times woollen stuffs were embroidered principally for use as hangings, covers and cushions, because of their efficiency as an insulation against cold. Stout woollens and felt were used for applied work and patchwork.

Due to its ease of working and its great strength, linen has always been the commonest ground material for embroidery. Embroidered linen covers have been used in churches since the Middle Ages. The Bayeux Tapestry (31–33) is also embroidered on linen; and linen was the usual foil for courtly embroideries and those made for domestic use. The material can serve as a visible background for the embroidery, or it can be completely worked over.

Silk stuffs were always regarded as the most beautiful and costly of ground materials. The sheen of silk was used to enhance the sumptuous effects of embroideries in silk and gold. This technique attained its highest expression in the gold embroideries of about the year 1000, worked on heavy twill silk materials of great strength and flexibility. Most later embroideries on silk required the support of an additional linen under-layer and in many cases the silk itself has been partly or wholly worn away in the course of centuries, thus exposing the linen (203–4, 231).

From the end of the thirteenth century onwards, plain silk velvet was sometimes used as a ground material. In order to make working more easy a thin, smooth cloth of silk or linen was laid over the velvet pile, as can be seen in an English embroidery in the Diocesan Museum at Vich (Catalonia).

Cotton, imported in increasing quantities in the seventeenth and eighteenth centuries as a result of the more active trade with the Near East and India, was also used as a basis for embroidery in Europe, possibly under the influence of Oriental work. For the thin, delicate whitework embroideries of the eighteenth and nineteenth centuries cotton cambric was employed.

Mixed materials were also used as a ground for embroidery. Silk and cotton mixtures are found in Fatimid work *(mulham)* and are recorded as "half-silks" in Medieval Europe. Linen and cotton mixtures were also woven.

Of the embroidery threads used, wool and linen threads were invariably spun, and sometimes plied as well, whereas for silk threads spinning was unnecessary. For particularly precious work, non-textile materials were also employed, especially metal thread. This again was of various kinds. Gold and silver thread usually consists of a fine strip of gold or silver, wrapped spirally round a silk thread, which is usually red, light red, yellow, or white. During the Middle Ages, and even before, the strips for the gold threads were cut from gold sheet of the finest quality, beaten very thin (*aurum battutum*). The degree of refinement attained in this work can be seen by looking at, for instance, the mantle of St. Kunigund at Bamberg, in which there are up to 56 such gold threads per centimetre, side by side (Colour Plate I). The gold threads of this period look particularly pale in colour; later gold threads, with a larger admixture of copper, look redder.

From the later Middle Ages onwards silver-gilt thread was the type most frequently employed (each type being named after the manufacturing centre), or else gilt membrane. The latter consisted of gold leaf adhering to a strip of vellum or other skin, which was wrapped spirally around a silk or linen thread. Metal is also used in embroidery in the form of flat or waved gold and silver strip, of wires (cf. back of Colour Plate III), and of spangles and small stamped plaques. Coloured glass beads seem to have been used mainly in Germany and Spain during the thirteenth century, while since the early part of the Middle Ages – and no doubt long before – pearls were employed "to enhance the design with noble craftmanship", as Hugo Falcandus says in describing the court workshops of Palermo in 1181 (Colour Plate VIII, 60-62). In regions where river pearls are found (Central and Southern Germany and Bohemia) this "enhancing of the design" was extensively practised until the eighteenth century. Coral beads were used in the same way. Thus together with references to silk-embroiderers we find others to pearl-embroiderers or bead-embroiderers.

We come now to some notes and observations on methods of work in former times. Besides needles of bone and wood, metal needles have been preserved from prehistoric times. Among other tools were tweezers, bodkins and thimbles – some have been found in the excavations of Pompeii. From earliest times, the cloth was frequently stretched on a frame before working to avoid folds and creases. This was also done when an artist produced a design for the embroidery, as we learn from the late fourteenth century *Trattato* of Cennino di Andrea Cennini, Chapter 164. Before the needlework itself was begun, a preliminary drawing of the subject, or an outline of the pattern, was sketched out on the ground material. Thus in gold embroideries of the eleventh and twelfth centuries the yellow and white lines of the preliminary drawing have been found in a few places. Preliminary drawings made with pen or brush, as described by Cennini can be very clearly seen in embroideries which were, never completed (129, 130), or in those where the stitches have been partly or wholly worn away (202, 204, 205–207). The

altar-frontal in the Louvre known as the *parement de Narbonne* (1373–1378) and the more or less contemporary mitre in the Musée de Cluny, Paris, are ornamented with paintings in *grisaille* which, in the characteristic fashion of the late fourteenth century, rival the delicacy of silk itself, but these were not intended as designs for execution in embroidery.

Cennini's instructions bear the mark of practical experience when he writes that for embroideries on velvet, although it is possible to make preliminary drawings in pen and ink on the velvet itself, it is less troublesome to draw the figures on white silk and then to cut them out and apply them to the velvet. We have already mentioned an example of this procedure in an English embroidery of about 1350.

The art of the embroiderer lies in the choice of stitches. In some types of work the stitches form a kind of outline drawing; in others, they are like brush-strokes and produce the effect of a painting. In others again the entire surface may be covered with stitches side by side, as in a mosaic. It is only by the study of these various methods of working that we can penetrate the creative and imaginative world of fine embroidery – which is quite independent of designs and preliminary drawings. To some extent a history of embroidery stitches would also be a history of embroidery as a fine art, for each period has found specific techniques suitable for the expression of its own particular style.

The following paragraphs describe the most important stitches used in the embroideries illustrated in this book. There are innumerable variants of these, especially in the field of peasant embroidery.

The linear stitches are running stitch and double running stitch, back stitch, stem stitch, split stitch and chain stitch.

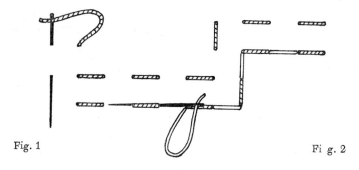

Fig. 1   Fi g. 2

Running stitch (Fig. 1) is the simplest of all stitches. The needle runs for equal distances over and under the ground material. Working a second row of running stitches in the intervals of the first row produces a continuous line. This "double running stitch" (Fig. 2) was used, for example, in Islamic embroideries, for patterns with stepped outlines, which persisted during the fifteenth and sixteenth centuries in Spanish and Italian silk embroideries on linen. These are known in England as "Spanish work" and in Germany as *Holbeinstickerei* (Holbein embroidery).

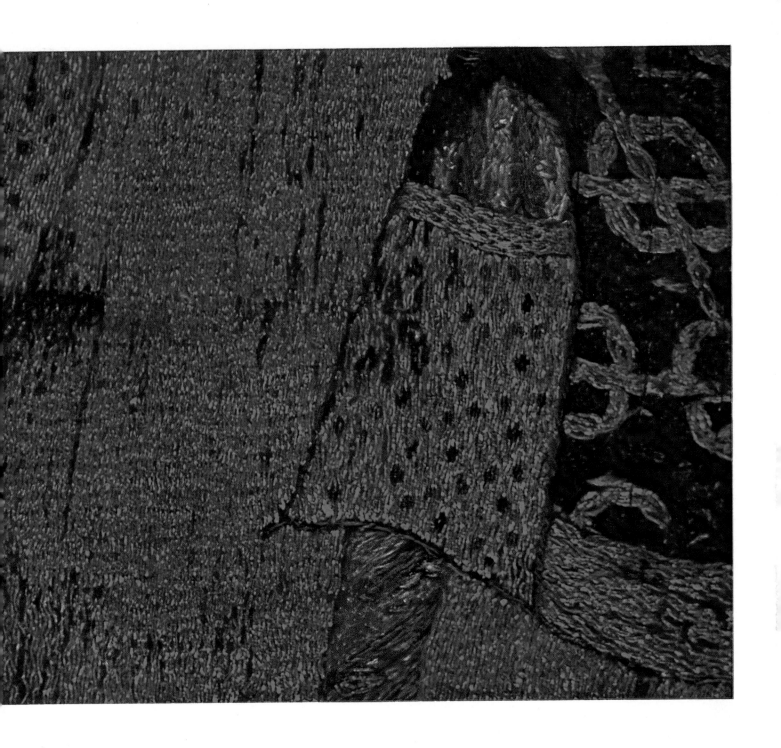

I The cloak of St. Kunigund, detail enlarged about six times.
South Germany, c. 1020.

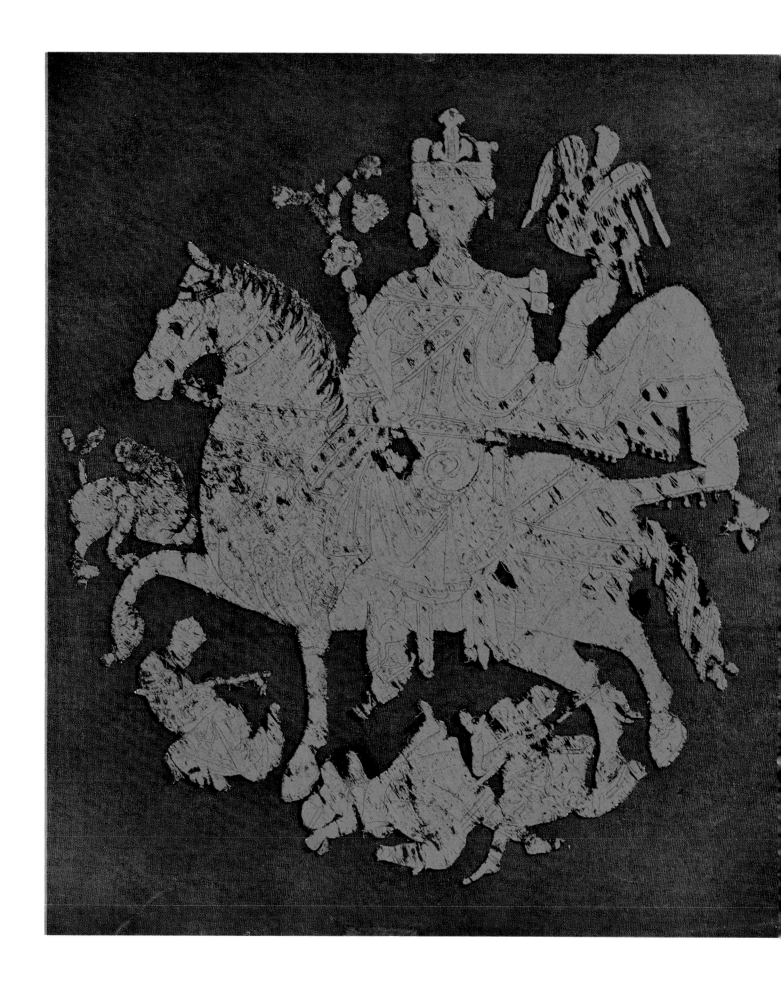

II So-called riding cloak belonging to Emperor Henry II detail, front.
Italy (?). c. 12th century.

III So-called riding cloak belonging to Emperor Henry II detail, back view.
Italy (?), c. 12th century.

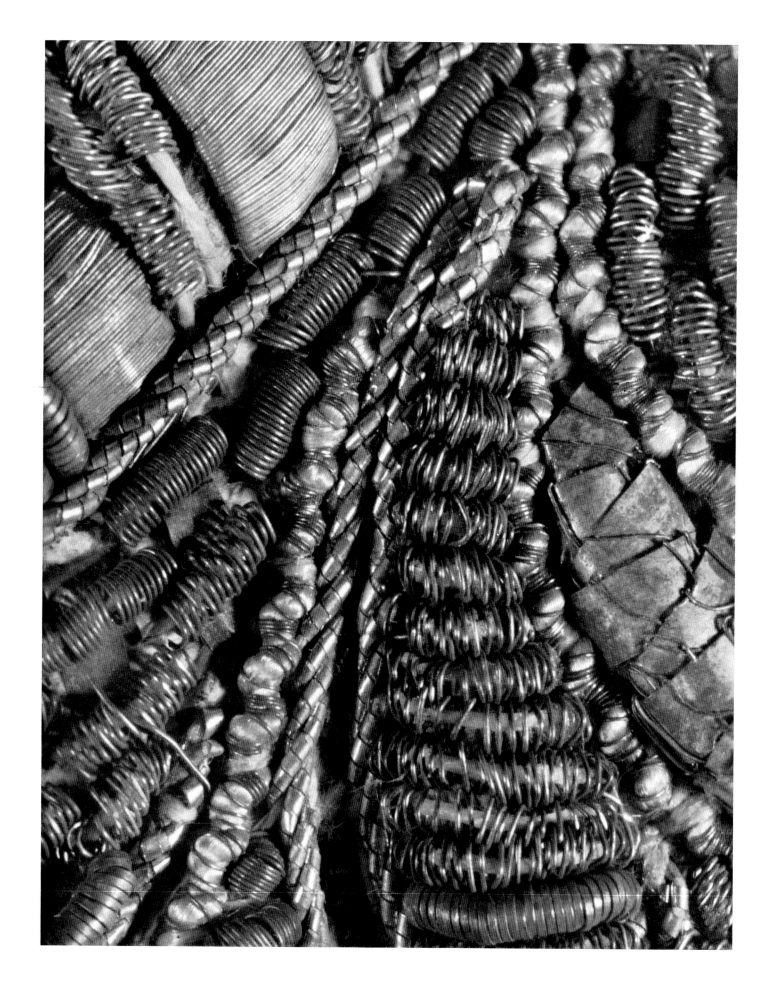

Detail of gold embroidery, enlarged about 15 times.
Paris, 1648.

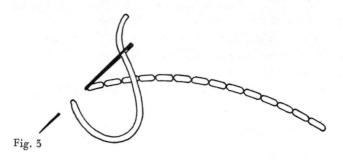

Fig. 3

Back stitch (Fig. 3) resembles double running stitch, but is worked in a single operation. The needle, passing up through the cloth, moves back the length of one stitch, then passes down through the cloth and forward the length of two stitches, before being brought up through the cloth again. The repetition of this cycle produces a series of firm, equal stitches which often served, especially in silk embroidery and quilting of the fifteenth to the eighteenth century, to form the outlines of an embroidered pattern, or of a pattern in reserve on a worked ground.

Fig. 4

Stem stitch (or outline stitch; Fig. 4) appears on the front of the work as a row of oblique, equal-sized stitches – the needle passes up through the cloth, moves forward the length of one stitch and then, passing down through the cloth, moves back for a shorter distance and passes up through the cloth again beside the stitch just made.

Fig. 5

Split stitch (Fig. 5) is similar except that at the end the needle, instead of emerging beside the thread, actually passes through it. Stem and split stitch are particularly useful for working curved lines.

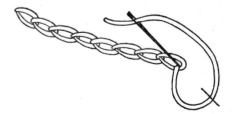

Fig. 6

In appearance, chain stitch (Fig. 6) is often almost indistinguishable from split stitch. This, however, is not a line-stitch but a loop-stitch, the thread being laid down in the form of a loop. The needle, passes down through the cloth at the point from which it last emerged, moves forward the length of the stitch required and emerges again within the loop.

Stem stitch, split stitch and chain stitch were used for outlines and inner drawing, or, arranged in parallel lines or spirals, they could also serve as a filling. Chain stitch was the most widespread in both space and time. It was the principal technique of the Chinese embroiderers, as is shown by archaeological finds in Turkestan and Mongolia, from the period about the beginning of our era. Fragments from classical times, found in graves at Kerch in the Crimea, also show figures and ornament worked in chain stitch. In Hellenistic wool embroideries and Coptic and Byzantine silk embroideries, chain stitch was much used, sometimes in conjunction with split stitch. The effectiveness of chain stitch for working very fine detail (e. g. for characterisation of faces) is demonstrated by superbly executed examples of about 1400. English embroideries – *opus anglicanum* – which excited universal admiration during the Middle Ages, made use of split stitch with masterly refinement, and beautiful work in split stitch is also to be found in the so-called Burgundian mass-vestments in the Schatzkammer in Vienna. Later, split stitch played a less important role and was generally used in conjunction with other techniques. But chain stitch remained in constant use down to the eighteenth century, especially in the simpler kinds of linen embroidery, together with numerous variants, such as open chain, twisted or double chain and feather stitch – all "openwork" stitches which could be used to spread a freely drawn mesh of pattern over the surface. The importation, during the seventeenth and eighteenth centuries, of "East Indian" embroideries, worked chiefly in chain stitch, helped to maintain the practice and popularity of the technique among European needlewomen. The stitch was often worked, not with an ordinary sewing needle, but with a fine hooked *tambour* needle.

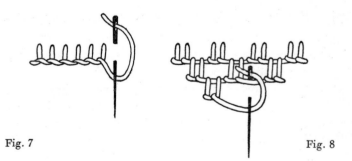

Fig. 7　　　　　　　　　　　　　　　　　　　Fig. 8

Buttonhole stitch (Fig. 7), a right-angled loop-stitch, and other stitches of this type serve for contours and as an ornament for edges. They are also commonly worked in interlocking rows (Fig. 8). Buttonhole stitch is very versatile as a filling stitch and, together with long-armed cross stitch and herringbone stitch, was much used in German and Swiss linen embroideries of the Middle Ages and the Renaissance, as well as in English and Italian silk embroideries of the sixteenth and seventeenth centuries.

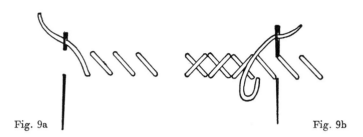

Fig. 9a   Fig. 9b

A further technical group arises from the crossing of stitches. The ordinary cross stitch – also known as *gros point* – consists of an oblique stitch which is crossed at the centre by a second oblique stitch of equal size (Fig. 9 a, b). Thus each complete cross stitch occupies a square. If the first oblique stitch is not crossed by a second, it is called half cross stitch or *petit point*. *Petit point* can also be worked by first making an oblique stitch (crossing one warp-thread of the ground material) upwards towards the right, and then carrying the needle obliquely downwards towards the left behind the material, so that it crosses two warp-threads before it emerges again (Fig. 11). This is the method used for "tent stitch", as found in English embroideries of the fourteenth century. Apart from these, cross stitch is very rarely seen in medieval embroideries, and did not come into common use until the sixteenth century. It was the obvious choice for European embroidered imitations of Oriental knotted carpets, while in the seventeenth century it was the most popular stitch for covers, wall-hangings and embroidered furniture.

Fig. 10   Fig. 11

Long-armed cross stitch (Fig. 10) differs from cross stitch in that one of the diagonal stitches is twice as long as the other, extending over two squares; the effect resembles a plait. Long-armed cross stitch, closely worked, was much used in the late twelfth and thirteenth centuries for silk embroidery worked on a linen ground. In later times long-armed cross stitch, like cross stitch, was chiefly employed in wool embroidery for covers, wall hangings and furniture.

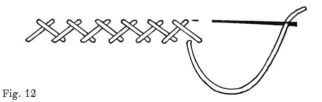

Fig. 12

A widely used form of cross stitch is that known as "herring-bone stitch" (Fig. 12), in which the intersecting stitches move in zig-zags over the ground material. A feature of this technique is that the thread is almost all on the right side of the material and is held only by very small stitches on the underside.

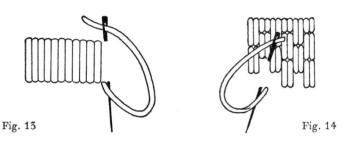

Fig. 13   Fig. 14

In satin stitch, parallel or radiating stitches are worked close together, completely covering the ground material both back and front. When satin stitches of equal length are worked parallel to the warp or weft of the ground material, forming straight lines which serve as a filling pattern (Fig. 13), the effect resembles that of a woven tapestry, and the stitch is called – applying a comparatively modern name to a much older technique – *Gobelin stitch*. Variants arise when the stitches are offset, like bricks, singly or in groups of two or three (Fig. 14).

Gobelin stitch occurs as a filling pattern in embroideries of the thirteenth and fourteenth centuries. In embroideries of the fifteenth century (e. g. in the Burgundian vestments in the Schatzkammer at Vienna or in Florentine embroideries in the style of Pollaiuolo) faces are worked, not in the split or chain stitch used in earlier examples, but with extremely thin silk thread in very fine brick stitch, over which the details of the features are added in the most delicate stem, split or chain stitches.

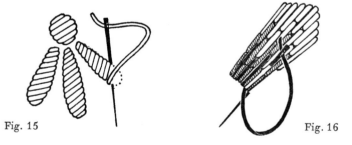

Fig. 15   Fig. 16

It may be noticed that in the fifteenth century satin stitch became more and more independent of the warp and weft directions of the ground materials (Fig. 15). Each embroiderer sought, as far as his artistic talents allowed, to translate exactly into needlework a pictorial model. With overlapping satin stitches of various lengths and colours extremely delicate effects of shading could be achieved (Fig. 16). This, too, like the finely shaded embroideries in chain, split and brick stitch, was a form of "needle-painting".

All the stitches described hitherto are worked with a single thread which is sometimes on the back and sometimes on the front of the ground material. In couching techniques, however, two threads are employed, one of which is laid on the top of the material only, and is caught down and fastened by a second or sometimes by a third thread. These techniques were used not only in the simplest types of work, but also – and with incredible perfection – in costly gold embroideries. A thread of any desired length may be fastened to the ground material by means of small couching stitches which emerge from the underside of the material at regular intervals and cross over the laid thread at right angles or obliquely. The laid thread can be employed for contours or for fillings. We find these couching stitches as early as the Scythian embroideries of the first century B.C.; later they were used in conjunction with other stitches. They are a characteristic feature of German pictorial hangings of the fourteenth to sixteenth century, worked in wool, and of linen embroideries, worked chiefly in Switzerland and on the Upper Rhine, from the fifteenth to the seventeenth century. These groups of embroideries have given rise to the name *Klosterstich* (convent stitch), which is now generally applied to this technique in Germany. When the two threads are of the same colour, embroideries of this type bear some resemblance to woven cloth.

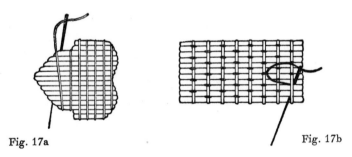

Fig. 17a   Fig. 17b

A related technique is that known as laid and couched work, a method which minimises the amount of embroidery thread remaining unseen on the back of the ground material – always a consideration of some importance when covering large surfaces. Threads are first laid down, side by side, from edge to edge of the particular area being embroidered. Then a second set of threads, with regular intervals between, is laid over the first set and at right angles to them. Finally this second set is fastened down by couching stitches made with a third thread (Fig. 17a, b). This is the technique employed, for example, in the Bayeux tapestry (31–33) and it lasted for centuries in Scandinavian and Icelandic embroideries (192). It was used, especially for less important details, in English medieval embroidery and in gold and silk embroideries of the fifteenth to the eighteenth century, and is also a characteristic feature of many Near Eastern embroideries.

Precious gold embroideries are the most distinguished examples of couched work. The gold thread is laid down in parallel lines from side to side of the area to be embroidered, and where

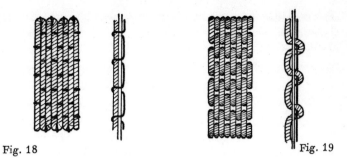

Fig. 18   Fig. 19

it turns round, on reaching the outline, it is fastened by a stitch. The gold threads on the surface are then fastened at intervals with a silk thread, the left hand pushing the needle up from beneath the work, while the right hand carries it over the gold thread and down again through the same needle-hole (Fig. 18). By varying the intervals between these stitches, or by grouping them together, it is possible to produce patterns on the gold surface, and by using thread of various colours, to differentiate the various parts of the subject represented (Colour Plates I, II, III). Many different effects can be achieved in this way; forms entirely in gold; inner drawings in colours; gold lines in reserve.

In underside couching (Fig. 19) the gold thread is fixed by being pulled through to the underside of the ground material and fastened there by means of a linen thread. Here again the intervals between the points of fixing may be so arranged as to produce a kind of dotted or engraved pattern on the gold surface. This technique is characteristic of Byzantine and Sicilian embroidery, as well as of *opus anglicanum*.

In the gold embroideries of the early Middle Ages, the work in gold thread is akin to the work of the goldsmith, and indeed, the surface of these gold embroideries was often hammered flat. From the twelfth century onwards, silk threads were added to distinguish certain details, for example the flesh of the figures. At the same time, the work was simplified by the use of gold threads in pairs. In the thirteenth century gold embroidery was used for gold backgrounds, in which the pictorial subjects were left in reserve to be worked in lustrous coloured silks. The patterns of these gold backgrounds were of geometrical type, foliage scrolls, or heraldic motifs, and were sometimes worked in slight relief.

To produce the effects of relief, the pattern was first laid out on the ground material in cotton, linen cords, or coarse embroidery, and then worked over with gold threads in couched work. For a higher relief a kind of applied work was used. Often the form to be represented in gold embroidery was first cut out in card or parchment; this foundation was then oversewn with gold thread (later with gold wire) and the edges sewn down to the ground material. The same method was adopted to produce the architectural canopies in relief which are frequently found from the fourteenth century onwards.

Another characteristic effect is that of *or nué* (shaded gold) embroidery. Already in medieval gold embroideries, it was a common practice to accentuate the shimmer of the gold threads by the use of couching threads of coloured silk. From about 1400 onwards this idea was extended so as to produce strong contrasts of light and shade. In the shadows the coloured couching stitches were worked so thickly that the gold was almost entirely hidden, while in the lighter areas the intervals between the stitches were gradually increased until, in the highlights, the gold was exposed in all its brilliance. The German term for this technique is *Lasurstickerei* (glaze embroidery), suggesting the effect of a painting in which an opaque background is overlaid by a succession of transparent glazes. The embroideries of the Burgundian vestments in Vienna and the Florentine embroideries in the style of Pollaiuolo mark the high-point of pictorial illusionism in this technique.

The late Gothic tendency towards three-dimensional realism gave rise, especially in Germany until the end of the sixteenth century, to relief embroideries which, by the use of a padding of tow or linen rags, or even of carved wooden blocks over which the embroidery was worked, reproduced the effects of sculpture in high relief. This type of work anticipates the embroidered pictures in "stump work" made in England during the second half of the seventeenth century. In these, large parts of the figure subjects are worked in a technique resembling needle-point lace.

In the gold embroideries of the seventeenth and eighteenth centuries the interplay between the gold thread and coloured silk couching stitches disappears. The principal effects are those produced by the juxtaposition of gold and silver thread of various types (back of Colour Plate III). In the execution of these embroideries we find all the stitches employed in earlier periods. Great technical skill and unfettered creative fantasy here combine to produce works in which the varied potentialities of gold and silver embroidery are superbly realised.

Sigrid Müller-Christensen

Historical Introduction

For Hanna Kronberger-Frentzen, with gratitude and devotion

De Laborde long ago put forward the view that a history of embroidery was urgently required, as a supplement to the history of painting. But a history conceived on these lines would inevitably give an incomplete and one-sided picture, since it would deal with only one section of the art of embroidery, a subject of such scope and variety that it is almost impossible to envisage, define and comprehend it as a whole.

Among the textile arts embroidery is unique, a law unto itself. Its sole purpose is to adorn, and it brooks no limitation of this function. Nothing escapes its play of line and colour. Its realm extends from the smallest personal possession, the handkerchief, to underwear and costume, from curtain, cover and cushion to suites of furniture and wall-hangings. It adorns the things of everyday life, yet is called upon for effects of splendour, and solemnity: the state robes and throne canopies of secular princes, ecclesiastical ornaments, and the vestments and baldachins of the princes of the church are the supreme creations of the art of embroidery.

It makes use of every kind of material which is soft and pliable, or in any way adaptable to the work of the needle: besides leather, wool, cotton, linen, silk and animal hair, it employs gold and silver, precious stones, pearls and enamels. These costly materials are partly responsible for the rarity of the fine embroidery of the past. Man, with his perpetual thirst for gold, often extracted or tore it out from rich textiles and embroideries. As recently as the early nineteenth century, in the lean times following the Napoleonic wars, English ladies extracted the gold thread from embroidered uniforms in order to melt down the metal.

The origins of embroidery are lost in obscurity; its earliest works have vanished as completely as the generations which created them, using primitive needles formed from fishbones or splinters of animal bone. But a comparatively early type is represented here by the applied work in leather and felt excavated from burial mounds in the Altai mountains. (4, 5)

These objects date from the fifth and fourth centuries B.C. and show cultural affinities with Achaemenid Persia. The sewing technique, employing horsehair and very fine needles, is highly developed, while the use of seven different kinds of cloth, of the finest wool, is indicative of an astonishingly sophisticated textile industry.

The remains of an embroidery on linen was recently found on the classical soil of Greece, in Attica; unfortunately all that can now be seen is the accurately executed design of lions, with upswept tails, within a lattice of lozenges (2). This forms an instructive contrast with the work of the nomads of the burial mounds. The highest perfection of needle-painting in wool is attained by the splendid and truly classical centaur (1), the extraordinarily lifelike head of a Hun (3) and the hanging with trees (7), each one of which has its own unmistakable individuality. These few rare pieces can be regarded indeed, to some extent, as a substitute for the lost paintings of antiquity.

In the civilisation of the *Mediterranean area* embroidery played a significant role from early times. Its circle of activity was very wide: among the *Islamic embroideries* illustrated here are examples attributed to Egypt, Mesopotamia, southern Italy, Sicily – with its wealthy capital, Palermo – and Spain. At these meeting-places of Orient and Occident the genius and craftsmanship of the Saracenic world enjoyed a glorious development, leaving relics behind which are characteristic and unmistakable.

The earliest of these embroideries (53, 54), found in Egyptian graves, show polychrome or monochrome needlework in very varied styles. These modest scraps of linen, though not particularly attractive for the ordinary observer, are of unique importance as evidence for the existence of a regular tradition-forming school of embroidery. As is indicated in the catalogue, the fragments show all kinds of stitches: running and double running (Holbein) stitch, stem, satin and weaving stitch – these most precisely executed. Gobelin, cross and long-armed cross stitch are also present and indicate that embroidery was practised by enthusiastic amateurs in house and harem. The zeal with which girls and women collected patterns is shown by the samplers (not illustrated) in Leipzig, Berlin and London – the earliest existing samplers apart from the similar specimens found by Lecoq at the oasis of Turfan in Central Asia, which he dates about 850. The Egyptian samplers are worked in black or dark blue silk with many geometrical patterns, chiefly in satin stitch. The patterns of these domestic embroideries migrated northwards by way of the Grecian archipelago – the well known Greek Island embroideries – to eastern and even to northern Europe, where they were adopted into peasant art.

The earliest dated Islamic embroidery of Spanish origin is the chasuble of St Thomas Becket at Fermo, which bears an inscription indicating that it was made in 1116 at Almeria (57, 58, 59). This is a superb princely mantle which was adapted subsequently for use as a chasuble. It bears no visible symbol of ecclesiastical use, nor could this be deduced from the entirely secular design worked in gold. It shows motifs of courtly art: noble falconers on horseback, ladies on elephants, enthroned princes with serving-women, and eagles attacking gazelles – a large number of figures, not all of which, owing to the defective preservation of the work, can now be identified. This magnificent work of art was made in one of the 800 workshops of Almeria, a town which was then at the height of its fame and which specialised, as we know from textual sources, in the production of costly mantles, brocades and silk textiles. The same type of composition is seen in the chasuble of Boniface VIII (72) of the end of the twelfth century. The most monumental work, perhaps not only of Islamic embroidery, but of embroidery as a whole, is the coronation mantle of the Holy Roman Emperors (62), a truly royal garment commissioned by King Roger II of Sicily in 1133 and completed in 1134. This, be it noted, was only 67 years after the Norman conquest of England and two generations after the Bayeux tapestry.

The confrontation of these two works conveys more clearly than words the tremendous superiority of Mediterranean culture and the high achievement of Saracenic textile art as compared with northern Europe in the twelfth century. But at the same time it demonstrates the mighty strength of these Northmen who were destined to win back Sicily for the West. In 1020 they had established themselves in southern Italy, a little later in Sicily, and in 1130 Roger received from the Pope the title "King of Sicily". The dates 1130 and 1133 are so close that it is tempting, especially in view of the fact that the embroidery was made, as the inscription proudly testifies, in the Royal Workshops, to see a connection between the two. Palermo is to this day an eloquent expression of Norman power and of that Saracenic culture which is apparent in the age-old Oriental motif of the mantle and in its superb artistic realisation. In the perfect accomplishment of its technique and its harmonious colour-composition of purple and gold, pearls and enamels, this mighty design can be fully experienced only before the object itself.

Several other garments were associated with the coronation mantle to form the set of imperial vestments which were worn by the Emperor Frederick II at his coronation in Rome in 1220. The dalmatic, details of whose apparels are shown here (65, 66) dates from the period of Roger II and may belong to the same set of vestments as the coronation mantle, while the alb was made in the Royal Workshop for King William II in 1181 (68-71). The gloves, with the single-headed Hohenstaufen eagle facing left, were embroidered for the coronation of Frederick II in 1220. The shoes, stockings and belt belonging to the imperial vestments (not illustrated) were also made in Palermo.

The persistent recollection during the Middle Ages of Charlemagne as an embodiment of imperial power is demonstrated by the unusually splendid medieval garments which are traditionally associated with his name. One of these is the mantle, converted into a cope, at Metz cathedral (63, 64) – a princely garment, not unworthy of comparison with the imperial coronation mantle, with a design of four motionless eagles, recalling in their implacable severity the world-renowned eagle-

silks, woven for the Byzantine Emperors about the year 1000, which must have been known to the designer. The tradition that this was an imperial mantle and a "gift from Haroun al Rashid to Charlemagne" testifies to the esteem and admiration in which foreign work was held from early times. It remains uncertain how and when the embroidery arrived in Metz.

Related to this piece is the dossal (76, 77) in the Treasury of San Francesco in Assisi, with griffins and birds in gold on yellow. The inventory of 1338 suggests that the embroidery was a gift from the Emperor of the Greeks, which indicates that it was greatly admired.

A great division – that of *Christianity* – separates the carefree embroideries of antiquity and the Islamic work just discussed from the circular panel with the Annunciation and Visitation (8), a Coptic (?) embroidery of the 7th-8th century, which is laden with religious significance. This marks the beginning of the period in which the church directed embroidery to sacred tasks and developed it gradually to the highest perfection. All artistic undertakings, even down to the details of craftsmanship, were borne up by the faith and the high seriousness of religion.

The subject-matter available in the Middle Ages was inexhaustible: not only the personages of the Old and New Testaments, but also the ever-growing host of the saints offered an infinite wealth of striking, interesting and miraculous happenings to edify, or sometimes to excite or terrify, the faithful. During the Middle Ages and down to the sixteenth century, embroideries were often based on holy tales and legends which were deeply rooted in the affections of the people, but which found no place in the official lives of the saints as approved by the church. On the other hand, they were also called upon to illustrate learned iconographical programmes in works produced for corporate institutions and clerical patrons. Allegorical and didactic elements played a large part in such work, so that many medieval embroideries are incomprehensible without their inscribed scrolls and other textual matter. Between 1174 and 1179, at the monastery of St. Afra and St. Ulrich at Augsburg, twelve wall-hangings were embroidered with an extremely complex programme of salvation, making use of a fantastic number of allegorical figures; one of these hangings, which are known only from literary records, was signed by a certain Brother Beretha as designer and embroiderer. Other examples of this German taste for didacticism are the well-known knotted pile carpet in Quedlinburg with the marriage of Mercury and Philology, based on the didactic poem of Martianus Capella, and the gigantic embroidered Heiningen carpet of 1516, in London, with the glorification of Philosophy (not illustrated). It would be easy to cite further examples of this kind. In convents, these tedious tasks were not without good reason and practical purpose. In the manner of modern work-therapy, they were intended to provide the inmates, during the long winter months, with a meaningful occupation and perhaps also with a change of ideas. In the fourteenth century profane subjects appear, such as Reynard the Fox (165-167), Tristram (193-195), Parsifal, the Wiles of Women (185-186, IX) and many others. Hunting, from earliest times the pleasure and passion of mankind, was a favourite subject, especially in the Gothic period and for centuries thereafter. This theme received its highest expression in the mature French Gothic style of the falconers embroidered on purses (214, 215). German delight in hunting is revealed in the boar-hunt of about 1330 (188) from the Upper Rhine, with its impressive freshness and simplicity of composition, colour and drawing. The wild men of the woods who are seen hunting in Upper Rhenish woven tapestries belong to the same circle of ideas; in embroidery, however, they are found, as far as I know, only in the hanging with lions from Wernigerode, the hanging with the Bortfeld arms from Marienberg (these two not illustrated here: see A. Fink, *Niederdeutsche Beiträge zur Kunstgeschichte*, Cologne, 1961, I, p. 169), and in the Kalchreuth hanging (XVIII, 301), where they are curiously associated with Biblical figures.

One of the most remarkable themes is a Dance of Death on the orphreys of a cope of about the middle of the sixteenth century from the Lower Rhine (370), an indication of the greatly diminished interest in saints' legends at this period. Classical mythology came into its own again (330, 331, 367, 377 – to name only a few examples). Landscape (343), the sky and the stars (337–339), and scenes of everyday life (340, 342) were now considered worthy of representation.

In the seventeenth century exotic themes from the Near and Far East began to appear, and became a prevailing fashion in the eighteenth century (416, 432, 437, 439). Finally there is a return to classical antiquity (455).

In Europe, *English embroidery* can be traced farther back than any other rational group. The so-called chasuble of St. Harlindis and St. Relindis at Maeseyck (9, 10) is the oldest known western European embroidery, datable to about 850 on grounds of its style, which is of Anglo-Saxon character and related to Irish miniatures. Literary records mention a whole series of aristocratic Anglo-Saxon ladies who distinguished themselves as embroideresses, and also some men, such as St. Dunstan, Archbishop of Canterbury. The stole and maniple of St. Cuthbert (11–13) provide eloquent testimony to the superb quality of Anglo-Saxon embroidery prior to the Norman conquest. They were commissioned by Aelfflaed, wife of Edward the Elder, for Frithestan, Bishop of Winchester, between 909 and 916. After the conquest, according to the reports of the chroniclers, Anglo-Saxon women continued to practise their embroidery, which was to attain the summit of its fame, as *opus anglicanum*, during the thirteenth and fourteenth centuries. At the Council of Bari in 1098 a splendid cope excited universal admiration as the most beautiful which had ever been seen in Italy.

But before the development of the delicate *opus anglicanum* we encounter, like an erratic block, the Bayeux tapestry (31–33), the most monumental – perhaps, indeed, the only really monumental – achievement of European embroidery which has survived. When, where and by whom it was made, remains uncertain. But the great undertaking, the powerful impact of the conquest, the enormous success of the mighty Northmen, is brought unforgettably before our eyes. It was the victors, not the vanquished, who wished to celebrate their great action, and it seems very likely that the hanging was made for Odo, Bishop of Bayeux and half-brother of the Conqueror, especially since it served to adorn his cathedral. The depiction of the battle is so spontaneous and alive that we can only suppose that the designer was himself one of the combatants and that the work dates from the years immediately following the conquest (1066–77).

Returning now to the gentle *opus anglicanum* we find that, though it includes gold embroidery, it is primarily silk embroidery of the utmost refinement, which was made not only in convents but also in secular workshops. Some of the most beautiful and interesting examples have been preserved since the Middle Ages in continental collections.

Thus Ascoli Piceno (101), Pienza (103) and Saint-Bertrand- de-Comminges (not illustrated) still possess the copes which were given to these, their native towns, by Popes Nicholas IV, Pius II and Clement V. It is known that other popes gave costly vestments "de opere anglicano" to St. Peter's and other churches and that both Edward I and Edward II sent embroidered copes to the reigning pope of their day. The examples reproduced here illustrate the stylistic development and the progressive modification and enrichment of the composition, from the earlier pieces with subjects in circles, eight-pointed stars and quatrefoils, to the later ones in which Gothic arches form tabernacles for the figures of the saints. The intervals are filled with flowering scrolls and a multitude of birds, beasts and horses, unparalleled elsewhere. The angel on horseback (not illustrated) is a particularly charming, very English conception. The forerunners of the polychrome silk embroideries, the true *opus anglicanum*, were embroideries in gold, at first somewhat awkward in design and execution, as in the mitre showing the martyrdom of St Thomas Becket (95, 96) and the so-called imperial mantle of Otto IV, but later acquiring nobility and elegance, in the dalmatic with centaurs, at Halberstadt, and the Clare chasuble (97, 98), and reaching their highest point in the pure Gothic style of the side panels of the Grandson altarfrontal (99). All these gold embroideries were executed in underside couching, a technique which was not practised in Germany.

The Christ in Majesty (100) and the Tree of Jesse (V) will perhaps reveal to the unbiassed observer the true quality of this subtle, delicate, polychrome embroidery, which for all its refinement makes a powerful, direct and deep impression – most of all in the Salvator Mundi (100) and in the Crucifixion of the Melk chasuble (Vienna, Österreichisches Museum für angewandte Kunst; not reproduced owing to its defective state of preservation).

After the decline of *opus anglicanum* – brought about chiefly by war and pestilence – there is a yawning gap in English embroidery of the sixteenth century. Ecclesiastical embroidery was no longer required. Existing stocks – and they were very great – were sold, cut up and used to adorn the interiors of great houses, where a small proportion has been preserved, by pious care, to this day. The far-seeing government and expansionist programme of the sagacious Queen Elizabeth led to increased wealth and prosperity among her subjects and hence to higher standards of life and greater comfort in the home. This conferred a new importance on the textile art of the period and not least on embroidery. For no other country in Europe does the embroidery of the late sixteenth and seventeenth century offer a more instructive political barometer than for England. The main concern was with life, with the present moment. Embroidery was called upon to supply the needs, not only of the court and the nobility, but also of the prosperous merchant class which was itself on the way to acquiring noble status. The great number of rich embroideries which have been preserved as honoured heirlooms in great English families and have often passed into the possession of the nation, speak an eloquent language (376–395). The works in *petit point* were mostly made at home, by the ladies of the family and the domestic staff, but a certain number of pieces, recognisable by their extremely regular execution, were also made by professional embroiderers. Besides cushions, bed-curtains, hangings, pin-cushions and purses, much time was spent on costume. Everything was embroidered: jackets, coifs, nightcaps and gloves, which, like the military scarves, were often presented as honorific gifts. Aprons appear rather later, at the beginning of the eighteenth century, worked in satin stitch and sometimes signed by the embroideress. In design, English embroidery of all periods shows a great taste for floral sprigs and scrolls, scattered animals, quadrupeds, caterpillars, butterflies, all naturalistically drawn and juxtaposed in rows. The great bed-curtains of the late seventeenth and eighteenth centuries (407, 423, 424), with undulating stems, acanthus-like foliage and exotic animals, are an expression of the "Oriental style" in England. The mutual influence and exchanges between England, India, China and Holland in the embroidered and painted hangings, or "palampores", are another interesting but complex chapter, as yet incompletely investigated. Towards the end of the seventeenth century in England, chairs began to be upholstered and covers were embroidered for them, with wool and silk, in *gros point* and *petit point* – a fashion which persisted until about 1760 (417, XXVI). Designs became lighter; silk was now favoured as a ground material. Quilting and withework became very fashionable, as is mentioned elsewhere. Embroidered copies of paintings were greatly admired, and won the approval even of Reynolds. In the late eighteenth century costume offered a fruitful field for embroidery – especially men's coats and waistcoats, but also to some extent ladies' dresses. From the degeneration into which it fell during the first half of the nineteenth century, embroidery was rescued by William Morris, who produced fine designs (462) and reawakened the old spirit of sound craftsmanship.

German embroidery opens at the beginning of the eleventh century with a magnificent diapason: the vestments of a group of royal saints – the Emperor Henry II, his wife Kunigund and her brother King Stephen of Hungary. The "star-mantle" of the Emperor Henry (1010–1020), the mantle of St. Kunigund (c. 1010), the cope of St. Kunigund (c. 1010) and the mantle of St. Stephen (dated 1031) are the most valuable and sacred relics of medieval embroidery which have been preserved in the care of the church. They are incomparable treasures. As a direct expression of a period whose religious sentiments had been deeply stirred by the Cluniac movement which is personified in the imperial couple, they represent for us the fruit of a brief span of time when the peace of God reigned, when the secular power and the church presided over the Empire in equilibrium and harmony.

The star-mantle of Henry II (Regensburg?, 1010–1020) is, according to ancient tradition, a symbol of dominion over all things terrestrial. It was given to the mighty imperial sovereign by Ismael, Duke of Apulia, probably when he visited Bamberg to seek the Emperor's aid against Byzantium. Christian subjects and representations of the constellations are scattered over the mantle, with Christ at the centre, about whom all things turn and towards whom all things gravitate. There are various inscriptions, including good wishes for Henry, "the ornament of Europe", around the edge, and captions for the constellation-pictures (cf. Catalogue 14-16). The mantle of St. Kunigund is of quite different type (17–22, I, IV). Here the subjects are enclosed in circles, which are arranged in rows as in the patterns of woven stuffs. The spaces between the circles are filled with foliage ornament. The impressive golden scenes are explained by the inscriptions around them. In the centre are subjects symbolising the Incarnation of Christ, and at the sides, scenes from the lives of St. Peter and St. Paul, the patron saints of Bamberg cathedral; the human types in these scenes demonstrate the German origin of the work. From the cope of St. Kunigund we reproduce only two details (29, 30) of the beautiful figure of an enthroned sovereign of Byzantine type, which is repeated 72 times on the cope, together with inscriptions which are no longer decipherable. These figures, about 8 inches high, are among the most expressive embroideries of this early period. Are they of Byzantine or of south German origin? The mantle of St. Stephen (23–26), originally a chasuble which was commissioned by Stephen and his wife Gisela in 1031, probably from a south German workshop, for the church of Székesfehérvár, was subsequently adapted to serve as the coronation mantle of the Hungarian kings. A host of figures is arranged in three zones, with a fourth zone of half-length figures around the edge. The two enthroned figures in the centre, distinguished from the throng by the mandorlas which frame them, dominate the whole. Lively miniature figures are scattered in ornamental fashion between the turrets of the architectural canopies. The composition would not be unworthy of some great apse. The iconographical programme, devised by a theologian and designed by great artists, has been made visible on the blue-purple ground by needle and gold thread and has been raised in the process, as in the most solemn rites of the church, out of the world of everyday life into the sphere of the sublime.

The most splendid of the garments associated with the name of Henry II, his so-called "rider-mantle" in Bamberg (27, 28, II, III), is a venerable relic of the medieval embroidery of Europe. It was long thought to be Byzantine work of about 1000. More recently, certain indications have suggested an Italian origin – southern Italy?, Venice? – and a later date, about 1200. It may be so. Its provenance remains problematic, like that of the exquisite Grandson altar-frontal in Berne (126, 127, VII) and of the late thirteenth century eucharistic veil (128). In the background of these distinguished works looms the high civilisation of Byzantium. The superb "dalmatic of Charlemagne" in the treasury of St. Peter's (140, 141), a work of the fourteenth century, is the only undoubted Byzantine embroidery of importance in our collection. It has always been considered as Byzantine work, even though its dating was uncertain.

Two of the earliest surviving German embroideries show the same motif: the flight of Alexander the Great. In the Würzburg piece (34–36), of uncertain date, the king, wearing a chasuble-like garment, floats in the air between two eagles who share a single tail; in the smaller piece, in Soest, (39), wearing a richly draped mantle and seated on a throne to which the eagles are attached, he entices them to fly upwards by means of pieces of meat on the spits which he holds in his raised hands. The origin of the embroideries cannot be definitely established, but may perhaps be indicated by the churches to which they belong – Würzburg cathedral suggesting Franconia and the church of St. Patroklus in Soest suggesting Westphalia. They are German transformations of Persian textile-patterns (cf. H. J. Schmidt, *Alte Seidenstoffe*, p. 115, Figs. 79, 80) transmitted through unknown intermediaries – textiles and possibly miniatures also. Equally problematic is the Ewald cover (46–51) which packs into a small space a gigantic iconographical programme – nothing less than the entire cosmos. This again is a puzzle as far as date and origin are concerned, though there is a relationship between the border pattern here and that of the Würzburg Alexander embroidery, with it serpent-heads and pairs of interlaced birds, reminiscent of double-headed eagles. The border of the Ewald cover consists of a row of beaded circles, after the Persian fashion, adorned with serpent-heads, and enclosing a pair of birds with interlaced necks;

this is a version of the pattern of a Byzantine woven silk from St. Peter, Salzburg, which Falke regards as provincial work of the twelfth century (Von Falke, II, p. 18, Fig. 254).

The representation of the cosmos links the modest little Ewald cover with the great Spanish Genesis hanging in Gerona (40–45). This presents the theme of the year in a magnificently comprehensive and detailed scheme, with summer and winter, day and night, sun and moon, and time itself culminating in Christ the ruler of the world, who appears at the centre, surrounded with scenes of the Creation. It is a composition characterised by grandeur, by unshakable earnestness, and by a remarkable and penetrating observation of nature. It is a passionate confession of faith, of monumental stature. At once typical and personal, it is marked by the influence of contemporary German and Byzantine miniature painting.

Compared to this, German Romanesque embroideries of the twelfth and thirteenth century appear reserved and unassuming; for example, a most beautifully designed and executed altar-cloth (81–85; destroyed by fire during the war), of linen embroidery, probably worked in the Rhineland, with scenes of the life of the Virgin, from the Annunciation to Pentecost. Of comparable distinction though quite different in appearance, worked in gold and silver on purple silk, is the altar-frontal from Rupertsberg, near Bingen, on the Rhine (78–80). This purple and gold altar-frontal was a valuable gift and was clearly recognised as such. All the personalities connected with the church and convent are depicted and named, illustrating the close family-feeling of the group, which was no doubt fostered by the kindly character, known to us from documentary evidence, of the convent's benefactress, the Duchess Agnes of Lorraine. Of the designer nothing is known. But both these embroideries are important works of art which are thoroughly to stand proxy for the wall-painting of the time.

German embroideries of the early Middle Ages are astonishingly varied. They are almost entirely of silk; gold is used sparingly, if not avoided altogether, as in the chasuble at St. Paul, Carinthia, and the set of vestments from Göss. It is hardly possible today to imagine the original effect of the colours. These old textiles are now no more than shadows of what they were, and it is only by examining the back of the work, where the light – their worst enemy apart from moth and dust – could not reach, that it is possible to reconstruct to some extent the freshness of their original colouring, and even then only if the original dyes were good. Unfortunately they were generally of very variable quality. Thus the chasuble at St. Paul (106–109, VI) has a very curious general tone, a mustard colour, which is found nowhere else. This chasuble, which is very regularly executed, chiefly in long-armed cross stitch, is divided, like the later example with the story of St. Nicholas (120–122), into many small square compartments so as to provide space for the maximum number of narrative subjects. The compartments are surrounded with ornamental borders or with inscriptions, in red on a white ground, which relate for the benefit of the faithful the legend of the saint. The vestment or altar-frontal is not conceived as a visual whole, nor it designed to produce a festive, joyful impression; it is intended above all to instruct and edify. Church and convent wish to penetrate the depth of the matter and for this purpose they needed explanatory texts and inscribed scrolls. The two chasubles from St. Blasien (there is also a third, not reproduced here, at St. Paul) are separated by several decades; the one showing the life of St. Nicholas, in animated scenes with many figures, is the later. It is uncertain whether these pieces were actually made in the convent of St. Blasien, though the subjects and saints represented indicate that they were made for that institution. But the existence of three vestments in the same technique from the same convent does suggest that they may have been made there, especially when one considers the evidence relating to Brother Beretha, mentioned above.

As for the Göss vestments, their embroidered inscriptions leave no doubts as to their origin. They were the pride of the convent, of the abbess and her nuns, and are quite unique of their kind. No convincing relationships with other contemporary work have been found. The whole set is completely uniform in style, materials and technique. The vestments are of remarkably large dimensions. The technique, with its large stitches, the glossy silk thread, the pure colours, all combine together, when seen on a bright summer day, to produce an effect of splendour reminiscent of stained glass windows. At first sight the ornament strikes one as a little odd in its heedlessness of symmetry. An attempt has been made to explain this in terms of the contemporary fashion for parti-coloured clothes, but the explanation is not immediately enlightening. Dreger pointed out that the ornament is of Oriental origin. The border-ornament composed of Z-shaped forms on the altar-frontal (near the three Kings) appears already on the garment of a Persian archer on an Attic bowl by Epiktetos, 520–510 B.C. (London, British Museum, E 135). The right-angled ribbon ornament forming a variety of square labyrinthine patterns is the basic ornament of tablet-weaving in northern Europe and was extensively used in Lower Saxon embroidery to form small-scale patterns on the clothing of the personages depicted. It probably reached northern Europe by overland routes, together with the technique of tablet-weaving, while it probably came to Styria by way of Venice and the Greek Islands, where some of the motifs are found in the local embroideries.

The only example in which these ribbon-ornaments are used to decorate a large complete object is the beautiful chasuble with the symbols of the Evangelists (132), probably of Venetian origin, but it must be admitted that they are used here in a quite different (and Italian) way, like the pattern of a woven textile. The forms are not meant to be seen individually, but as small rhythmically arranged elements in the diagonal stripes.

In Lower Saxony the aristocratic convent of Quedlinburg has preserved the earliest European woven tapestries, from the twelfth and thirteenth centuries, and – a major monument of Romanesque textile art – fragments of the only European pile carpet surviving from the Middle Ages (not illustrated). It is all thus all the more inexplicable that from the thirteenth century onwards only embroideries were made in Lower Saxon convents; the earliest example is a fragment of a wall-hanging of about 1180–1200 (110).

Opus teutonicum was the name applied in the middle ages to *whitework embroidery* from Germany. White linen thread, sometimes with the addition of a little light-coloured silk or dyed wool (159, 167) to emphasise haloes and other details, was worked on white linen in a great variety of stitches, with openwork effects of cross-stitch type, and patterns such as letters, stars and rosettes worked in darning stitch on drawn-thread backgrounds. Was it a sign of poverty, of lack of means, especially in north German convents, for purchases of costly foreign silk, that this kind of linen embroidery, *opus teutonicum*, was considered the typical German embroidery? Should not the polychrome *beadwork* of Lower Saxony be interpreted in the same sense? These were certainly substitutes for work in pearls, precious metals and the coveted Byzantine enamels, but they are artistic substitutes and they do not fail to make their effect; for example in the charming specimens at Halberstadt (VIII) and in the Kestnermuseum at Hanover (180). And do not (to anticipate another subject) the woollen embroideries, which are so numerous in Lower Saxony, point in the same direction – even allowing for the fact that many such embroideries must have suffered destruction in other countries?

The whitework embroideries were made for the service of the church, as altar-cloths, chalice-veils and Lenten veils, of which the largest collection is preserved at Kloster Lüne (near Lüneburg). These Lenten veils were intended to conceal the altar and the choir from the congregation during Lent and they are of considerable size. The Lenten veil from Lüne, a detail of which is reproduced here (146), measures 113 × 383 cm. The cloth, when extended during Lent, showed Christ on the Cross at the centre, flanked on either side by Pilate, the Flagellation, the Resurrection and Limbo, with Eve in the foreground. Above was the figure of Christ in Glory between apostles and saints. The figures, left in reserve in the linen, hover like puppets in a shadow-show against the transparent mesh of the drawn-thread ground; the subjects were worked in reversed order so that, when the front of the work faced the altar, they appeared to the congregation in correct sequence.

One of the most individual embroideries of the secound quarter of the thirteenth century is the Magdalene hanging in Wernigerode (142, 143). This is the only example in which an attempt was made to reproduce, in the draperies of the principal figures, the agitated, jagged style of drawing current in Lower Saxony at this period, but it remains uncertain whether the misunderstanding was due to the artist or the embroiderer. The style is not inappropriate to the spiritual content of the subject and the group of Christ and the Magdalene has a rare strength and sincerity.

The dating of the early linen embroideries is uncertain for want of firmly dated comparative material and only approximate indications can be given. The designs of this early whitework are sometimes clumsy, but the sewing and the drawn-thread work show astonishing ability and great accuracy, especially when one considers the primitive nature of the tools, such as the sewing needles made from wire. (Germany, however, had a reputation for good needles; England was importing sewing needles from Germany as late as the sixteenth century, in the time of Queen Mary). Most of the Lower Saxon linen embroideries are still in the convents where they were made – Wienhausen, Isenhagen, Ebstorf, Lüne – and likewise the silk-embroidered altar-cloths – at St. Marienberg (Helmstedt) and Drübeck – but much was handed over from the convents to the Welfenmuseum in Hanover in 1864 and is now in the Kestnermuseum. The designs of the embroideries must often have been made for the nuns by wandering craftsmen and painters. – The whitework embroideries of Hesse are distinguished by their figure-subjects, which were designed by artists and are later than those of Lower Saxony – for example, the beautiful altar-cloth in the Metropolitan Museum, New York (160–164), the dainty one in the Cleveland Museum of Art (154–157), and a third (not reproduced) in the Kunstgewerbemuseum, Frankfurt. These come from a convent which was intimately associated with St. Elisabeth, the convent of Altenberg on the Lahn, where they were no doubt made.

To judge from the small number of whitework embroideries preserved in Italy, there seems to have been less interest in such work in that country. The earliest example is a tablecloth, a unique object in the Museo Sacro Vaticano in Rome (85) whose style, ornament, origin and period are all problematic, since no related textiles are known. The design is not of a textile type; the primitive ornament is comparable with metalwork, with the gold filigree-work of the eleventh century. The same may be said of the eagles, which are the only representational motif present and throw no light on the origin of the work. There is no trace of a Christian symbol, which seems to suggest that this very large embroidery was originally made as a secular table-cover and was used as an altar-cloth only at some later date.

The "Lenzulo della Beata Benvenuta" an altar-hanging of the end of the thirteenth century from Friuli (131, 133, 134), has a strong compositional structure, quite unlike the German works, and is organised in the manner of a painted altarpiece. St Ursula, however, whom this embroidery especially honours, is isolated, like her virgins, each in a separate compartment of the border. The next of our Italian whitework embroideries (330), made about 1500, is remote from ecclesiastical ideas in both subject and technique; it represents Orpheus sitting amid foliage scrolls, accompanied by birds, and playing his fiddle for some friendly, attentively listening animals, including a bear, a lion and several dragons. To the Italian, in the intense light of his climate, work in colour comes more naturally than pure white linen embroidery, which reflects back the full glare of the day. A new and gay type of embroidery was therefore evolved, in which the principal forms are left in reserve in the linen, while the inner drawing, outlines and background are worked in coloured silk – the background commonly in long-armed cross stitch in red, green or yellow, and the outlines in back stitch. The illustrations show various stages in the meticulous execution of these domestic embroideries, which must have been very popular in the sixteenth century, to judge from the large number of surviving examples (327–329).

The term *Swiss linen embroidery* designates the embroidery of the burgher-class of German-speaking Switzerland, worked on white linen in white linen thread, sometimes with details in blue and brown thread. Its development runs from the first half of the thirteenth century down to the year 1640, but it flourished especially in the fifteenth and above all in the second half of the sixteenth century. It may be considered as a continuation of *opus teutonicum* which, after reaching its zenith in the late Romanesque and early Gothic period, was generally abandoned in fifteenth century Germany in favour of embroidery in coloured silk. It is not possible in every case to make an absolutely clear division between Swiss and south German embroideries. There was a continuous interchange between the two countries and currents of influence ran in both directions. Thus the finest late Gothic hanging (306–309) seems to be from the Upper Rhine rather than from Switzerland. As is often the case, the earliest works are artistically the most distinguished, for instance a tablecloth 6½ yards long from the first half of the thirteenth century (Zürich, Schweizerisches Landesmuseum; Verena Trudel, Pl. I) and the Gothic tablecloth from Feldberg (151–153). We know from texts that these embroideries were worked by women of the patrician and burgher classes, and by nuns, and that the designs were drawn out on the material by painters. The designs were based on woodcuts and especially on Bible illustrations; the Tobias embroidery of 1563 (336), for example, is derived from an illustration by the younger Holbein. Illustrations by Tobias Stimmer, Jost Amman, Hans Sebald Beham, Virgil Solis and Bernhard Salomon were also used. The fine hanging of 1575 showing "Virgil's Trap for Adulterers" (356) looks as if it is based on a woodcut, but the artist is unfortunately not known.

Woollen embroidery formed a most attractive complement to linen embroidery in Switzerland. The two were intimately related, though the technique of the woollen embroidery was much simpler, being restricted as a rule to couched work, cross-stitch and long-armed cross stitch and generally to only one of these. It is astonishing that with these limited means the embroideresses were able to render in so lively a fashion such scenes as the Washday (342) and Women breaking flax (340).

The view of Bischofszell (343), about 1530, is as far as I know the only woollen embroidery with a faithful rendering of an actual landscape. Most of these woollen embroideries come from Schaffhausen, Zürich and St. Gall. They include table-covers, hangings and a very few altar-frontals. Like the linen embroideries, they continue into the seventeenth century, down to the Baroque style. But under the increasing dominance of French taste, the Swiss women evidently ceased to take pleasure in the forceful, almost rustic effects of these embroideries. The latest example, dated 1700, from the convent of Rheinau (430) and probably made in Schaffhausen, is in the fashionable style of the time and seems to reflect influences reaching Switzerland from France and the Netherlands.

Carpets for floors and tables were still comparatively novel phenomena in Renaissance Europe. In England, floors were still covered with rushes and skins. But evidence from paintings shows that prosperous European families were using knotted pile carpets imported from Turkey as floor and table carpets. In view of the high cost of these it was natural to call on embroidery to provide substitutes and our illustrations show three woollen embroideries of this class (357–359), which are related not only in pattern but also in their technique of cross and long-armed cross stitch. They come from Switzerland (1533), Alsace (1539) and England (undated) and their interlace patterns are all interrelated: the small interlace ornament in the main field of the Swiss example recurs in the border of the English piece, while the latter so obviously resembles the example from Alsace that one can only suppose that their large octagonal motifs and the arrangement of large flowers in lozenge-shaped or square compartments must have been derived from some common source which has not yet been identified.

It may be mentioned here that liturgical embroidery played a very subordinate role in Switzerland, owing to the lack of great secular and ecclesiastical patrons. But silk embroidery was practised in the nunnery of Engelberg, which was later transferred to Sarnen. The well-preserved and decorative cope in the Benedictine convent of Engelberg (174, 175) was presumably made there and is clearly dated 1318. But the inscription on the cope is partially destroyed and can no longer be read, though an attempt has been made to interpret it as referring to Queen Agnes, the great benefactress of the convent. The large hood with its reference to Abbot Walther (1317–1331) is evidently of the same period as the body of the cope, but differs from it in style and perhaps belonged to another vestment. Two further embroideries from Engelberg are the altar-frontals from the Iklé collection (St. Gall, Museum für Industrie und Gewerbe, Catalogue Nos. 1197, 1198), of which No. 1197 has an inscription with another reference to Abbot Walther (not illustrated).

Woollen embroidery was no less important in Germany than whitework embroidery and was practised above all – to judge from the number of examples which are preserved there – in Lower Saxony. The polychrome woollen hangings served not only as decoration but also as a protection against the cold; some are of enormous size, for use in church and refectory, and some have been enlarged subsequently by the addition of sections of other hangings, cut up for this purpose, as at Wienhausen. For the most part they illustrate sacred themes – the life of the Virgin, Passion subjects and, of course, the popular saints – for which the Golden Legend served as the principal source. But an indication that apocryphal literature was also familiar and popular in the convents, despite ecclesiastical prohibitions, is provided by the bench-covers with the life of St. George, at Lüne (not illustrated). These are based on a Latin version of a Greek popular work of the fifth century. The Easter hanging from Lüne, now in Hamburg (not illustrated) is particularly interesting as a late re-working of the theme of the year, already seen in the early medieval hanging at Gerona (40–45) and in the Ewald cover (46–51). Secular themes were very popular and their sources are no less interesting. The two medieval Tristram hangings illustrated here, the well-known one at Wienhausen (193–195) and the other in the Victoria and Albert Museum, London (230), are based on the original version, then still current in Lower Saxony, of this most popular of all medieval romances, whereas the Tristram scenes in the hanging of 1539 from Alsace, now in Leipzig (359), follow the chap-books of 1484 and 1498, which are derived from Eilhard von Oberg.

At the beginning of the sixteenth century the production of embroidered hangings came to an end in Lower Saxony. It is true that Lüne and Heiningen were still undertaking major works as late as 1516, but these are no longer the gay naive romances and the stories of the saints. The tendency towards didacticism and abstract theology predominates in these late works and stifles artistic imagination.

The Icelandic wall-hangings, less familiar in Europe than the north German examples, are a kind of distant echo of the latter, merging into peasant art; they preserve medieval motifs down to a late date and they employ the technique of the Bayeux tapestry (189–191).

Southern Germany, to judge from the number of woollen embroideries preserved there, seems to have been less attached to this type of work. Examples in Erfurt and on the Wartburg (not illustrated) may be referred to in passing, and mention must be made of Regensburg, with its hanging of pairs of lovers, about 1370–1380 (229, XII), and of Franconia, with beautiful examples from the second half of the fifteenth century (298, XVIII, XIX). On the Upper Rhine, the charming Malterer hanging (185, 186, IX) and the fragments of a wall-hanging with the arms of a noble family from Breisgau (187, 188), both about 1310–1330, are among the attractions of Freiburg. In these, the subjects and the dimensions, suitable for comparatively small rooms, clearly suggest a middle-class environment. The fragmentary piece, with its simplified drawing and strong unshaded colours, is a perfect expression of the Gothic style. The Malterer hanging takes a favourite theme of the embroideresses of south Germany and Switzerland, the wiles of women, and arranges it humorously as a moral tale to amuse the nuns.

There is a wide gulf between these secular works and such liturgical embroideries as the Bamberg altar-frontal of about 1300 (170, 171), a work without predecessors or successors, and the wonderful gold-embroidered rationale (shoulder ornament) of about 1320–40 in the treasury of Regensburg cathedral (182-184). It has been said that this was destined for Bishop Berthold of Eichstätt (1354–1365), Burgrave of Nuremberg, and the perfection of the design and the workmanship certainly suggest that it was made to the order of some great lord, in an important workshop.

In the fourteenth century, the embroidery of the heart of Europe attained unexpected heights, inheriting the leading position previously held by *opus anglicanum*, but embarking on new and different courses. *Austria, Bohemia* and *France* were the main centres. The predominant types were silk embroidery and needle-painting, following very closely the models provided by the painters of the time. The most important example of this collaboration is the exquisite altar-frontal in Berne with scenes from the life of Christ (X, 196, 197, 201, 202) a gift of Duke Albrecht II of Austria (d. 1358) to the convent of Königsfelden, the residence of his sister Agnes, dowager Queen of Hungary. In parts the embroidery has been worn away, revealing on the linen ground the most delicate, softly shaded grisaille painting (visible only in the original, not in reproductions). We see here the beginnings of a movement which came to maturity a hundred years later, achieving its highest perfection in the Burgundian-Netherlandish vestments of the Order of the Golden Fleece.

Painter and embroiderer share the same high level of accomplishment. The close collaboration between embroiderer and painter in the Middle Ages is a subject which has not yet been explored, but this, though a very desirable aim, is one which is perhaps hardly attainable. According to Maurer, the designer of the altar-frontal stands close to the Master of the Hohenfurt altar and the Kaufmann Crucifixion. A striking feature is the emphasis on the architectural elements in the composition of the frontal, with plastically rendered, projecting towers, the continuous podium and crenellations, and interiors with perspective effects as settings for the figure subjects. In the altar-band, too, the ceiling with its beams is consistently rendered from a low viewpoint. Together with this work we may consider the great altar-frontal from Salzburg cathedral, now in the Österreichisches Museum für angewandte Kunst in Vienna (205–207), unfortunately less well preserved than the other, so that the impression which it makes is somewhat impaired. This altar-frontal, with its double row of barbed quatrefoils with raised frames, and with figure subjects in the intervening spaces, was designed for a great church and a large altar. The composition of the scenes and the rendering of the human types, some of which are very delicately conceived, are unusually sensitive and pictorial, as, for example, in the youthful kings who form the central point of the whole, and in the Annunciation.

The restrained emphasis laid on architectural elements, such as steps, forms a link with the frontal in Berne, while the needle-painting is perhaps even more delicate than in that work. That it was regarded as something of special quality appears from the fact that the names of donor and artist are placed in a very prominent position on the plastically treated chalices held by the kings. This, now a disturbing element, must have merged, in the original state of the work, into the sheen of silk and precious metal.

The embroidery of the eagle-dalmatic (208–210), one of the coronation vestments of the Holy Roman Emperors, must, in accordance with its high purpose, have been commissioned from the workshop of the principal master of the time. Dürer showed it in his painting of Charlemagne, of 1512, as one of the symbols of imperial rank.

Bohemian embroideries of the second half of the fourteenth century form an individual group, reflecting the refined culture of the country under the French-educated Luxemburger Charles IV and the rich artistic gifts of the people. They are distinguished by great ability in design and craftsmanship and by a special charm which emerges in their individual, light-hearted conception and lively rendering of the traditional themes of church art. On the chasuble-orphrey of the church at Rockycany, near Pilsen (240), the Virgin of the Annunciation looks like a sacred Bohemian peasant girl, with her mantle drawn like a kerchief over her broad head. Above, in a charming composition, she appears between two angels, with enormous gaily coloured wings, in the guise of a young crowned princess squatting calmly on her haunches and reaching out a hand to steady her frisky baby. A similar individual rendering of the subjects is found in the chasuble-cross (241) with the Annunciation, Visitation and Adoration of the Kings; the Virgin receives the Kings seated on her bed, while Joseph, leaning on the other side of the bed, is an interested spectator. The altar-frontal from the Marienkirche in Pirna, of about 1360 (232–235), has long been well-known, but is unfortunately much damaged; with its dignified saints of Bohemian type, it seems to be the only Bohemian frontal which survives. In this late Gothic period of European art, the spiritual links run unseen in all directions, and it is not yet possible to make a clear division between Austrian, Bohemian and east German embroidery, even though certain connections and types can be identified. Thus, for example, the Christ in the Winepress (237), the Mary Magdalene and the Evil Desires (251) and St John and St Peter (252) all show Bohemian influence. The fine John the Evangelist (XIII), however, is derived, in physical type as well as style, from Austria. The taste for architectural forms and an architectonic framework is common to Austrian, Bohemian and east German embroideries (196, 205, XIII, 240, 241, 247, 252). Ideas originating in Paris, the cultural centre of Europe, were picked up in Prague and retransmitted to the eastern areas. There is, however, a marked difference between French embroideries and the Bohemian works, with their healthy familiarity with the natural world.

French embroidery – judging from the surviving examples – was at its best in the fourteenth century. What remains excites admiration, and regret that time has spared so little of the early heritage of this gifted people. The purses reproduced here (214–218, XI, 221, 222) reflect the sunset of the old traditions of chivalry, still, in the fourteenth century, embodying in most beautiful forms the ideals of courtly love and of tender reverence for women. They allow us a glimpse of the literary taste of high society; the purse in Sens (218) illustrates a subject from the romance of the Châtelaine de Vergy. The contemporary mitres from northern France and Paris (219, 220, 223–225) are well preserved and of fine quality. The severe stylisation of the early fourteenth century mitre of Jean de Marigny stands in sharp contrast to the over-elaboration of that from the Sainte Chapelle in Paris, to whose minute craftsmanship reproductions do less than justice. The mysticism of the High Gothic style finds expression in the Man of Sorrows of the folding altarpiece in the treasury of Chartres cathedral (226, 227) which, with its small dimensions, may have served for a travelling altar. It is one of the very great masterpieces of embroidery and of uniquely French character, though it has not yet been possible to identify the designer.

The lively heraldic leopards (212, 213), which have escaped from Hesse to the Musée de Cluny in Paris, cannot be passed over without a mention. Their origin is not yet established. Perhaps they were once a splendid horse-trapper for use in a knightly tournament and, when no longer needed for this purpose, were converted into a chasuble and given, according to the pious medieval custom, to the church. The droll figures sporting among the foliage recur in the engraved ornament of Israel von Meckenem at the end of the fifteenth century.

The monumental John the Baptist (228) is a giant, a new and startling apparition, clad in a camel-skin with the head hanging between his legs and a mantle falling from his shoulder in long slow folds, and gazing lovingly at the tiny lamb which he holds in the crook of his arm. This figure belongs to northern France or perhaps to the *Netherlands*. The drawing and execution of the face, with its animated expression, place it very close to the figure of God the Father in the dossal of the Golden Fleece, in the second quarter of the fifteenth century.

With the embroideries of the Order of the Golden Fleece (254–268, XIV, XV) we reach the summit of European embroidery. It has come as close to painting as it sought to do, and yet it

has remained entirely itself by virtue of the subtlety of its technique of *or nué*, or shaded gold. This technique deliberately renounces all rivalry with painting by allowing the gold to shimmer everywhere through the coloured silks, thereby producing a fantastic, other-worldly effect which is perhaps best compared to that of translucent enamel on gold. Such unique artistic achievements are possible only in exceptionally fortunate combinations of circumstances, when powerful creative artists coincide with powerful, artistically minded patrons, representing the highest culture of their age; such patrons as the wealthy Dukes of Burgundy, who, despite their political failure, gained great and lasting renown through the artists and scholars of their court. To this same Burgundian cultural enviroment belong the embroideries of the cope with the arms of the Count of Romont, a devoted follower of Charles the Bold (269–273, XVI). They come from the same Netherlandish workshops as the embroideries of the Golden Fleece.

Of equal rank with the Burgundian vestments, both as artistic creations and as embroidery, are the embroidered panels designed by Antonio Pollaiuolo (325, 326) executed between 1466 and 1479 as ornaments for a set of vestments commissioned by the Arte dei Mercatori, the Florentine merchants' guild, for use in Santa Maria del Fiore, the cathedral of Florence. The *or nué* technique of these embroideries, which depict the story of St John the Baptist, excels at times, as in the Burgundian vestments, the effects of painting itself. Seen by candlelight, with the solemn movements of the priest, they must have made a magnificent impression. It was no accident that these splendid vestments were produced in Florence, for that rich town seems to have been the main centre of embroidery in Italy. *Opus florentinum* had a great reputation. The Dukes of Burgundy were great customers and amateurs of "ouvraige de Florence", which figures in the inventories of Philip the Bold in 1404 and Philip the Good in 1420, as well as in that of the Duke de Berry in 1401. Florentine merchants at Toulouse and Avignon are mentioned among the suppliers of the Duke of Burgundy in 1388 and 1393, and it may be supposed that they included Florentine embroideries among their shipments (Grönwoldt). These precious embroideries are lost. But we still possess two examples whose Florentine origin is attested by inscriptions: the great altar-hanging by Geri di Lapo at Manresa in Spain (319) and the altar-frontal of 1336, by Jacopo Cambi, in the Museo degli Argenti in Florence, with the Coronation of the Virgin, and scenes from the Life of the Virgin in the altar-band. In reproductions (320–323), Florentine embroideries, with their many figures, look like frescoes and it was the aim of Italian embroidery to approximate as closely as possible to painting. Designs for embroidery were produced by important painters. Antonio Pollaiuolo has already been mentioned; Francesco Squarcione, Mantegna's master, was an embroiderer until his twenty-ninth year, while Sassetta, Botticelli, Raffaelino del Garbo, Pierino del Vaga, Bacchiacca, Paolo

Veronese, Alvise Vivarini and others are mentioned by Vasari as designers for embroidery. Florentine embroidery of the fifteenth century seems very unassuming when compared with the stately ecclesiastical work of the late sixteenth century, designed, like the chasuble and *paliotto* of Cardinal Alessandro Farnese (334, 335), to be seen from a distance. In these examples, painting enters into deliberate rivalry with embroidery and actually replaces the delicate figure-work of needle-painting: but though painting is here a substitute, it is employed with admirable skill and taste and does not fail to produce the desired effect.

Siena and Venice were also known for their embroideries, but no details can be given, since no examples have as yet been positively identified. Dreger attributed to Venice two fragments which formed the ends of a delicate linen cover (Vienna, Österreichisches Museum für angewandte Kunst and Frankfurt a. M., Kunstgewerbemuseum), worked in the most delicate double-sided needle-painting with the Loves of Neptune and Jupiter, as related by Ovid (331, XX). These form a happy contrast to the severe ecclesiastical work of Florence and their graceful decorative conception is well suited to the light material.

Spanish embroidery is indebted to painting in the same way as Italian and Netherlandish embroidery. In the late fourteenth century, the altar-frontal of the former convent of San Juan de las Abadesas, in Catalonia (274–278), shows the influence of French painting, but in the fifteenth century the influence of Netherlandish painting is dominant, as in the altar-frontal of Henry IV of Castile (279). The dramatic intensity of the fight of St. George and the dragon (280–282) is unparalleled in the decoration of altar-frontals; probably this was in accord with the chapel to which it belonged, and with the wishes of the patron. In contrast to this, the scenes on the two following altar-frontals, one with the Pieta, of about 1480 (284, 285), the other with the Three Marys at the Sepulchre, Valencia work of 1474 (286, 287), are characterised by a noble calm. The latest of our selection (288–291), Castilian work of 1483–1495, indicates by its name, "Frontale rico", its unusual splendour of pearls and precious stones. Common to all this figure-embroidery is the sharp definition (sometimes, indeed, the hardness) of the drawing, the delight in the decorative effect of patterned costumes, and the clear characterisation of the human types. The same features are still apparent in the lectern-cover (369), about a century later, which follows an Italian compositional scheme.

The desire for realism and forceful expression led embroiderers to employ raised work, or embroidery in relief. The important altar-frontal of the Eucharist (332, 333), Brabant work of the first third of the sixteenth century, is the most artistic example of the use of raised work in conjunction with *or nué*. Such work was already being produced in widely separated areas in the fifteenth century, for example, in south Germany about 1430

(283) and in Catalonia about 1460 (280–282), but the most productive period was the sixteenth century. We may mention here the Julius banner of 1512 in Basle (317), the Leipzig chimney hanging of 1571 with its unique satirical subject (352, 353), and the shields of the guilds of Passau, made in 1574–1575 by Wolf Popp (354, 355). The chalice veil (372), a gift of Henrietta Maria, widow of Charles I of England, shows the technique rising to effects of supreme elegance in seventeenth-century France.

It is curious how many types of embroidery flourish for a time, disappear, and then, through some influence, are resurrected again. Generally speaking, this is true of the ancient technique of *applied work* (190, 230, 304, 398), though admitted applied work in coloured wools has never been forgotten, in the peasant art of Sweden and north Germany. Its revival in Europe was inspired by the war-booty taken from the Turks in the seventeenth century, including tents worked all over with flowers and foliage in the most delicate applied work; these tents were greatly admired and no doubt exercised considerable influence.

Quilting also reached Europe from the East, transmitted by the imported Indo-Portuguese silk-embroidered quilts, which enjoyed their maximum popularity between 1570 and 1652. Spanish quilts appear in the inventories of Louis XIV in 1672 and 1701. Various types of quilting and whitework were fashionable throughout Europe in the eighteenth century for linen garments (401, 425, 427), curtains, fashion accessories and silk dresses. As the century advanced these techniques lost their early heaviness and a very delicate form of whitework embroidery was evolved which could vie with lace. Indeed, so admirably did it imitate this desirable commodity, which in the seventeenth and eighteenth centuries was considered suitable only for the nobility, that it made the conquest of the Paris *salons* and was sold by the privileged lace-merchants of the capital, as *point de Saxe* or *point de Dresde*.

Sweden has long cultivated the textile arts with special love and understanding and can boast of a remarkable wealth of textiles, carefully preserved for many centuries, including medieval examples and, above all, oriental pieces of the seventeenth and eighteenth centuries. A small selection of Swedish embroideries, from the fifteenth to the eighteenth centuries, may be indicated here (190, 294, 295, 398, 401-2, 404-5, 435-6). The embroidered chasuble from the workshop of "pictor Albertus" represents the silk embroidery of the late fifteenth century; applied work in various styles is illustrated by a fifteenth century example (190) and by the noble velvet cover of 1630 with the arms of Horn and Oxenstierna; finally the suit of Gustavus Adolphus, 1617, the lady's dress of 1750–1760 and the elegant man's suit of about 1770 show the rich costume of court and society in Stockholm.

We have run on too far and must turn back again. In the sixteenth century Italy discovered the grotesque style, for which France cherished a strong and lasting affection. The manner in which French wit played with this theme is illustrated by two embroideries of the second half of the sixteenth century (365, 366, 368).

In the Baroque period, French embroidery was entirely in the service of architecture and performed architectural tasks. In the course of the king's grandiose building activities it attained extraordinary perfection, succeeded in reproducing architectural motifs, perspectives, and marble, ceased to be treated as a mobile, flexible surface and was incorporated into the solid wall. This stretching of embroidery on the wall persisted in the Rococo style of the following century, as in the bedroom and the small diningroom of Schloss Favorite, about 1720–1730 (442, 443). The three wall-panels from Dresden (429, XXVII), with characters from the *commedia dell'arte* and figures in the manner of Callot, transport us to the court of Dresden between 1711 and 1719 and to the early days of porcelain. The amusing hangings for a bedroom, Austrian work of only slightly later date, about 1720–1740 (440, 441), produce an artistic and tasteful effect by the simplest means – applied work in chintz. A great contrast with these is provided by our latest wall-panels (453); these, worked in chenille thread, are a last soft exhalation of the Louis XVI style, about 1800.

We have reached the end of our story. It concludes with the last attempt to find a new style. *Art nouveau*, in its endeavour to evolve new forms, assigned to embroidery a responsible role in this creative work, which is now coming to be regarded once more with respect and understanding.

Marie Schuette

1 Centaur, fragment. Hellenistic.
4th–5th century.

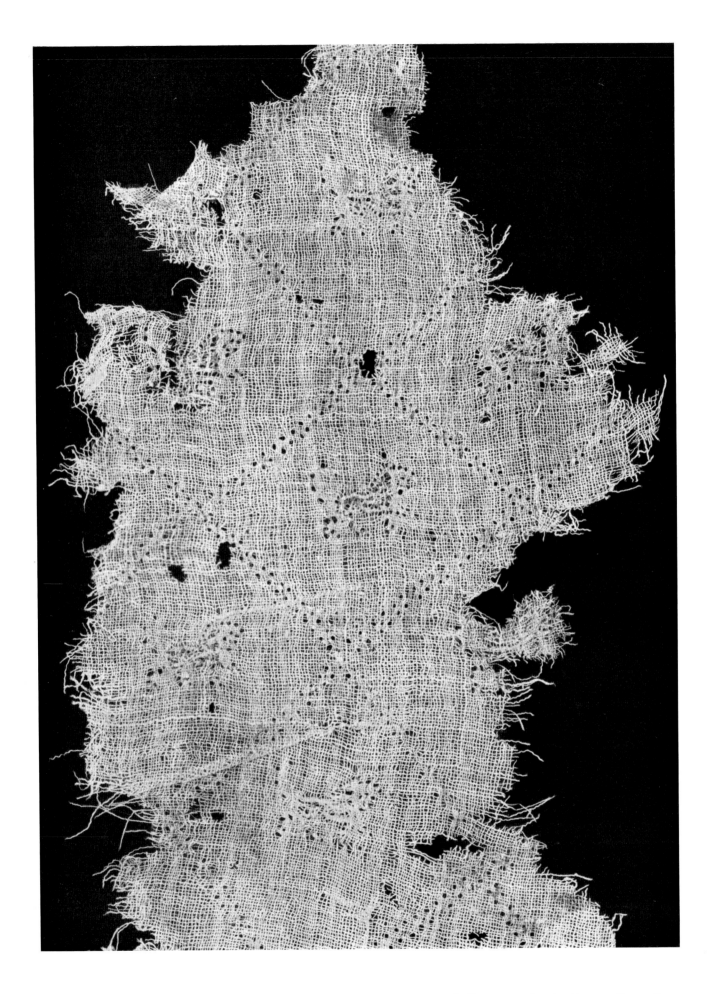

2 Fragment of embroidery on linen: lions.
Attica, late 5th century B. C.

3 Fragment of tapestry: Hun's head.
Northern Mongolia, Noin-Ula, 1st century B. C.

4 Saddle cloth, detail: griffin.
Altai, 4th–3rd century B. C.

5 Tapestry, detail: rider.
Altai, 4th–3rd century B. C.

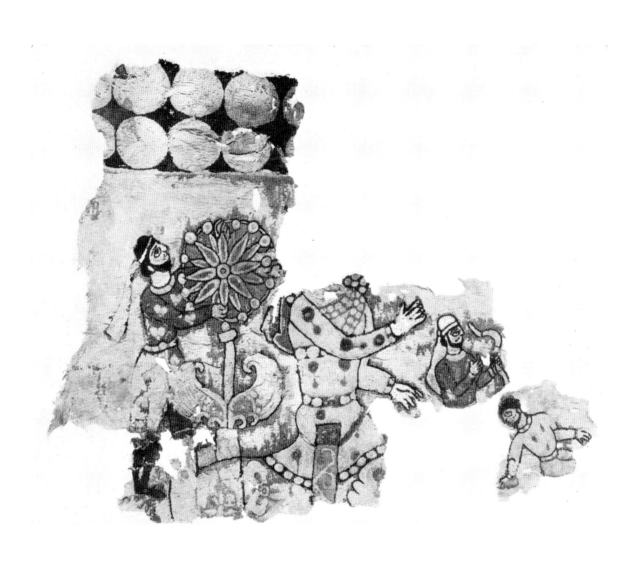

6 Fragment of embroidery.
Persia, Sassanian, 6th–7th century.

7 Fragment of tapestry with trees.
Probably Eastern Mediterranean area, 4th–5th century.

8 Roundel: The Annunciation and Visitation.
Coptic art, 6th–7th century.

8

9/10 So-called chasuble of St. Harlinde and St. Relinde, details.
England, c. 850.

10

11/13 Stole and maniple of St. Cuthbert, details.
England, between 909 and 916.

14 Starred cloak of Emperor Henry II.
South Germany, c. 1010–1020.

15 Detail from the starred cloak of Emperor Henry II.
South Germany. c. 1010–1020.

16 Detail of a star from the cloak of Emperor Henry II.
South Germany, c. 1010–1020.

17 The cloak of St. Kunigund, detail.
South Germany, c. 1020.

18 The cloak of St. Kunigund.
South Germany, c. 1020.

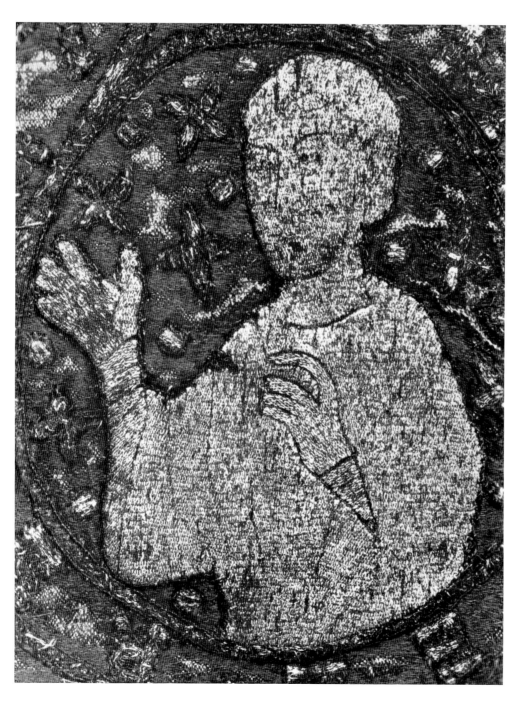

19/20 The cloak of
St. Kunigund,
details.
South Germany,
c. 1020.

IV The cloak of St. Kunigund, detail.
South Germany, c. 1020.

21/22 The
cloak of St.
Kunigund, de-
tails of border
and below:
Virgin an Child.
South Germany,
c. 1020.

23/24 The cloak of St. Stephen.
South Germany, 1031.

25/26 The cloak of St. Stephen, details.
South Germany, 1031.

27 Riding cloak of Emperor Henry II.
Italy, 12th century.

28 Detail of riding cloak of Emperor Henry II.
Italy, 12th century.

29/30 The Cope of St. Kunigund, Christ's head and Christ enthroned.
South Germany, c. 1010.

31/32 The Bayeux tapestry, details.
Normandy or England, 1066–1077.

ET FRANCI: INPRELI

33 The Bayeux tapestry, detail.
Normandy or England, 1066–1077.

34–36 Ornamental hanging, flight of eagles belonging to Alexander the Great.
South Germany, 10th century.

37 Front of a pouch.
France, 11th–12th century.

38 Standard of San Oth, detail.
North Spain, 12th century.

39 Cushion cover, flight of eagles
belonging to Alexander the Great.
Germany, first half of 12th century.

40/41 The Creation tapestry, complete and detail.
Catalonia, 11th–12th century.

42 The Creation tapestry, detail of sungod.
Catalonia, 11th–12th century.

43–45 The Creation tapestry, details.
Catalonia, 11th–12th century.

46 Cloth of St. Ewald, detail.
Germany, mid-9th (?) to 12th century.

47–50 Cloth of St. Ewald, complete and details.
Germany, mid-9th (?) to 12th century.

51 Cloth of St. Ewald, detail.
Germany, mid-9th (?) to 12th century.

31

52 Fragment showing harpy.
Mesopotamia or Egypt. Fatimid period,
11th–12th century.

53 Fragment of robe.
Egypt, 13th–14th century.

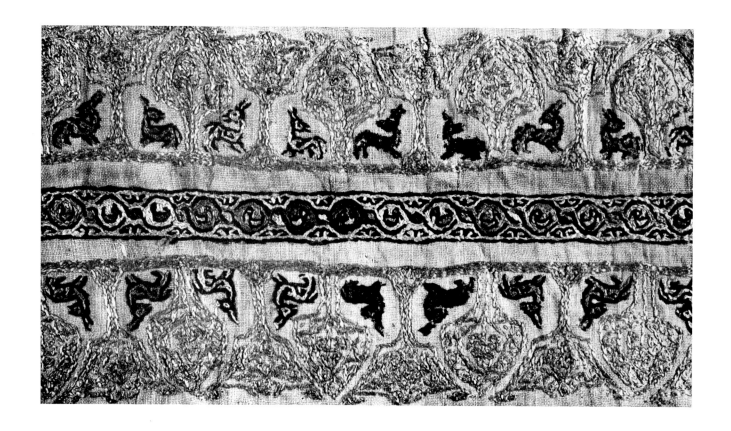

54 Detail of embroidered robe.
Egypt, 12th–13th century.

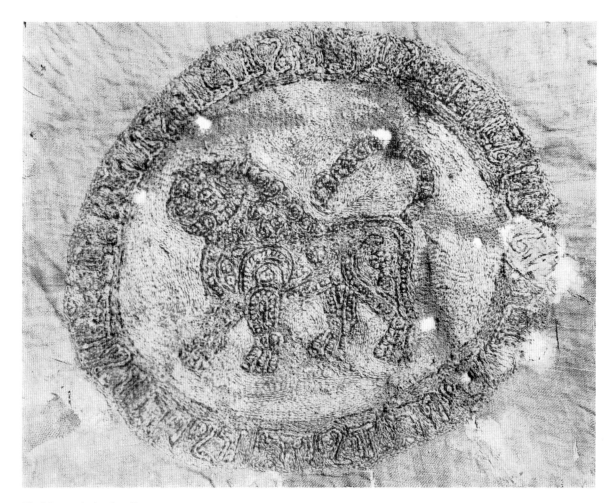

55 Linen cloth, detail.
Egypt, Fatimid period, 11th–12th century.

56 Fragment: Four Apostles.
Egypt, 12th century.

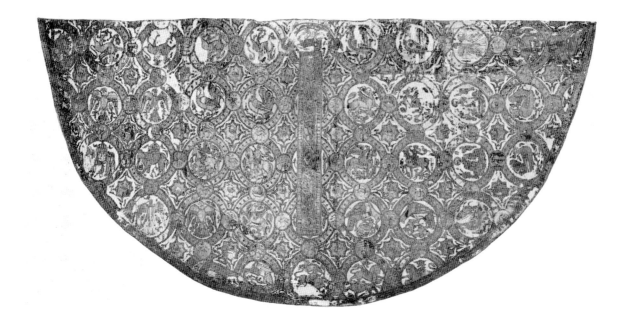

57/58 The chasuble of St. Thomas Becket.
Spain, Almeria, 1116.

59 The chasuble of St. Thomas Becket, detail.
Spain, Almeria, 1116.

60/61 Coronation mantle
of the Holy Roman Empire, details.
Sicily, Palermo, 1133–1134.

62 Coronation mantle of the Holy Roman Empire. Sicily, Palermo, 1155–1154.

65 The so-called coronation cloak of Charlemagne, detail of eagle.
Sicily or Spain, c. 1200.

64 The so-called coronation cloak of Charlemagne. Sicily or Spain. c. 1200.

39

65 Cuff of a dalmatic, part of insignia of the Holy Roman Empire.
Sicily. Palermo. 1130–1140.

66 Lower border of the dalmatic, part of insignia of the Holy Roman Empire.
Sicily, Palermo, 1130–1140.

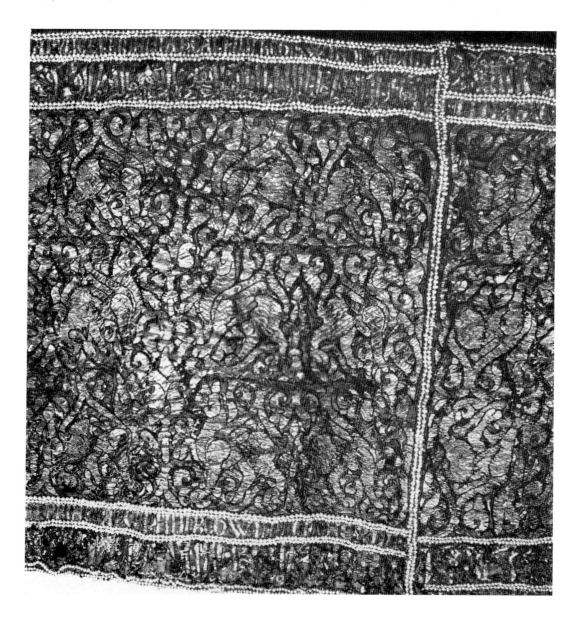

67 Lower border of the alb, part of insignia of the Holy Roman Empire.
Sicily, Palermo, 1181.

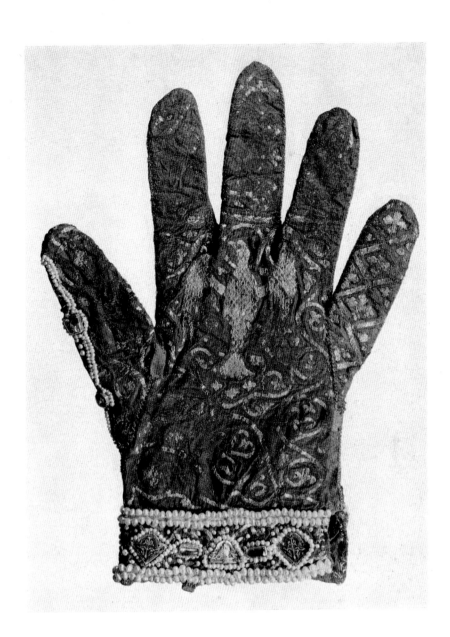

68 and 70 Gloves of the Emperor Frederick II,
part of insignia of the Holy Roman Empire.
Sicily, Palermo, before 1220.

69 and 71 Lower cuff of the alb,
part of insignia of the Holy Roman Empire.
Sicily, Palermo, 1181.

72 Chasuble of Pope Boniface VIII, detail.
South Italy or Sicily. c. 1200.

73 Medallion: Christ Pantocrator.
Byzantine, c. 1200.

74/75 Reliquary pouch, front and back.
Byzantine, 12th century.

46

76 Dossal, detail of eagles.
Italy, Sicily (?), beginning of 13th century.

77 Dossal, detail of griffins.
Italy, Sicily (?), beginning of 13th century.

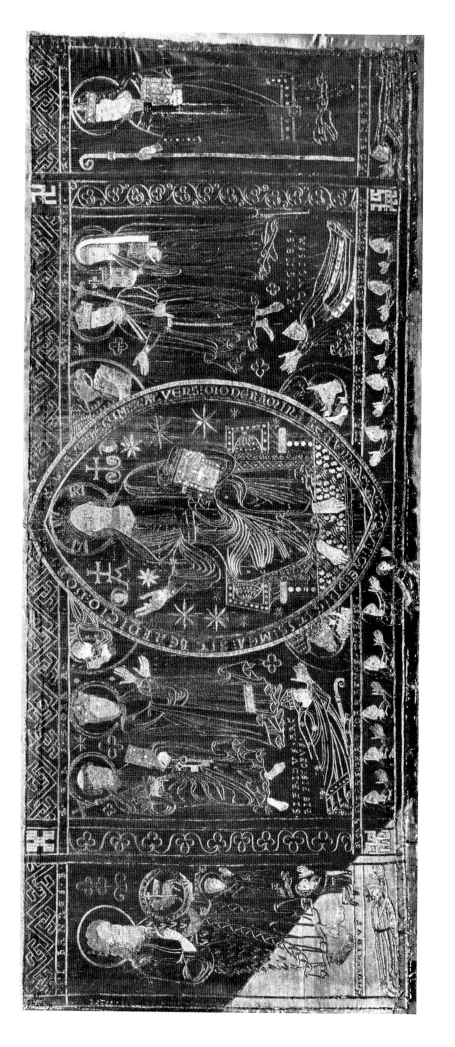

78 The Rupertsberg altar frontal.
Rhineland, first third of 15th century.

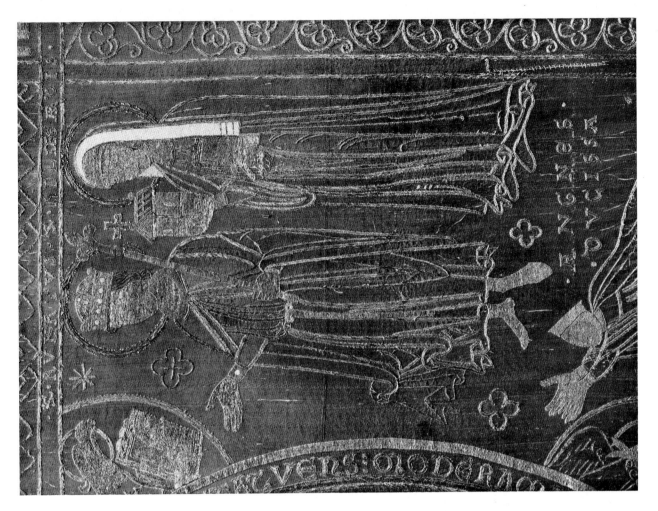

79/80 The Rupertsberg altar frontal, two details.
Rhineland, first third of 15th century.

49

81/82 Altar cloth, fragment, two details.
Rhineland (?), end of 12th century.

GABRIEL · S MARIA

83 Altar cloth, detail of the Annunciation.
Rhineland (?), end of 12th century.

84 Altar cloth, detail of the Ascension.
Rhineland (?), end of 12th century.

85 Altar cloth, corner detail.
Lombardy, end of 12th (?) century.

86 The so-called cloak of the Emperor Otto IV.
England, c. 1200.

87–90 The so-called cloak of the Emperor Otto IV, details.
England, c. 1200.

91 Dalmatic with centaurs and stags.
England, beginning of 13th century.

92 Dalmatic, detail of stag.
England, beginning of 13th century.

93 Dalmatic, detail of centaur.
England, beginning of 13th century.

94 Dalmatic, detail of lion.
England (?), c. 1200.

95/96 Mitre.
England, end of 12th century.

97　The Clare Chasuble, front view.
England, late 13th century, before 1294.

98 The Clare Chasuble, back view.
England, late 13th century, before 1294.

99 The Grandson altar frontal, side section.
England, c. 1300.

100 Christ in Majesty, embroidered panel.
England, c. 1300.

101 Cope.
England, c. 1275–1280.

V Chasuble, detail of orphrey showing the stem of Jesse.
England, c. 1330.

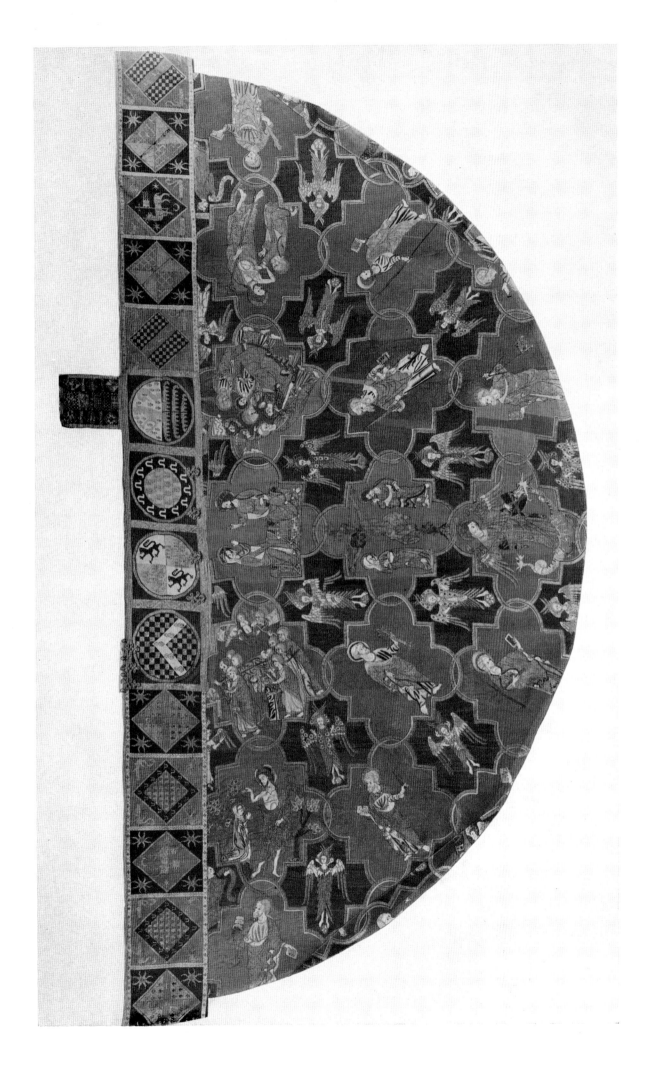

102 The Syon Cope.
England, c. 1300.

65

103 Detail from a cope.
England, second quarter of the 14th century.

104 The Vatican Cope, detail.
England, c. 1280.

105 Cope, detail of St. Andrew.
England, beginning of 14th century.

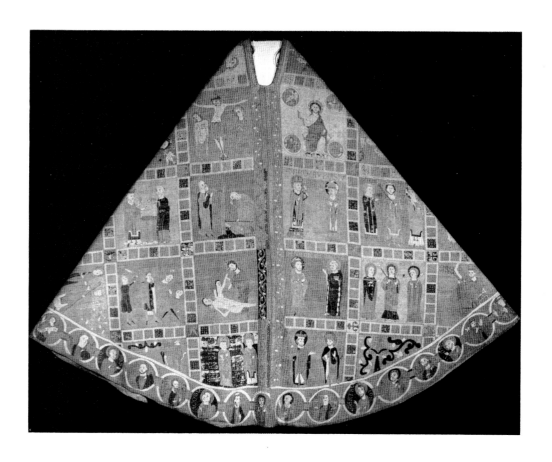

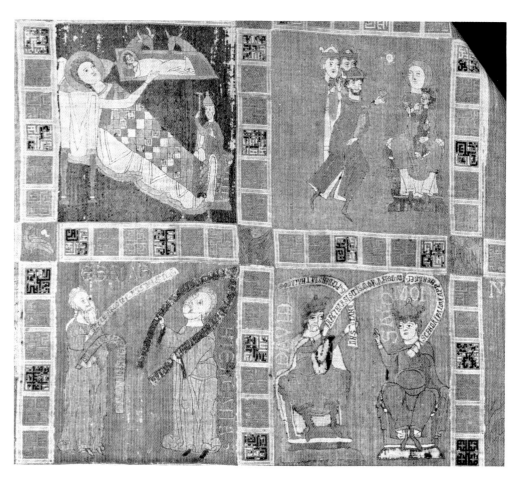

106/107 Bell chasuble, below: detail of back.
South-west Germany, end of 12th century.

VI Bell chasuble, detail showing the creation of woman.
South-west Germany, end of the 12th century.

108/109   Bell chasuble, details of back.
South-west Germany, end of 12th century.

110 Tapestry, detail.
Lower Saxony, c. 1180.

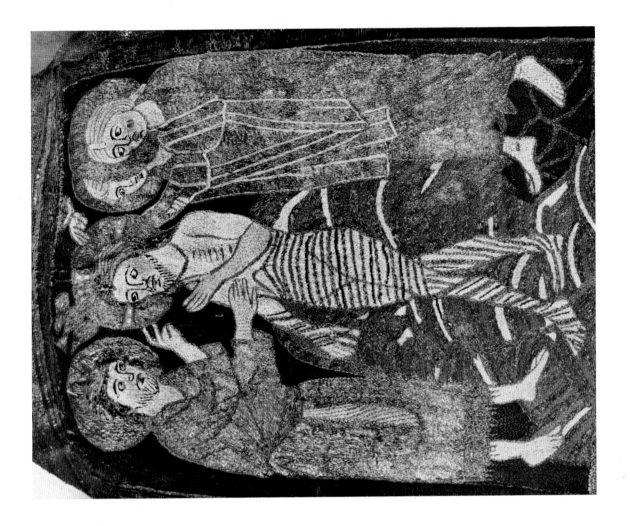

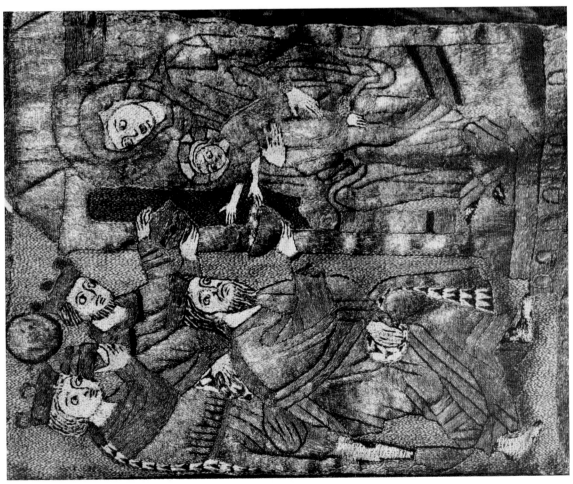

113 Chasuble, back view.
Göss (Styria), second to third quarter of the 13th century.

114–116 Altar curtain, complete and details.
Göss (Styria), mid-13th century.

74

117/118 Dalmatic, front and back.
Göss (Styria), mid-13th century.

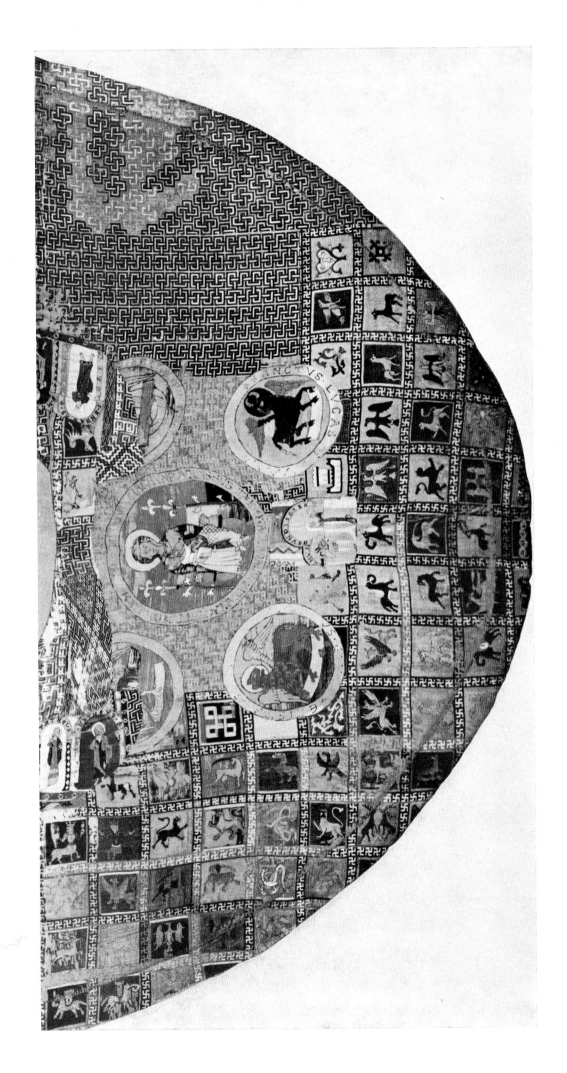

119 Cope.
Göss (Styria), mid-15th century.

75

120/121 Bell chasuble, details.
Upper Rhine, latter half of the 15th century.

122 Bell chasuble.
Upper Rhine, latter half of the 15th century.

77

123/124 Altar curtain, complete and detail.
Rome, c. 1300.

125 Altar curtain, detail.
Rome, c. 1300.

126/127 The Grandson altar curtain, complete and detail.
The work of a Greek artist working in the West.
Beginning of 13th century.

VII The Grandson altar curtain, detail of St. Gabriel.
Work of a Greek artist working in the West.
Beginning of the 13th century.

128 Eucharist cloth.
Byzantine, end of 13th century.

129/130 Linen strip with tracings and unfinished embroidery. Italy, Umbria, mid-14th century.

131 "Il lenzuolo della Beata Benvenuta Bojani", altar curtain, detail.
Friaul, end of 13th century.

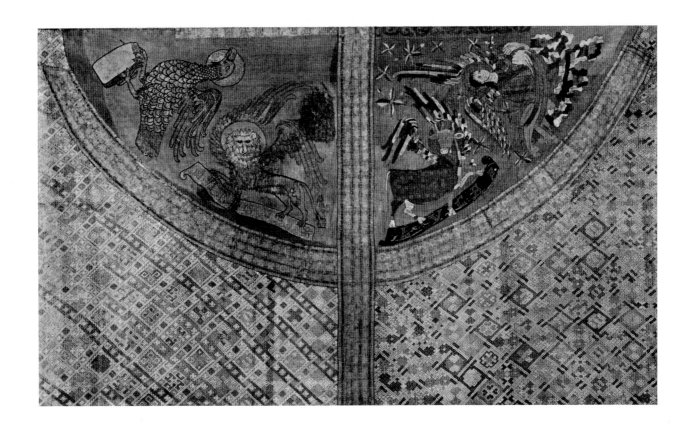

132 Chasuble, detail showing symbols of the Evangelists.
Venice, beginning of 13th century.

133 ''Il lenzuolo della Beata Benvenuta Bojani'', altar curtain, detail.
Friaul, end of 13th century.

134 "Il lenzuolo della Beata Benvenuta Bojani", altar curtain, detail.
Friaul, end of 13th century.

85

135/136 Altar curtain of Jacopo di Cambi, complete and detail.
Florence, 1336.

137/139 Altar curtain of Jacopo di Cambi, details from the border.
Florence, 1336.

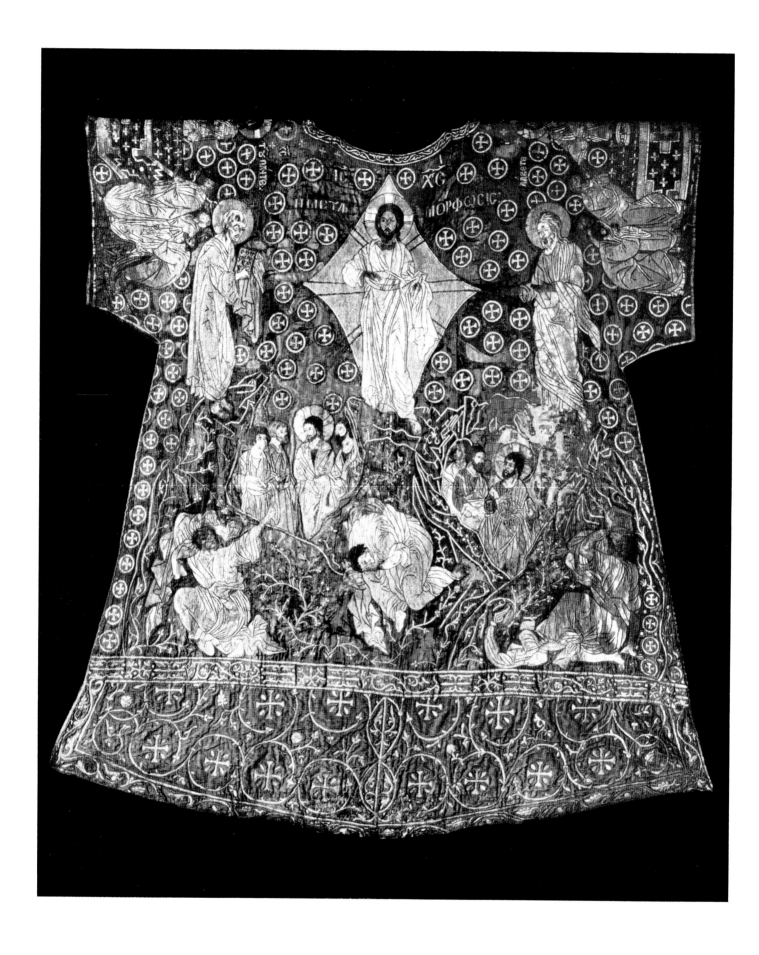

140 So-called dalmatic of Charlemagne, back view.
Byzantine, 14th century.

141 So-called dalmatic of Charlemagne, detail.
Byzantine, 14th century.

142 Linen hanging, detail.
Lower Saxony, mid-13th century.

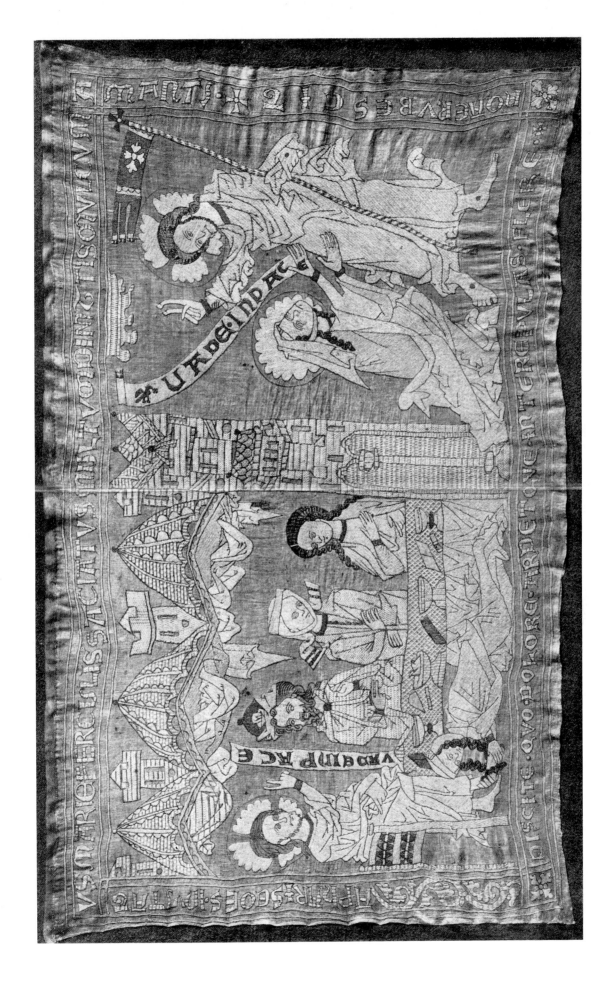

145 Linen hanging.
Lower Saxony, mid-15th century.

144/145 Altar frontal, complete and detail.
Lower Saxony, c. 1250.

146 Lenten altar cloth, detail.
Lower Saxony, mid-13th century.

147/148 Altar curtain, details.
Lower Saxony, turn of the 13th/14th centuries.

149/150 Altar curtain, details.
Lower Saxony, turn of the 13th/14th centuries.

151 Table cloth, left half.
Switzerland, 14th century.

152/153 Table cloth, right half and detail.
Switzerland, 14th century.

154/155 Altar cloth, complete and detail.
Hesse, c. 1300.

156/157   Altar cloth, details of border.
Hesse, c. 1300.

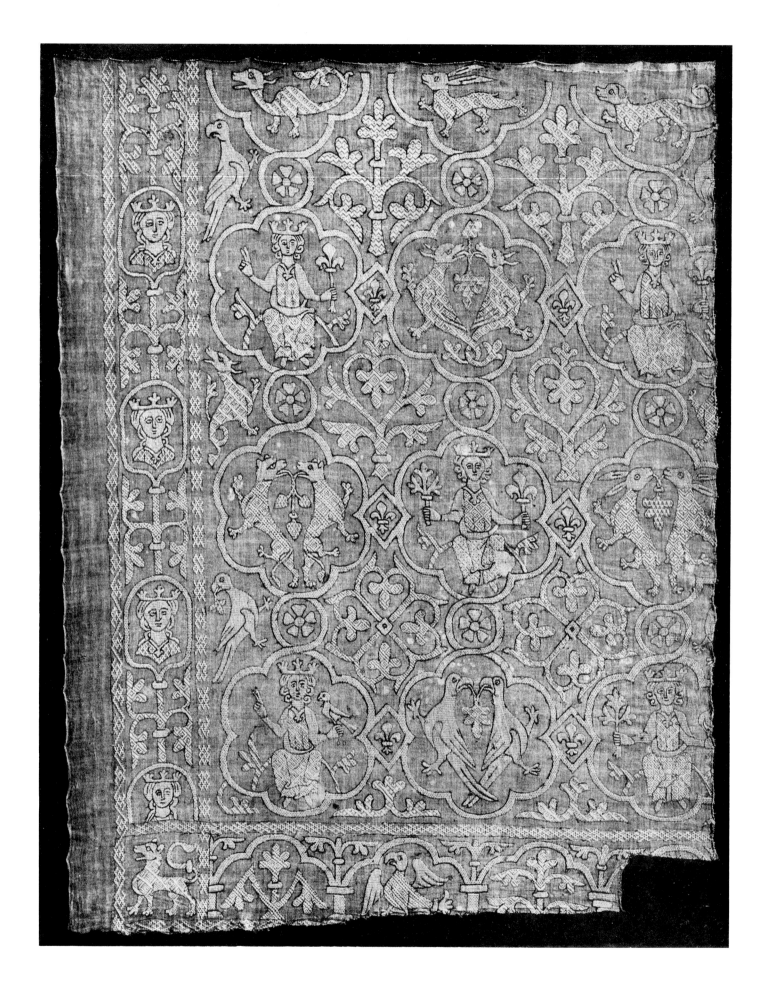

158 Altar cloth, fragment.
Lower Saxony, c. 1300.

159 Linen cloth.
Lower Saxony, second quarter of the 14th century.

160/161 Altar cloth, complete and detail.
Hesse, c. 1350.

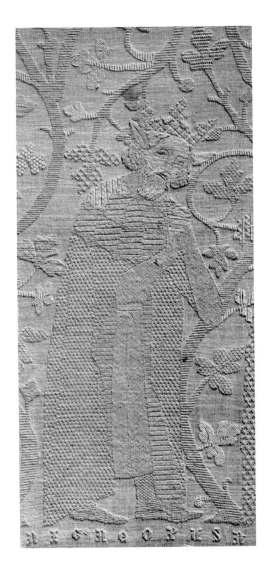

162/164 Altar cloth, details.
Hesse, c. 1350.

165/167 (top and bottom left)
Lectern cover, details.
Probably Lübeck. 14th century.

104

168 Altar cloth, detail.
Westphalia, 14th century.

169 ''Coperta Guicciardini'', quilted cover, detail.
Sicily, c. 1400.

170/171 Altar frontal from Bamberg cathedral complete and detail.
South Germany, c. 1300.

172 Altar curtain.
Upper Rhine (?), first half of the 14th century.
173 Altar curtain showing arbor vitae, right half.
Rhineland, end of 14th century.

107

174 Cope, detail of the hood.
Switzerland, 1318.

175 Cope.
Switzerland, 1318.

176 Hanging, detail from scenes of the legend of St. Nicholas. Lower Saxony, latter half of the 14th century.

177 Hanging. Detail: from the legend of St. Margaret. Lower Saxony, c. 1290.

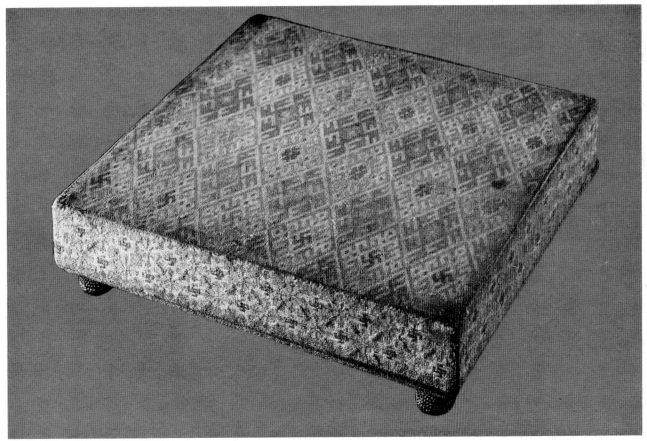

178/179 Cushion and corporal box.
Westphalia, 14th century.

111

180 Altar curtain, detail.
Lower Saxony, 14th century.

VIII Altar frontal, detail: The Coronation of the Virgin.
Lower Saxony, latter half of the 13th century.

181 Tapestry, detail with Prophets Hosea and Jonah.
Lower Saxony, c. 1300.

113

182/183 Rationale, details.
South Germany, c. 1320–1340.

184 Rationale.
South Germany. c. 1320–1340.

185/186 The "Malterer
tapestry", details.
Upper Rhine,
c.1310–1320.

IX The "Malterer tapestry", detail.
Upper Rhine, c. 1310–1320.

187/188 Backcloth, heraldic tapestry.
Upper Rhine. c. 1550.

189 Tapestry, detail.
Iceland, 14th century.
190 Panel of a canopy.
Sweden, 15th century.
191 Tapestry, detail.
Iceland, 16th century.

192 Altar curtain, scene from the Life of the Virgin.
Iceland, 14th century.

119

193 The Tristram tapestry.
Lower Saxony, c. 1300.

194 Tristram tapestry, detail: Tristram in the skiff.
Lower Saxony, c. 1300.

195 Tristram tapestry, detail: Tristram bathing (1:1).
Lower Saxony, c. 1300.

196/197 Altar curtain showing "The seven ages of Our Lord". Above: detail of the Ascension. Austria, 1340–1350.

X Altar frontal, detail: Christ before Pontius Pilate, from "The seven ages of Our Lord".
Austria, 1340–1350.

198/199 The Königsfeld altar curtain, detail and complete.
Upper Rhine, between 1334 and 1365.

200 The Königsfeld altar curtain,
detail showing St. Margaret.
Upper Rhine, between 1334 and 1365.

201/202 Altar curtain showing "The seven ages of
Our Lord", details from the border.
Austria, 1340–1350.

203/204 Altar curtain of Giovanni di Nicosia. Below: detail of the Coronation of the Virgin.
Pisa, 1325.

127

205/206 The Salzburg altar curtain, both halves.
Austria, c. 1520.

207 The Salzburg altar curtain, detail of the Pietà.
Austria, c. 1320.

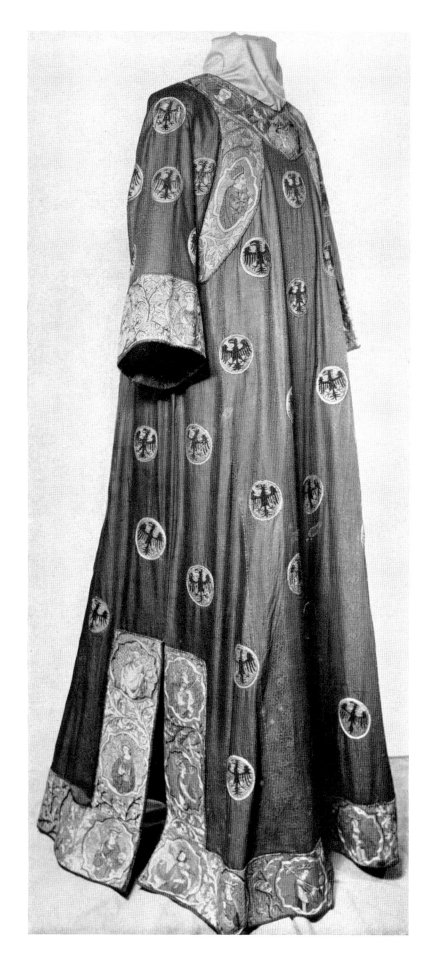

208/209 Dalmatic, insignia of the Holy Roman Empire. Right: detail of orphrey.
Upper Germany, c. 1520.

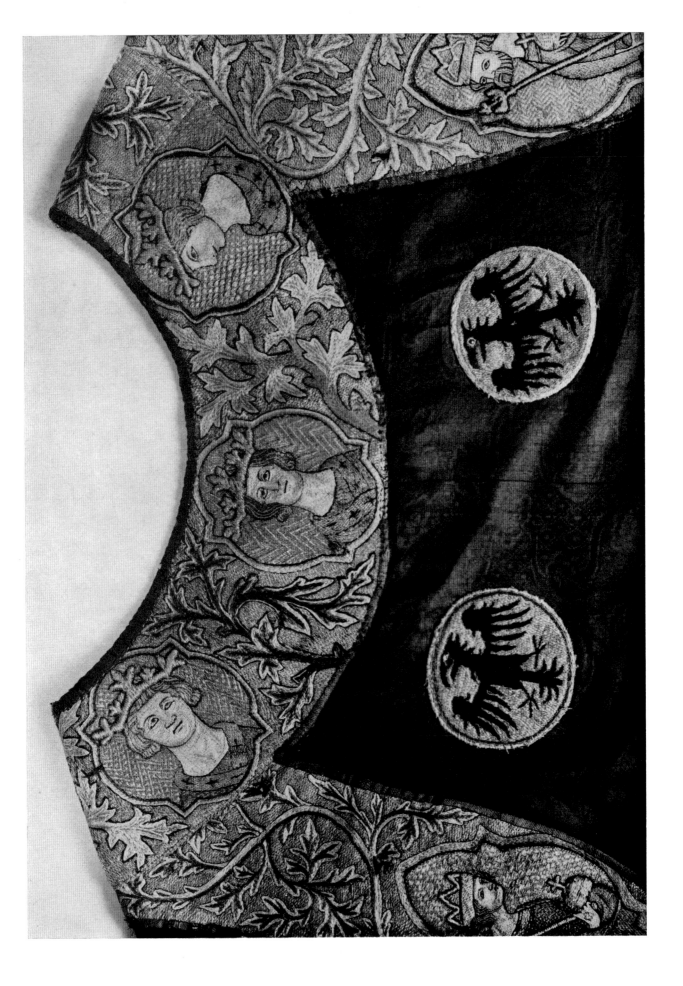

210 Dalmatic, insignia of the Holy Roman Empire, detail.
Upper Germany, c. 1520.

211 Chasuble, embroidered with eagles.
Germany, latter half of the 13th century.

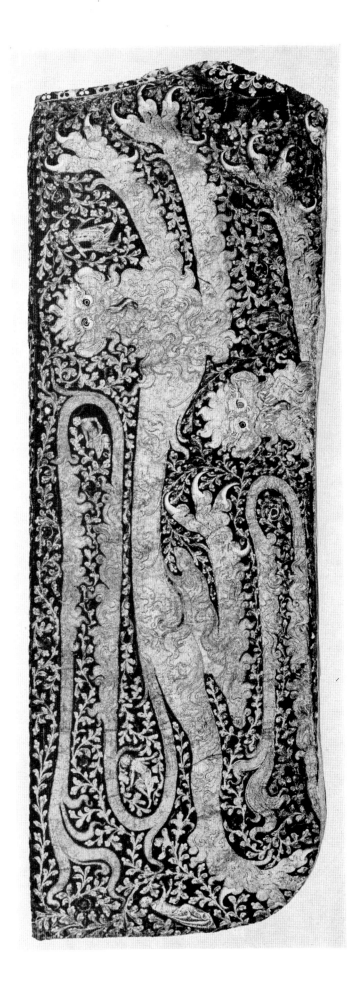

212/213 Two fragments of a coat-of-arms.
Lower Rhine or southern Netherlands, mid-14th century.

214 Embroidered pouch, front, detail: Lady and falconer.
France, Paris (?), latter half of the 14th century.

215 Embroidered pouch. Back, detail: Falconer.
France, Paris (?), latter half of the 14th century.

216 Almoner pouch with lovers.
France, Paris (?), c. 1340.

217/218 Almoner pouch with lovers, front and back.
France, mid-14th century.

XI Pouch showing lovers (Aumônière).
France, Paris (?), c. 1340.

219/220 Mitre of Jean de Marigny,
front and back.
North France, mid-14th century.

221 Alms purse, (Aumônière), with musicians.
France, Paris (?), mid-14th century.

222 Alms purse (Aumônière).
France, Paris (?), mid-14th century.

139

224 Mitre.
Paris, c. 1380.

223 Mitre from the Sainte Chapelle, Paris, back view.
Paris, c. 1380–1390.

225 Mitre from the Sainte Chapelle, Paris, front view.
Paris, c. 1380–1390.

226/227 Embroidered triptych. Below: detail of the Passion.
Paris, c. 1410.

142

228 St. John the Baptist.
France, c. 1400.

229 Tapestry with lovers, detail.
Bavaria, c. 1570–1380.

XII Tapestry showing lovers, detail.
Bavaria, c. 1370–1380.

230 Tapestry showing the Tristram legend.
North Germany, latter half of the 14th century.
231 Embroidered picture, detail.
Bohemia, c. 1370.

232/233 The Pirna altar frontal. Below: detail of a bishop. Bohemia, c. 1360.

234/235 The Pirna altar frontal, details of both halves.
Bohemia, c. 1360.

236 Altar hanging, detail.
Southern Bohemia, c. 1370–1380.

257 Ornamental hanging: Christ in the wine-press and the mercy-stool. Franconia. c. 1580.

258/259 Chasuble. Right: detail from orphrey.
Bohemia, end of the 14th century.

240 Chasuble.
Bohemia, c. 1380–1390.

241 Chasuble, detail from orphrey.
Southern Bohemia, beginning of the 15th century.

XIII Chasuble cross, detail.
Bohemia or Eastern Germany, c. 1410.

242 Embroidered hood of a cope.
Bohemia, early 15th century.

243–246 Chasuble belonging to Bishop George of Liechtenstein. Details from orphreys.
Austria or Bohemia, c. 1410.

247/248 Trimming on dalmatic belonging to Bishop George of Liechtenstein.
Austria or Bohemia, c. 1410.

249 Lid of a pyx: Agnus Dei.
South Germany, c. 1450–1470.

250 Embroidered velvet cloth.
Danzig, late 15th century.

251 Morse of a cope, detail: St. Magdalen.
Probably Danzig, early 15th century.

252 Border of an altar curtain.
Detail of St. Peter and John the Evangelist.
Danzig, mid-15th century.

253 Angels as supporters, detail from a coffin covering.
Netherlands, end of 15th century.

254 Altar frontal, central section. Mass vestments of the Order of the Golden Fleece.
Netherlands, probably Brussels, mid-15th century.

255 Mantle of the Virgin, detail. Mass vestments of the Order of the Golden Fleece.
Netherlands, probably Brussels, mid-15th century.

XIV Mantle of the Virgin, detail: St. Barbara. Mass vestments of the Order of the Golden Fleece.
Netherlands, probably Brussels, mid-15th century.

256 Mantle of the Virgin. Mass vestments of the Order of the Golden Fleece. Netherlands, probably Brussels, mid-15th century.

257 Dossal. Mass vestments of the Order of the Golden Fleece. Netherlands, probably Brussels, mid-15th century.

258 Altar frontal. Mass vestments of the Order of the Golden Fleece. Netherlands, probably Brussels, mid-15th century.

259 Dossal, detail showing the mercy-stool.
Mass vestments of the Order of the Golden Fleece.
Netherlands, probably Brussels, mid-15th century.

260 Dossal, detail of God the Father.
Mass vestments of the Order of the Golden Fleece.
Netherlands, probably Brussels, mid-15th century.

261/262 Dossal and altar frontal, details of the prophets Micha and David.
Mass vestments of the Order of the Golden Fleece.
Netherlands, probably Brussels, mid-15th century.

265/264 Dossal and Mantle of Christ, details of St. Peter and prophet. Mess vestments of the Order of the Golden Fleece. Netherlands, probably Brussels, mid-15th century.

167

265 Dalmatic. Mass vestments of the Order of the Golden Fleece.
Netherlands, probably Brussels, mid-15th century.

XV Meßornat des Ordens vom Goldenen Vlies, Tunicella, Ausschnitt: Der heilige Eustachius.
Niederlande, wahrscheinlich Brüssel, zweites Viertel des 15. Jahrhunderts.

266 Mantle of Christ, detail. Mass vestments of the Order of the Golden Fleece.
Netherlands, probably Brussels, mid-15th century.

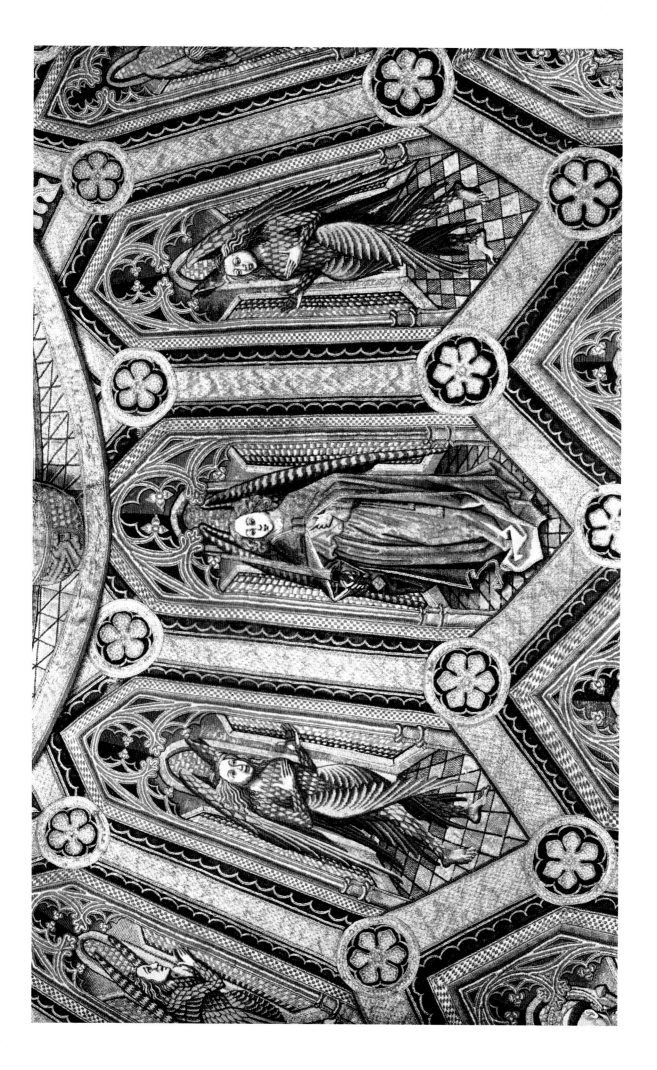

267 Mantle of Christ, detail. Mass vestments of the Order of the Golden Fleece. Netherlands, probably Brussels, mid-15th century.

268 Mantle of Christ. Mass vestments of the Order of the Golden Fleece. Netherlands, probably Brussels, mid-15th century.

269–272 Four pictures of the sacraments
from the morse of cope.
Netherlands, third quarter of the 15th century.

XVI Embroidered hood of a cope, detail: the Sacrament.
Netherlands, mid-15th century.

273 Embroidered hood of a cope. The Sacrament.
Netherlands, third quarter of the 15th century.

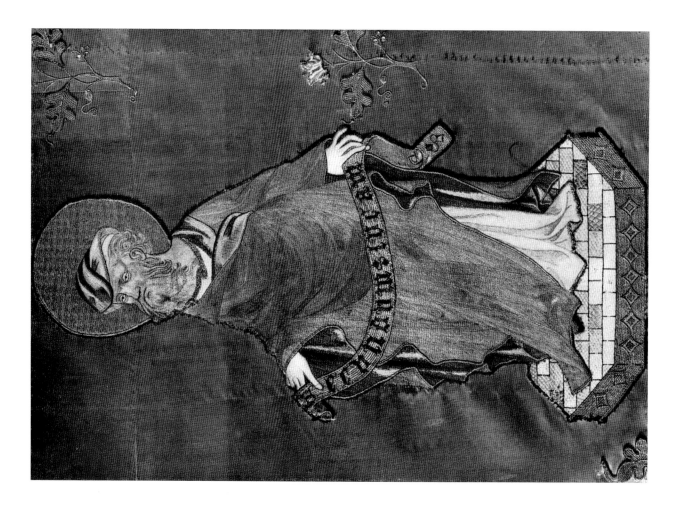

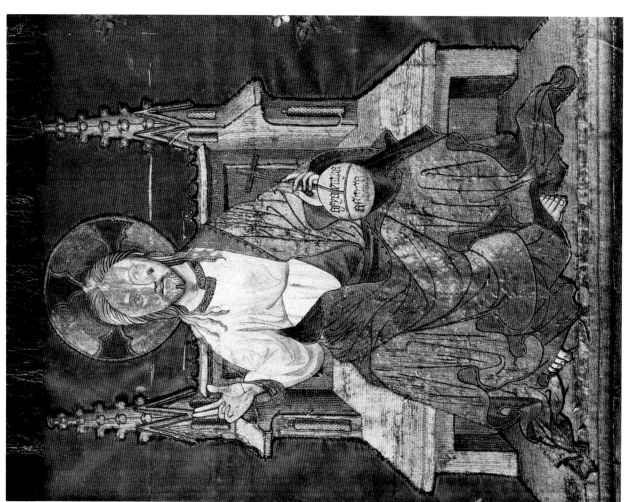

274/275 Altar frontal. Details of Christ enthroned and St. Luke.
Catalonia, c. 1400.

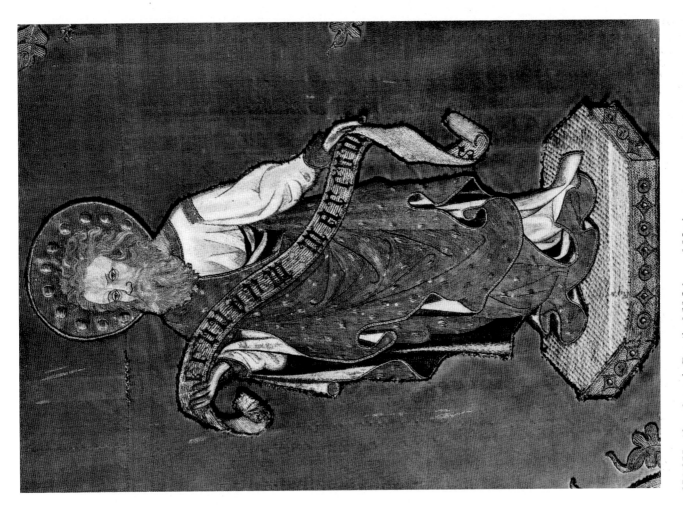

276/277 Altar frontal. Detail of SS John and Mark.
Catalonia, c. 1400.

278 Altar frontal. Detail of St. Matthew.
Catalonia, c. 1400.

279 Altar frontal of Henry IV of Castile, detail.
Spain, mid-15th century.

280/281 Altar curtain by Antonio Sadorni:
St. George and the Dragon.
Below: detail of crowd.
Catalonia. c. 1460.

282 Altar curtain by Antonio Sadorni, detail.
Catalonia, c. 1460.
283 Badge of the Order of the Dragon.
South Germany, c. 1450.

179

284/285 Altar curtain, complete and detail.
Catalonia, c. 1480.

286/287 Altar curtain, details.
Valencia, 1474.

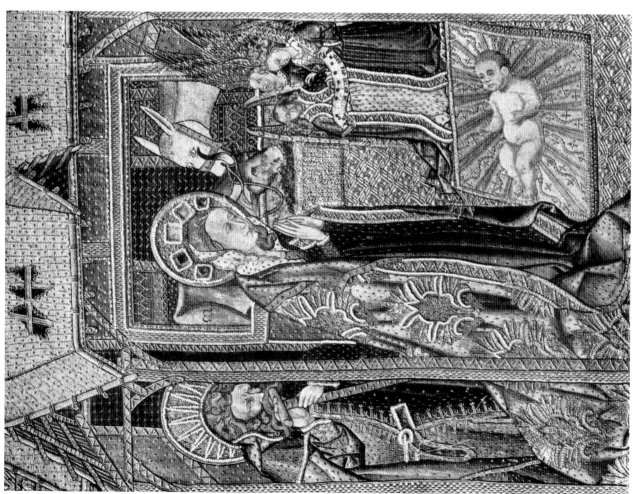

288/289 "Frontale rico", details of the Nativity and the Epiphany. Castile. 1485–95.

290/291 "Frontale rico", details of Joseph and a King. Castile, 1485–95.

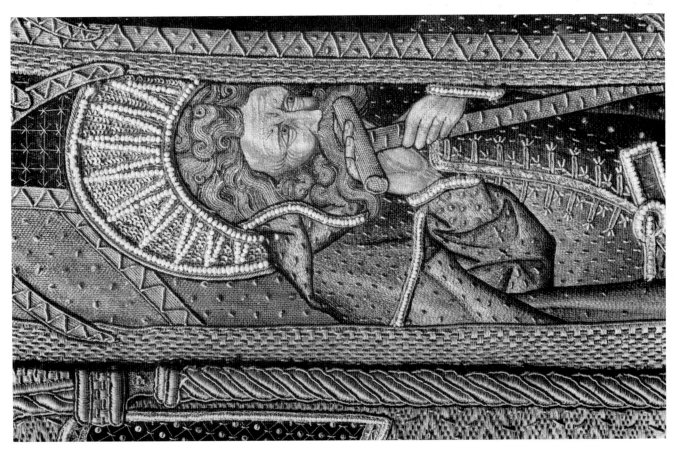

292 (top left) Orphrey of a chasuble, detail.
Spain, c. 1470.
293 (bottom left) Angel from the orphrey of a cope.
Spain, mid-15th century.
294 St. George, fragment.
Stockholm, mid-15th century.

295 Embroidered chasuble, detail: Virgin and Child. Studio of the painter Albertus.
Stockholm, end of 15th century.

hir gift em de konig den lear an the em late buwen en pallas ko

m arm des konigues broder in keyt he wedder up van dode hur is d

296 The Thomas tapestry, detail.
Lower Saxony, end of 14th century.

297 The Thomas tapestry, detail.
Lower Saxony, end of 14th century.

298 Tapestry, fragment showing lovers and musician.
Franconia, c. 1470.

XVII Elizabeth tapestry, detail: Elizabeth's nightly flagellation.
Lower Saxony, Convent of Wienhausen, late 15th century.

299/300 Desk cover or curtain.
Germany, Upper Rhine, 1500–1510.

301 Backcloth.
Franconia. c. 1480.

302 Tapestry: St. Sebastian.
Franconia, end of 15th century.

303 Long cushion cover.
South Germany, third quarter of the 16th century.

304 "Tapestry of Death" – a shroud.
Upper Rhine, latter half of the 15th century.

XVIII Backcloth, detail.
Franconia, c. 1480.

XIX Tapestry picture: Adoration of the Magi.
Swabia or Franconia, c. 1450.

305 Tapestry: Adam and Eve.
South-east Germany, beginning of the 16th century.

306/307 Embroidered linen. Below: detail of central panel.
Upper Rhine, late 15th century.

308/309 Embroidered linen, two details of end panels.
Upper Rhine, late 15th century.

195

510/515 Chasuble of the Palatine Count, Peter Kmita, details from the life of St. Stanislaus. Cracow, 1504.

314/315 Two wings of an altar reliquary.
South Germany, Franconia (?), 1519.

316 Chasuble, detail from embroidered orphrey.
Austria, c. 1470.

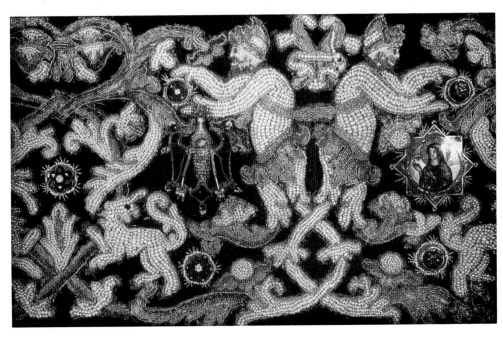

317 Corner square of the Julius banner of Basle.
Upper Rhine, 1513
318 Paliotto, detail.
Sicily, c. 1520–1540.

319 Altar curtain by Geri di Lapo,
detail.
Florence, between 1322–57.

320 Chasuble, detail:
Marriage of the Virgin.
Florence, towards mid-15th century.

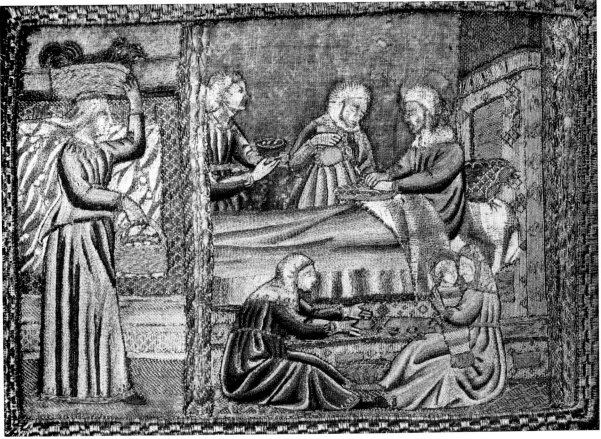

321–322 Altar frontal, details of the frieze.
Florence, mid-15th century.

523 Cope with embroidered hood and orphreys.
Florence, c. 1420–1450.

524 Dalmatic, detail of border showing the Presentation of Christ. Umbria, end of 15th century.

325 Salome with the head of John the Baptist, after a design by Antonio Pollaiuolo.
Florence, 1466–1479.

326 The birth of St. John the Baptist, after a design by Antonio Pollaiuolo.
Florence, 1466–1479.

327 Unfinished embroidery in silk on linen, detail.
Italy, mid 16th century.
328 Embrodery in silk on linen, detail.
Italy, mid-16th century.

329 Embroidery in silk on linen, detail.
Italy, latter half of 16th century.
330 Linen cloth, detail.
Italy, c. 1500.

551 The Loves of Jupiter, fragment. Italy, mid-16th century.

XX The Loves of Jupiter, detail: Asteria and Jupiter as an eagle.
Italy, mid-16th century.

332/333 Altar curtain, the Eucharist. Below: detail of left hand panels.
Brabant, first third of the 16th century.

334 Chasuble, detail from orphrey.
Florence, late 16th century.

555 Paliotto.
Florence, third quarter of the 16th century.

336 Linen cloth,
detail: Tobias and the Angel, after Hans Holbein the Younger.
Switzerland, 1563.
337 Linen cloth: the signs of the heavenly bodies and zodiac.
South Germany, mid-16th century.

212

538/539 Linen cloth, details: the signs of the heavenly bodies and zodiac.
South Germany, mid-16th century.

340 (top) Tapestry: women gathering flax.
South Germany, 1544.
341 (below left) Tapestry, detail: David and Bathsheba.
Switzerland, Zürich (?), 1522.
342 (below right) Tapestry: the weekly wash.
Switzerland, 1556.

344 Embroidered songbook cover.
Augsburg, 1530.
345 Linen cloth with embroidery in silk, detail.
Italy or Spain, 16th century.

XXI Sampler.
Bavaria, 1706.

346/347 Handkerchief. Below: detail of figures.
Moravia (?), 1560.

348 Tapestry, family tree of St. Ulric, detail.
Switzerland, Zürich, 1568.
549 Frieze showing the coat-of-arms of the Archduke Ferdinand, Count of Tyrol (1529–1595).
South Germany. Second half of the 16th century.

Von MARIA IST GE- BOREN IHS CHS MA I IVI

Ioleph.

MARIA

IHS

350 Linen embroidery, detail: The Holy Family.
Upper Germany or Switzerland, 1591.
351 Tapestry: Children at play.
South Germany, 1553.

ICH BIN FRANTZOSE WOL BEKANT
MEINEM HERRN DEM DIENE ICH
BEI MEINER KLEIDVNG BLEIBE ICH

...CHSEINEMSTANTSDAN...

SO BIN ICH DER HOHE DEVTSCHE GEN...
ALLER NATION KLEIDVNG GEFELT MIR WOL
WEIS DOCH NICHT WIE ICHS MACHEN SOL
MIR DOCH EINE BAS DAN DIE ANDER GEFELT
DAMIT ICH EIN ANSEHEN...HAB ALS EIN HELT
SO WIL ICH HIN ZVM...WERCK MAN GAN
VND IM DIE SACHE SE...BERZEIGEN AN

352/353 Chimney hangings, two details.
Germany, Leipzig (?), 1571.
354/355 Shields of the guilds, relief embroidery
by Wolf Popp. Passau, 1574–1575.

556 Linen hangings: The wizard of Virgil's trap for marriage breakers.
Switzerland, 1575.

357 Tapestry carpet, corner detail.
England, mid-16th century.
358 Tapestry carpet.
Switzerland, Schaffhausen, 1533.

559 Tapestry, detail of the Tristram legend.
Alsace, 1559.

360 Dress coat.
Persia, 17th century.

361 Cover.
North-west Persia (Caucasian Provinces),
16–17th century.

XXII Dress coat, detail.
Persia, 17th century.

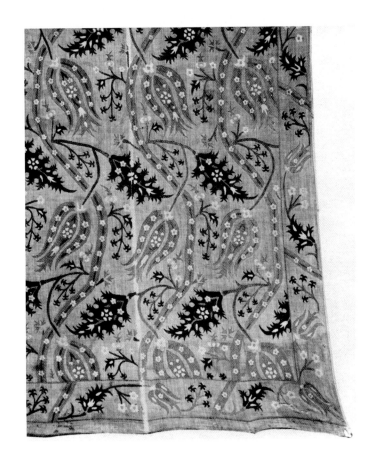

362 Cloth, corner detail.
Turkey, 17th to 18th century.
363 Cloth, corner detail.
North-west Persia, 17th century.
364 Wall hanging, detail.
Turkey, 18th century.

365 Hanging. detail with grotesques.
France, latter half of the 16th century.

366 Part of bed hangings.
France, c. 1560.

367 Tapestry: Jeanne d'Albret as Venus.
Paris, c. 1600.
368 Bed hangings, detail.
France, c. 1560.

369 Lectern cover, detail: Birth of St. John the Baptist.
Spain, latter half of the 16th century.

370 Embroidered morse of a cope, detail: Dance of the Dead.
Netherlands, early 16th century.
371 Gold embroidery.
Italy, 1557.

230

572 Chalice cover.
France, c. 1668.

574 Chasuble of Bishop C. Madruzzo.
Italy, between 1600–1629.

375 Chasuble of the Elector Casimir Anselm of Mainz.
Germany, second quarter of the 17th century.

576 The Bradford table carpet.
England, late 16th century.

577 Tapestry, banquet of Lucretia. England, late 16th century.

378–380 Valence from a bed canopy, details.
England, end of the 16th century.

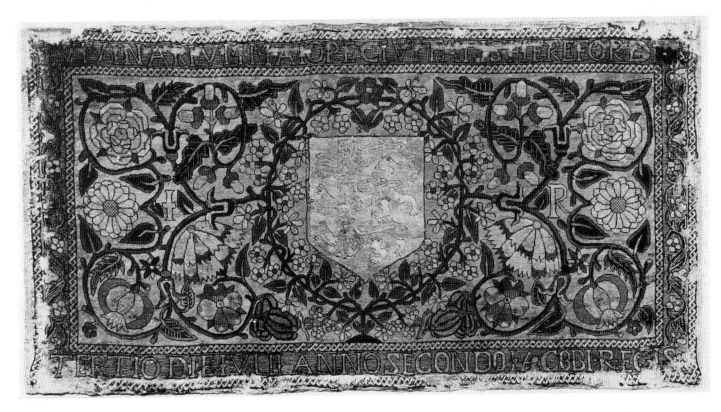

381 Long cushion worked by Mary Hulton.
England, early 17th century.
382 Long cushion cover bearing the Arms of the City of Hereford.
England, 1604.

238

384 Camisole.
Denmark (?), c. 1640.

239

585 Pin-cushion.
England, late 16th century.
386 Three purses, one with a pin-cushion, the third like a bunch of grapes.
England, early 17th century.

XXIII Gloves, pin-cushion and prayer book of Elizabeth Stuart.
Netherlands (?), beginning of 17th century.

387 A pair of lady's mittens.
England, 16th to 17th century.
388 Lady's gloves.
England, early 17th century.

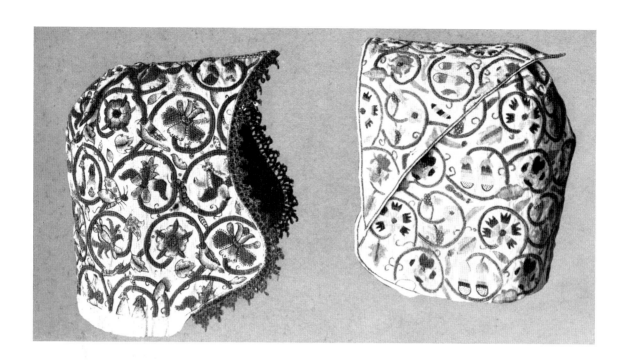

389 Lady's coifs (made up).
England, late 17th century.
390 Lady's bodice.
England, late 16th century.

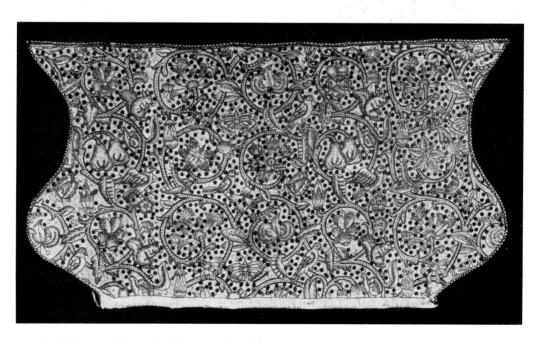

391 Lady's embroidered hood (not made up).
England, late 16th century.
392 Lady's coif (not made up).
England, c. 1600.

393 Long cushion cover.
England, 16th–17th century.
394 Pillow cover.
England, late 16th century.

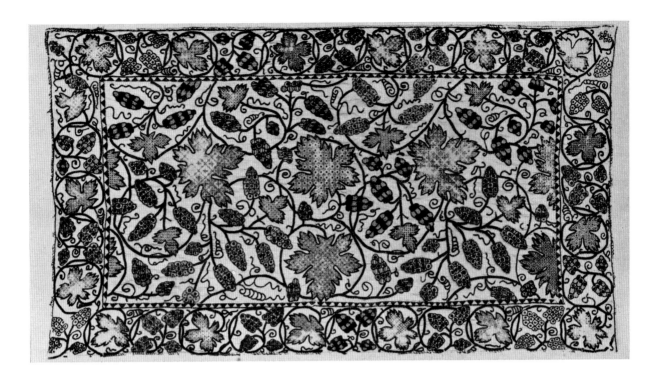

395 Pillow cover with embroidery in black silk.
England, latter half of the 16th century.
396 Embroidered picture: David and Bathsheba.
England, 1656.

597 Wedding robe of Duke William V of Bavaria.
Munich, 1568.

398 Cloth with appliqué work.
Sweden, 1630.

399 Lady's bodice.
England, latter half of the 17th century.
400 Embroidered dress, detail.
England, beginning of the 18th century.

401 Linen cloth with piqué embrodery, detail.
Sweden, beginning of the 18th century.

402 Coronation robe of King Gustav Adolf II of Sweden, back view.
Stockholm, 1617.

403 Court dress.
Dresden, beginning of 17th century.
404 Suit belonging to King Gustav Adolf II of Sweden.
Stockholm, 1617.

405 Coronation dress of King Gustav Adolf II of Sweden.
Stockholm, 1617.

406 Cover with scattered flowers, detail,
England, early 17th century.

XXIV Sash, detail.
England, 1630–40.

XXV Sleeve of a lady's bodice.
France, c. 1640–1650.

407 Bed with hangings worked by Abigail Pett.
England, latter half of the 17th century.

408 Lady's bag.
Regensburg. 1604.

409 Hunting pouch belonging to the Elector Maximilian I of Bavaria.
Munich, 1620–1630.

410 Toilet bag.
Netherlands, mid-17th century.

411/412 Embroidery on a valance.
Italy, c. 1700.

413 Tapestry.
England, c. 1675.

414 Tapestry, detail of flowers, buds and animals.
England, c. 1675.

415 Tapestry from Hatton Gardens.
England, late 17th century.

XXVI Embroidered cover of settee.
England. 1700–1720.

416 (above) Cover for a chair back.
Germany, early 18th century.
418 (below) Armchair with embroidered covering.
Germany, first half of the 18th century.

417 (above) Back of an arm-chair.
England, c. 1700.
419 (below) Arm-chair with embroidered covering.
England, 1470.

261

420 Dress coat.
India, Mogul period, early 17th century.

421 Knuckle protector against shield grip.
Indian, Mogul period 17th century.

422 Prayer mat.
India, Mogul period, c. 1700.

423 Bed curtain, detail.
England, latter half of the 17th century.

424 Bed curtain, detail.
England, late 17th century.

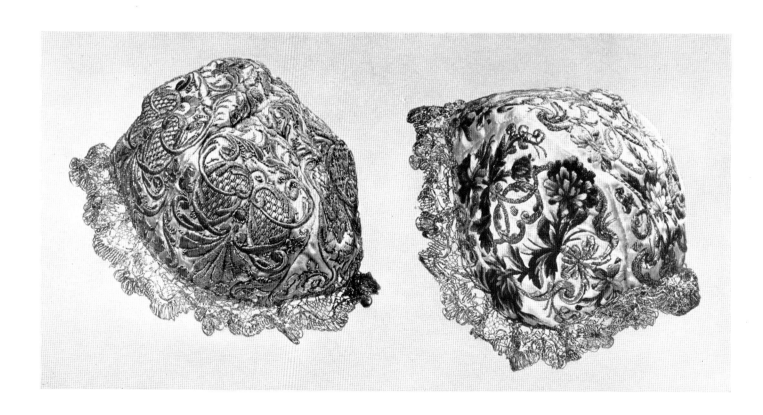

426 Christening bonnets for a boy and a girl.
Munich, 1717.

427 Christening robe.
North Germany, c. 1700.
428 White embroidery, detail.
Holland, 1694.

429 Wall hangings.
Dresden, between 1711 and 1719.

XXVII Wall covering, detail.
Dresden, between 1711 and 1719.

430 Floral tapestry.
Switzerland, 1700.

431/432 Two embroidered pictures from a set representing the eight Tâoistic immortals.
China, Ming period, probably 14th century.

455 Congratulatory rug, detail.
China, 17th century.

434 Chinese embroidered lady's dress copied from a European pattern, detail.
China, c. 1720.

455 Lady's embroidered silk dress.
Sweden, 1750–1760.

436 Gentleman's suit with silk embroidery.
Sweden or France, c. 1770.

457 Prayer carpet.
Persia (Resht), 19th century.

459 Christening shawl, detail.
Franconia. c. 1752.

458 Fire-screen.
England, 18th century.

277

440 Tapestry, part of Chinoiserie room decor.
Austria, c. 1720–1730.

441 Tapestry, detail.
Austria, 1720–1750.

442/443 Wall hangings in Favorite Castle near Rastatt.
Germany and France, c. 1720–1750.

XXVIII State bed with curtains embroidered with mythological scenes.
France, beginning of the 18th century.

444 Tapestry depicting market scenes.
Southern Netherlands, beginning of 18th century.

445 Tapestry.
Paris, 1683–84.

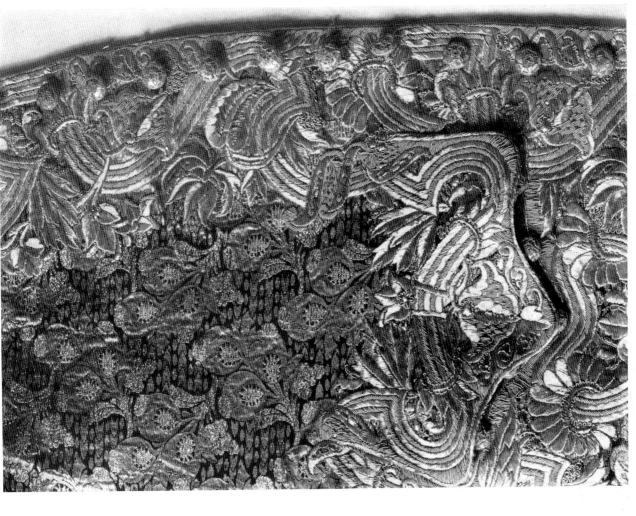

447 Suit of King Christian VI of Denmark, detail of pocket. Copenhagen, 1745.

446 Court dress of August the Strong of Saxony. 1719.

448 Chasuble embroidered with gold thread.
France, c. 1700.

449 Chasuble belonging to Cardinal Damian Hugo of Schönborn.
Germany, c. 1740.

450 Paliotto, detail.
Bologna, mid-18th century.

451 Cope lavishly embroidered with gold thread. North Italy, c. 1700.

452 Silk hangings.
North Italy, c. 1740.

XXIX Silk hangings.
North Italy. c. 1740.

453 Wall covering.
France, c. 1800.

454–456 Embroidery patterns for a gentleman's suit
and a lady's dress.
Lyons, end of the 18th century.

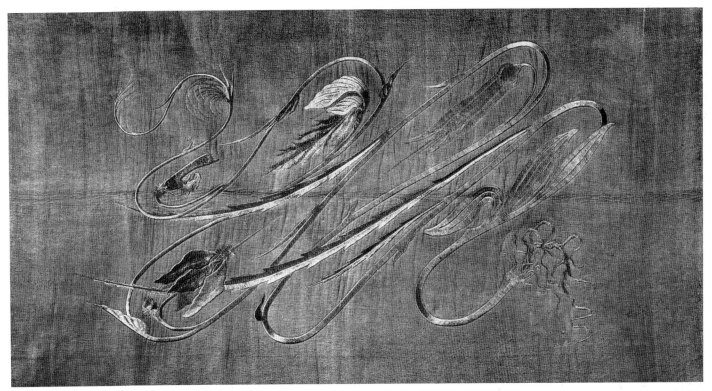

460 Tapestry: "Whipping", designed by Hermann Obrist.
Florence or Munich, c. 1895.
461 Cloth, design by Hermann Obrist, detail.
Munich, c. 1895.

294   462 Tapestry, design by William Morris.
England, 1875–1880.

463 Tapestry, design by Aristide Maillol.
France, 1896–1898.

295

464 Cover for a sofa cushion, design by Thorwald Bindesböll.
Beginning of 20th century.

1 CENTAUR, Fragment
Hellenistic, 4th–5th century
Lyon, Musée historique des Tissus (30457a)
34 × 18 cm
Red woollen twill. Red, green and brown woollen thread and white linen thread. Stem and chain stitch.

2 FRAGMENT OF EMBROIDERY
Attica, late 5th century B.C.
London, Victoria and Albert Museum (T. 200–1958)
Lozenge: 35 × 41 mm, Lion: 8 × 13 mm
Fine linen. The embroidery thread has fallen out and the pattern is traceable only from the holes left by the needle. A pacing lion with tail and one forepaw raised appears in a regular lattice of lozenges. The technique of the embroidery cannot be determined. Traces of gold and silver have been discovered by analysis and these, in conjunction with remains of textile fibres, suggest a metal strip wound round a thread. The fragments, which are said to have been found in a bronze kalpis at Koropi near Athens, are the first textiles of antiquity to be found in Attica.
Lit.: J. Beckwith, in Illustrated London News, 23rd January, 1954

3 FRAGMENT OF A WALL HANGING: HEAD OF A HUN
Noin-Ula, Northern Mongolia, 1st century B.C.
Leningrad, Hermitage
20 × 14 cm
Dark red woollen rep. Plied woollen thread in beige, brown and black tones. Laid and couched work. Other embroideries, including larger fragments of a frieze with horsemen, show stylistic and technical connections with the Chinese Empire and the classical world. They were found in the tombs of princes of the Hunnish Empire. Considered by Roman Ghirshman to be an import from Iran.
Lit.: C. Trever, Excavations in Northern Mongolia, 1924–25. Memoirs for the Academy of History of Material Culture III. Leningrad 1932, p. 29 – S. Umehara, Studies of Noin-Ula Finds in North Mongolia, Tokyo, 1960 – S. I. Rudenko, Kultura chunnow i noinulinskie kurganji. Moscow-Leningrad 1962 (russ.), p. 105 – R. Ghirshman, Iran, Munich 1962, p. 109

4 SADDLE COVER, detail: A GRIFFIN
Altai, South Siberia, 4th–3rd century B.C.
Leningrad, Hermitage
20 × 22 cm
Patchwork and applied work in dyed felt. The design is emphasised by couched cords.
Lit.: M. Griaznow, L'art ancien de l'Altai. Leningrad 1958, p. 20

5 WALL HANGING, detail: RIDER
Altai, South Siberia, 4th–3rd century B. C.
Leningrad, Hermitage
About 130 × 110 cm
The complete hanging (4.5 × 6.5 m) shows three bands with seated goddesses and horsemen and served to adorn a burial chamber (Kurgan) at Pazyryk (Siberia). Applied work in red, blue, yellow and black felt on a beige felt ground.

Lit.: S. J. Rudenko, Der zweite Kurgan von Pazyryk. Berlin 1951, pl. 88 – M. Griaznow, L'art ancien de l'Altai. Leningrad 1958, p. 21

6 FRAGMENT OF EMBROIDERY
Persia, Sassanian Empire, 6th–7th century
Athens, Benaki Museum (7001)
38 × 39.5 cm
The mounted prince is accompanied by archers and is followed by a man bearing a symbol of his rank. Linen; with white, red, green and black woollen thread. Chain stitch.
Lit.: A. Apostolaki, Kentimata Mallina. Athens 1956, p. 43

7 WALL HANGING WITH TREES, Fragment
Probably Eastern Mediterranean, 4th–5th century (?)
London, Victoria and Albert Museum (T. 233–1917)
157 × 96 cm. Trees: 17 to 25 cm
Linen ground. Woollen thread in three shades of green, dark blue, yellow, pink and violet. Chain and stem stitch. Said to have been found at Shaikh Shata near Damietta.
Lit.: Victoria and Albert Museum, London, Catalogue of Textiles from Burying-Grounds in Egypt, I Graeco-Roman Period, by A. F. Kendrick, London 1920, p. 46, No. 22
There is a hanging with the same pattern in Berlin.

8 CIRCULAR PANEL: ANNUNCIATION AND VISITATION
Coptic (?), 7th–8th century (?)
London, Victoria and Albert Museum (814–1903)
Diameter: 17.5 cm
Linen. Lustrous silk thread. Colours: light, shaded tones of green, blue, red, yellow and flesh colour. Split, satin, cross and couched stitches. The surface is completely embroidered. Well preserved, apart from four holes.
Lit.: Victoria and Albert Museum, London. Catalogue of Textiles from Burying-Grounds in Egypt, III Coptic Period, by A. F. Kendrick, London 1922, p. 57, No. 777

9/10 SO-CALLED "CHASUBLE" OF SAINTS HARLINDIS AND RELINDIS
England, Anglo-Saxon period, c. 850
Maeseyck Collegiate Church
Bands, 10 × 66 and 62 cm
Two details. Linen ground. Background of untwisted silk thread in blue, red, yellow and green. The gold thread is a metal strip wound on brown transparent animal-hair. White linen thread ground for the seed pearls, which are now missing. Couched work of fine silk thread, and minute satin stitch. Poor state of preservation. The so-called "chasuble" of Saints Harlindis and Relindis, who founded the convent of Aldeneyck in the 8th century, was discovered, together with other textiles, in their shrine; it has practically no resemblance to a chasuble. Four strips – two with a row of nine arches and two smaller ones each with two rows of five circles – are sewn to the "chasuble" which, according to an old local tradition which cannot be verified, was made by Saints Harlindis and Relindis. The embroideries are in the Anglo-Saxon style and are to be considered, according to Calberg, as an import from Great Britain during the 9th century. They are the oldest known English embroideries.

Lit.: M. Calberg in Bull. Soc. Roy. d'Archéologie de Bruxelles, October 1951, p. 1 ff.

11–13 STOLE AND MANIPLE OF ST. CUTHBERT, details
England, between 909 and 916
Durham Cathedral
Stole originally 304 × 6.5 cm. Manible 81.5 × 6.5 cm.
The fragmentary stole originally showed the sixteen major and minor prophets (three are now lost), while the maniple showed Popes Sixtus II and Gregory VI with their deacons Laurence and Peter on either side of the hand of God. On the terminal panels, half-length figures of saints; on the back, an inscription: AELFFLAED FIERI PRECEPIT – PIO EPISCOPO FRIDESTANO (Ethelfleda ordered this work for the pious Bishop Frithestan). Ground, silk taffeta (destroyed); stem and split stitch in coloured silks; the inner drawing, haloes and background in gold thread, couched with red silk. Queen Ethelfleda died in 916; Bishop Frithestan held the see of Winchester 909–31. In 934 King Athelstan (924–40) presented to the shrine of St Cuthbert at Chester-le-Street a stole, maniple and girdle which are probably identical with those now preserved at Durham.
Lit.: C. F. Battiscombe, The Relics of Saint Cuthbert, Oxford 1956, p. 375, The Stole and Maniples: a) E. Plenderleith, Technique, b) C. Hohler, Iconography, c) R. Freyhan, The Place of Stole and Maniples in Anglo-Saxon Art of the 10th Century.

14–16 STARRED CLOCK, SO CALLED "STAR-MANTLE" OF THE EMPEROR HENRY II.
South Germany; Regensburg (?), c. 1010–1020
Bamberg, Cathedral Treasury
Diameter: 297 cm. Height: 154 cm
The semi-circular mantle shows scenes from the Life of Christ together with symbols of the heavenly bodies (Fig. 15, celestial hemisphere with constellations; Fig. 16, Hercules and the Lernaean Hydra) and fourteen medallions containing nimbed busts. Latin inscriptions. Around the lower edge a dedicatory inscription in large capitals: O DECUS EUROPAE CESAR HEINRICE BEARE ANGEAT (augeat) IMPREIUM (Imperium) IBTI (tibi) REX QUI REGNA (regnet) WNE (in evum) = Ornament of Europe, Emperor Henry, Happiness be with thee, may the King who reigns to all eternity increase your Empire. Above this in small capitals: PAX ISMAHELI QUI HOC ORDINAVIT. Gold embroidery in couched work on dark violet silk twill. Very fine gold strips wound on reddish yellow silk; silk thread in white, red, blue and green. On the outlines of the figures, red couching stitches; the inner drawing and other patterns on the figures in couching stitches of other colours. Inner drawing of some figures in silk; stem stitch. In 1503 the embroideries were cut away from the ground material and re-mounted on blue Italian silk damask. At that time the cut edges were partly concealed by a thick white silk thread and partly oversewn with red silk. The original arrangement of the motifs may have been confused at that time. The mantle was given to the Emperor by Duke Ismahel of Bari (d. 1020 in Bamberg) and was probably given to Bamberg Cathedral by Henry II or his wife St. Kunigund. It was used as a cope.
Lit.: E. Bassermann-Jordan und W. M. Schmid, Der Bamberger Domschatz, Munich 1914, p. 1, No. 4 – S. Müller-Christensen, Sakrale Gewänder des Mittelalters, Ausstellungs-Katalog, Munich 1955, p. 18 – P. E. Schramm und F. Mütherich, Denkmale der deutschen Könige und Kaiser. Munich 1962, p. 163, No. 130

17–22 COLOUR PLATES I AND IV. MANTLE OF ST KUNIGUND
South Germany, c. 1020
Bamberg; Cathedral Treasury
Diameter: 286 cm. Height: 162.5 cm. Detail on Colour Plate IV: 27 cm high
In the middle of the back, the figure of the Youthful Christ emerging from the Gate of Heaven and surrounded by subjects relating to prophecies of his Advent and Coronation (Fig. 18: view of the whole. Fig. 20: bust with inscription: O EMANUEL REX. Colour Plate IV: Moses and the Burning Bush. Fig. 22: Virgin and Child). On the front, scenes from the lives of Saints Peter and Paul, the patron saints of Bamberg Cathedral (Fig. 17: Peter resuscitating Tabitha. Fig. 19: corner of the border, with a half circle showing Peter between the Widows. Fig. 21: corner of the border, with half circle showing Nero eaten by wolves). Gold embroidery in couched work on blue silk twill. Very fine gold strip wound on silk; silk thread in white, red, and light and dark blue. The gold threads (up to 56 threads per cm) are perpendicular to the direction of the motifs and are couched with various patterns. (Colour Plate I: enlargement from Fig. 17). Inner drawing in stem stitch with silk thread of various colours. The mantle of St. Kunigund is listed among the relics of Bamberg Cathedral as early as 1448 and was probably a gift from the Empress. In the course of a restoration in the 16th century the gold embroideries were applied to new blue satin. At that time the cut edges were covered with outlines in red silk thread. Hence the red tonality is now stronger than it was originally.
Lit.: E. Bassermann-Jordan und W. M. Schmid, Der Bamberger Domschatz, Munich 1914, p. 9, No. 13 – S. Müller-Christensen, Sakrale Gewänder des Mittelalters, Ausstellungs-Katalog, Munich 1955, p. 20 – P. E. Schramm und F. Mütherich, Denkmale der deutschen Könige und Kaiser. Munich 1962, p. 163, No. 131

23–26 MANTLE OF ST. STEPHEN
South Germany, 1031
Diameter: 268 cm. Height: 135 cm
Christ Victorious and Christ in Majesty, surrounded by Prophets, Apostles and Martyrs (Fig. 23). The medallions include portraits of King Stephen and Queen Gisela of Hungary, who commissioned this chasuble and gave it in 1031 to the Church of Székesfehérvár ("casula hec operata et data ecclesiae Sancta Maria sitae in civitate alba anno incarnationis Xpi MXXXI"). Fig. 24: St. Vincent. Figs. 25 and 26: Prophets and Apostles. Gold embroidery in couched work on dark blue silk twill. Very fine gold strip wound on yellowish silk. Red, brown, blue and green silk thread. The inner drawing of figures is in red stem stitch, in reserve in the gold embroidery. Details in coloured chain, stem and feather stitches in the architectural parts and in the wings of the angels and birds. A great variety of patterns in the couching of the gold threads. The inscriptions are in part in reserve in the gold embroidery. Queen Gisela was a sister of the German Emperor Henry II. The chasuble belongs stylistically and technically in the artistic ambience of the Emperor Henry. It was subsequently altered (considerable parts of the front edge were lost at this time) and utilised as the Coronation Mantle of the Hungarian Kings.
Lit.: É. Kovács, Casula Sancti Stephani Regis: Acta historiae artium V. Budapest 1958, p. 181

27/28 COLOUR PLATES II AND III. RIDING CLOAK, SO-CALLED "RIDER MANTLE" OF THE EMPEROR HENRY II.
Italy (?), 12th century
Bamberg, Cathedral Treasury
Diameter: 307 cm. Height: 156 cm
Semi-circular mantle with thirteen large medallions (diameter: 48 cm), in part intersected by the edge, with representations of a prince on horseback. In the spaces between the circles palmettes and birds (Fig. 28). Gold embroidery in couched work. Fine gold strip wound on silk; silk thread in red, pink, blue, yellow-green, olive-green, dark green, brown and black. The gold threads (45 threads per cm) are parallel with the warp threads of the dark blue silk twill. The embroidery was re-mounted on new ground material in the 16th

century and again in 1954. Thanks to the colours of the silk couching threads, the rich inner drawing originally made a very strong impression (Colour Plates II and III: front and back of an embroidered horseman). The combination of a crowned victor, riding over the conquered enemy, and of a princely falconer hunting lions is an unusual one, which has no parallel in Byzantine art.

Lit.: E. Bassermann-Jordan und W. M. Schmid, Der Bamberger Domschatz, Munich 1914, p. 6, No. 9 and p. 55 – S. Müller-Christensen, Sakrale Gewänder des Mittelalters, Ausstellungs-Katalog, Munich 1955, p. 20 – A. Grabar, Kunstchronik VIII, Munich 1955, p. 315 – P. E. Schramm und F. Mütherich, Denkmale der deutschen Könige und Kaiser. Munich 1962, p. 186, No. 189

29/30 COPE OF ST. KUNIGUND, DETAIL: CHRIST ENTHRONED

South Germany, c. 1010
Bamberg, Cathedral Treasury
Height of the figure: 20 cm

On the semi-circular mantle are seventy-two identical figures wearing a crown with pendants, holding an orb in the left hand and a labarum in the right hand; the figures are arranged in rows, with Latin verses between. Embroidery in gold and silk. The faces, hands and feet are completely embroidered with couched gold thread, while the robes and thrones are worked in outline only. Eyes, mouth, beard, the jewels on the crown and labarum and the patterns on the stole, cuffs and shoes are worked with red and black silk. Probably a gift from the Emperor Henry II, whose name is decipherable in the inscription, or from his wife St. Kunigund, to Bamberg Cathedral. (A restoration of the mantle during which the figures were replaced in their original arrangement was completed in 1960).

Lit.: E. Bassermann-Jordan und W. M. Schmid, Der Bamberger Domschatz, Munich 1914, p. 8, No. 12 – S. Müller-Christensen, Sakrale Gewänder des Mittelalters, Ausstellungs-Katalog, Munich 1955, p. 17 – P. E. Schramm und F. Mütherich, Denkmale der deutschen Könige und Kaiser. Munich 1962, p. 163, No. 132

31–33 THE BAYEUX TAPESTRY

Normandy – England, 1066–77
Bayeux, Musée de la reine Mathilde
Height: 0.5 to 0.55 m. Length: 70.35 m
Size of details reproduced: Fig. 31, 50 × 90 cm; Fig. 32, 50 × 97 cm: Fig. 33, 50 × 45 cm

The subject is the Conquest of England by William, Duke of Normandy, in 1066. Earl Harold travels to Normandy to visit Duke William (Figs. 31, 32). Returning to England, he allows himself to be chosen as King, but is conquered by William in the Battle of Hastings (Fig. 33). White linen. Plied woollen thread in yellow, green, red, blue and black. Inscriptions, faces, hands and outlines in chain, stem and split stitch. The remaining embroidered surfaces in laid and couched work. Probably the most famous of all embroideries, not only on account of its size and artistic importance but also as a representation of an historical event. It is not known for whom the work was executed, but it may have been for Bishop Odo of Bayeux in whose cathedral (consecrated 1077) the hanging was suspended on feast days.

Lit.: F. Stenton (ed.), The Bayeux Tapestry, London 1957

34–36 HANGING: FLIGHT OF ALEXANDER THE GREAT

South Germany, 10th century
Würzburg, Mainfränkisches Museum
58 × 100 cm

White linen. Silk in blue, red and yellow. The ground is embroidered with interlace patterns in white. Chain, stem and gobelin stitch. The border, containing a Latin inscription, is preserved only on one side. From the Treasury of Würzburg Cathedral.

Lit.: S. Müller-Christensen, Sakrale Gewänder des Mittelalters, Ausstellungs-Katalog, Munich 1955, p. 14

37 PURSE

France, 11th – 12th century
Sens, Cathedral Treasury
20 × 14 cm

On the front, a mounted knight. Linen ground, embroidered throughout with silk in blue, green, red and yellow. Split stitch. The back shows an eagle with a hare.

Lit.: M. Symonds and L. Preece, Needlework through the Ages, London 1928, p. 171, Pl. XXIV, 4

38 STANDARD OF SAN OTH, BISHOP OF URGEL, Detail

North Spain, 12th century
Barcelona, Museo des Artes Decoratives
105 × 72 cm; detail about 29 × 18 cm

On each of the three pendent strips at the bottom of the banner appears the figure of a donor (?) carrying a book and looking up to the figure of Christ in Majesty on the main panel. (Inscription: ELIS AVA ME F(E)CIT). Linen; silk thread in white, red and dark blue. Chain and stem stitch. From the Cathedral of Seo de Urgel in the Pyrenees.

Lit.: J. Gudiol Ricart, Arts de España: Cataluña. Barcelona 1955, p. 42 – A. C. Floriano, El Bordado. Barcelona 1942, p. 40

39 CUSHION-COVER

Germany, first half of the 12th century
Soest, St Patroklus
30 × 30 cm

On the front, the Flight of Alexander the Great. On the back, the Lamb of God. White linen twill. Preliminary drawing in red. Split stitch. The ground is white, the outlines and foliage scrolls red, the robe of Alexander yellow. The cushion served as a support for the skull of St. Patroklus.

Lit.: A. Schnütgen, Zeitschrift für christliche Kunst XV, 1902, p. 117

40–45 THE GENESIS HANGING

Catalonia, 11th century
Gerona, Cathedral
365 × 460 cm (original size: about 500 × 500 cm)

In the middle, a circle with Christ as Ruler of the World (Fig. 44) surrounded by scenes from the Story of the Creation (Figs. 41, 43 and 45); above the figure of Christ, the Dove of the Holy Ghost. All this is enclosed within a circular inscription. The border shows, at top centre, a figure of the Year (Annus) between squares showing the Four Seasons, Samson and a man with a sheep. In the two top corners, Rivers of Paradise; in the side borders, representations of the Months, together with circles showing Dies Solis (Fig. 42) and Dies Lunae; at the bottom, the Discovery of the Cross. Terracotta-red woollen twill with embroidery of plied woollen thread in yellow, yellow-grey, red, green and light and dark blue, with white linen thread. The ground is densely embroidered with stitches whose technique is not clear (probably a type of couched work), while the subjects are worked in stem, chain and a little satin stitch. A strip has been cut away on the right-hand side and the scene of the Discovery of the Cross is only fragmentarily preserved. The inscriptions indicate that the piece was made in the border-country of Spain; the style of the subjects betrays an acquaintance with contemporary German and Byzantine miniature painting. The history of the hanging prior to 1884 is unknown.

Lit.: P. de Palol, Une broderie catalane d'époque romane: La Genèse de Gerona, Cahiers Archéologiques, VIII, Paris 1956, p. 175, IX, 1957, p. 219 – A. C. Floriano, El Bordado. Barcelona 1942, p. 37

46–51 THE EWALD COVER

Germany; the dating varies from the middle of the 9th to the 12th century.
Cologne, St. Kunibert
83 × 310 cm. Centre panel: 130 cm. Side panels: each 90 cm long
Blue linen. The side panels faded to pale green. Embroidered with silk thread in two tones of red, two of blue, two of brown, and grey. Gilt leather strip couched with red silk. Stem, chain and knitting stitches with couched work. Restored. The central panel has an endless swastika pattern. The side panels show figure subjects: 1. Sun and Moon, holding torches, in a circle of stars, which is linked by chains to the four corners; (figs. 50 and 51) all within the circle of the Zodiac. 2. An enthroned figure of the Year (Annus), holding Day and Night in his hands, between four fiery wheels (Ezekiel, Chapter I); (fig. 46) in the inner circle, the four seasons and the four elements, in the outer circle, the twelve signs of the Zodiac. Below, the sea and the earth. Above: Alpha and Omega. Border with inscription: POPULUS QUI CONSPICIT OMNIS ARTE LABORATUM. This cloth, which is apparently a cover for a lectern or an altar, comes from the shrine of the two Anglo-Saxon martyrs, Black Ewald and White Ewald, in St. Kunibert, Cologne.
Lit.: According to W. Nyssen, in Wallraf Richartz Jahrbuch 1956, p. 70 ff. the work is late Carolingian, approximately contemporary with the Folchard Psalter or not much later, and closely connected with St. Gall, if not made there. According to Schnitzler, Rheinische Schatzkammer, Düsseldorf 1951, p. 42, 11th to 12th century. "In favour of a later dating is the widespread use of this subject matter in Romanesque floor mosaics and wall hangings (Gerona, see figs. 40 to 45). The earlier elements which appear in certain motifs and forms, e. g. the initials reminiscent of Late Carolingian and Ottonian work, are not surprising in textiles, which are often characterised by conservation of archaic elements."

52 FRAGMENT SHOWING HARPY

Mesopotamia or Egypt, Fatimid period, 11th – 12th century
Athens, Benaki Museum
23 × 32 cm. Width of the border: 11 cm
A harpy in a cartouche between scroll ornament. Silk taffeta, now of brownish colour. Gold thread with a high proportion of copper. In the ground the gold thread is laid vertically, in the figures it follows the direction of the outlines. Couched work. From Egypt. Strong resemblance to embroideries on the mitre of St. Valero in the Cathedral of Roda, Spain (illustrated by Antonio C. Floriano, El Bordado, Barcelona 1942, Fig. 2)

53 FRAGMENT OF ROBE

Egypt, 13th–14th century
Berlin, Staatliches Museum (J. 3175)
56 × 42 cm
Thin cloth with dark grey silk embroidery. Running and double running stitch.
Lit.: E. Kühnel, Islamische Stoffe, Berlin 1927, p. 56

54 FRAGMENT OF A ROBE OR CUSHION-COVER

Egypt, 12th–13th century
Berlin, Staatliches Museum (J. 4915)
Width of band: 16 cm
Hares between trees; central band with small ducks in interlace. Linen: silk thread in salmon pink, yellow, light green and black. Chain stitch.
Lit.: E. Kühnel, Islamische Stoffe. Berlin 1927, p. 51

55 LINEN CLOTH, Detail

Egypt, Fatimid period, 11th–12th century
Athens, Benaki Museum
100 × 66 cm. Detail: Diameter 19 to 21 cm

At the two narrow ends, three pairs of stripes with foliage scrolls and Kufic inscriptions between. In the middle, between six heart-shaped compartments with hares and foliage ornament, two medallions with lions. Linen. Silk embroidery in stem and chain stitch in white, blue, red and black; the background of the medallions is densely embroidered with yellow-brown chain stitch.

56 FRAGMENT OF AN EMBROIDERY WITH FOUR APOSTLES

Egypt, 12th century
New York, Metropolitan Museum of Art. Gift of Mrs. E. S. Harkness, 1929 (Inventory Number 29.106)
15 × 30 cm
Linen. Gold embroidery (gilt membrane) with a little black wool and white silk. Couched work, satin and stem stitch.
Lit.: M. S. Dimand, Festschrift Strzygowski, Klagenfurt 1932, p. 38

57–59 THE CHASUBLE OF ST. THOMAS BECKET

Spain, Almeria, 1116
Fermo (Italy), Cathedral
Height: 160 cm. Diameter of the medallions: 20 cm
Semi-circular chasuble. In the circles, enthroned princes, horsemen, sphinxes, griffins and animals. In the middle of the back, a broad vertical band with a border containing a Kufic inscription. Blue silk twill (rather worn). Gold thread (gilt membrane) in couched work; silk embroidery in chain and split stitch, in red, blue, white and brown. The black outlines have to a large extent disappeared. The place and date of the work is indicated by the Kufic inscription ("In the name of Allah . . . in the year 510 in Mariyya"). According to tradition St. Thomas of Canterbury wore this garment as a chasuble.
Lit.: D. S. Rice, The Fermo Chasuble. The Illustrated London News, October 3, 1959, p. 356 – G. Menéndez Pidal, Boletin de la Real Academia de la Historia, Madrid CXLVIII, 1961, p. 169

60–62 CORONATION MANTLE OF THE HOLY ROMAN EMPIRE

Sicily, Palermo, 1133–1134
Vienna, Weltliche Schatzkammer
Diameter: 342 cm
Semi-circular mantle of red silk twill with "incised" pattern. In the centre, a stylised Tree of Life. On either side symmetrical representations of a lion attacking a camel. Embroidery in gold thread and red, light-blue, yellow, dark brown (or black) silk. The sumptuous effect is enhanced by the double row of pearls forming the outlines and by the use of applied ornaments of goldsmiths' work, with enamels and precious stones. Gold embroidery in underside couching; the couched gold threads are arranged in pairs; the couching thread is invisible. The inner drawing of palmettes and rosettes which now appears in reserve in the gold embroidery, was originally worked throughout in coloured silk, in chain stitch. All the outlines are black, as are the claws of the lion. Most of the silk threads have fallen out. The Kufic inscription round the border indicates that the mantle was made "in the Royal Workshop of the capital of Sicily in the year 528 of the Hegira". The mantle was probably made for King Roger II (1130 to 1154) and later became part of the coronation insignia of the German Kings and Emperors.
Lit.: H. Fillitz, Die Insignien und Kleinodien des Heiligen Römischen Reiches. Vienna-Munich 1954, p. 47 – P. E. Schramm und F. Mütherich, Denkmale der deutschen Könige und Kaiser, Munich 1962, p. 182, No. 179

63/64 COPE: SO-CALLED "MANTLE OF CHARLEMAGNE"

Spain or Sicily, c. 1200
Metz Cathedral,
Diameter: 304 cm. Height: 142 cm

Red silk twill, with embroidery in gold and silk. The gold threads are couched in pairs and the couching threads sometimes form zigzag and interlace patterns. Silk in white, red, green, blue and brownish black. Outlines in silk threads, couched with silk threads of a different colour. The garment, originally a princely mantle, has been converted for use as a cope. In the process it has been curtailed at the lower edge and an embroidered orphrey has been attached to the front edge; this shows angels with the instruments of the Passion and was made in the Netherlands in the 16th century.

Lit.: W. F. Volbach, G. Salles, G. Dutuit, L'Art Byzantin, Paris 1931, No. 99 – J. Beckwith and D. T. Rice, Masterpieces of Byzantine Art. Exhibition Edinburgh-London 1958, No. 226

65/66 DALMATIC, PART OF THE INSIGNIA OF THE HOLY ROMAN EMPIRE
Sicily, Palermo, Royal Workshop, 1130–1140, Period of King Roger II.
Vienna, Weltliche Schatzkammer
Cuff: 21 cm wide. Lower border: 21 cm wide

Two details. The dalmatic is of deep purple silk. The apparels illustrated, however, – a cuff and the lower border – are made of a silk material resembling that of the Coronation Mantle. The gold thread is underside couched, but on the cuff the gold is in the form of minute tubes with the couching thread passed through them. Pearls, gold plaques, enamels and filigree work. According to Fillitz the garment may belong to the same set of vestments as the Coronation Mantle.

Lit.: H. Fillitz, Die Insignien und Kleinodien des Heiligen Römischen Reiches. Vienna-Munich 1954, p. 58, Figs. 27, 28 – P. E. Schramm and F. Mütherich, Denkmale der deutschen Könige und Kaiser, Munich 1962, p. 182, No. 181

67, 69, 71 ALB OF KING WILLIAM II OF SICILY,
PART OF THE INSIGNIA OF THE HOLY ROMAN EMPIRE
Palermo, Royal Workshop, 1181
Vienna, Weltliche Schatzkammer
Lower border: 30 cm wide. Cuff: 10 cm wide

Details: lower border and cuff. The borders are adorned with rich gold embroidery and pearls. The lower border shows two motifs in dense gold embroidery; pairs of confronted lions on a white ground and pairs of confronted griffins on a purple ground. Along the upper and lower edge of the border run a Latin and an Arabic inscription indicating that this garment was one of those made for King William II in the Royal Workshop. The cuff is made of the same purple silk material with similar gold embroidery (pairs of griffins). But part of the embroidery was restored in the Hohenstaufen period, in the 13th century.

Lit.: H. Fillitz, Die Insignien und Kleinodien des Heiligen Römischen Reiches, Vienna-Munich 1954, p. 58, figs. 27, 28 – P. E. Schramm und F. Mütherich, Denkmale der deutschen Könige und Kaiser, Munich 1962, p. 183, No. 180

68, 70 GLOVES OF THE EMPEROR FREDERICK II.
PART OF THE INSIGNIA OF THE HOLY ROMAN EMPIRE
Sicily, early 13th century, before 1220
Vienna, Weltliche Schatzkammer
Circumference of the wrist opening: 24 (25) cm
Length from the wrist to the point of the middle finger: 25.5 (27) cm
Red silk. Gold embroidery in couched work. The back of the hand is richly embroidered with pearls, rubies, sapphires and enamelled plaques (four of the latter have been lost and replaced by others). On the inner side, a single-headed nimbed eagle. The gloves were made for the Emperor Frederick II and were worn by him at his coronation in 1220.

Lit.: H. Fillitz, Die Insignien und Kleinodien des Heiligen Römischen Reiches. Vienna-Munich 1954, p. 59, figs. 31, 32 – P. E. Schramm und F. Mütherich, Denkmale der deutschen Könige und Kaiser, Munich 1962, p. 190, No. 200

72 CHASUBLE OF BONIFACE VIII.
Southern Italy or Sicily; late 12th century
Anagni, Museo del Duomo
Height: 110 cm. Width: 68 cm. Height of the detail illustrated: 55 cm, width: 40 cm

Chasuble of red silk twill, with pattern of circles embroidered in gold. Within the circles, griffins, double-headed eagles and addorsed birds. Orphrey with half-length figures of Apostles in star-shaped compartments. The gold thread is couched in pairs on the body of the chasuble, with the couching thread sometimes forming patterns; the fillings in the wings of the eagle and in the frames of the medallions are worked in split stitch with red, white and blue silk. The gold embroidery of the orphrey is somewhat less densely worked; the silk embroidery of the faces and garments, now much worn, is in split (and chain?) stitch. The embroidery of the chasuble and of the matching cope and two dalmatics is stylistically and technically reminiscent of works like the "Pappagalli" chasuble at St. Corona, Vicenza, and the dossal in Assisi (Figs. 76, 77). The vertical borders of the chasuble orphrey are of later date. These vestments belong to a great donation of Pope Boniface VIII (1294–1303) to the church of his birthplace (cf. Figs. 123–125 and 173) and correspond with a description in an inventory of the 14th century: "unum pluviale de samito rubeo laborato ad acum de auro battuto ad grifos, pappagallos et aquilas cum duobus caputibus".

Lit.: B. de Montault: Annales Archéologiques XVII, XVIII, Paris 1857 and 1858, p. 235 and p. 23, 26 – A. Santangelo, Tessuti d'arte italiani. Milan 1958, p. 16

73 MEDALLION: CHRIST PANTOCRATOR
Byzantium, c. 1200
Speyer. Cathedral Treasury
Diameter: 21.5 cm

Light brown silk twill. Gold thread, and silk in light and dark brown and lilac. Face, hands and inner drawing of the garment in split stitch. Halo, garment and frame of the medallion in underside couched gold embroidery; the couching thread on the back of the work is of linen. This medallion, with another representing the Virgin in prayer, is applied to the mantle of King Philip of Swabia (d. 1208), which was found when his tomb was opened in the Cathedral of Speyer.

Lit.: S. Müller-Christensen, Die Tunika König Philipps von Schwaben. 900 Jahre Speyerer Dom. Speyer 1961, p. 219 – P. E. Schramm and F. Mütherich, Denkmale der der deutschen Könige und Kaiser. Munich 1962, p. 187, No. 190

74/75 RELIQUARY POUCH
Byzantium, 12th century
Nuremberg, Germanisches Nationalmuseum (KG. 562) 14.8 × 12.5 cm
Front: violet-purple silk twill with applied silver-gilt plaques, interlaced rosettes of gold wire, gems and embroidered gold strips. Back: scarlet silk twill with underside couched gold embroidery; outlines in brown silk in stem stitch.

Lit.: S. Müller-Christensen, Sakrale Gewänder des Mittelalters, Ausstellungs-Katalog, Munich 1955, p. 27, No. 43

76/77 DOSSAL
Italy (Sicily ?); early 13th century
Assisi, S. Francesco, Treasury
600 × 122 cm

Yellow silk twill with rows of twelve-lobed circles occupied by pairs of griffins and pairs of birds alternately; in the intervening spaces, leopards. Gold embroidery in couched work; outlines in silk, part of which has fallen out. Some ornamental details, e. g. eyes and joints, worked with red, black and blue silk in satin, stem and chain stitch. Mentioned in the inventory of 1338 as a gift from an "Imperator Graecorum", perhaps Baldwin II (1229–37).
Lit.: U. Gnoli, Il tesoro di San Francesco d'Assisi, II: Dedalo II, Milano-Roma 1921–22, p. 564 – A. Santangelo, Tessuti d'arte italiani. Milan 1958, p. 11

78–80 ALTAR FRONTAL FROM RUPERTSBERG, NEAR BINGEN
Rhineland; first third of the 13th century
Brussels, Musées Royaux d'Art et d'Histoire (7248)
102 × 235 cm
Purple Byzantine silk twill. Gold and silver thread. Silk in pale colours: white, pink, light blue, light green. Satin, stem and Gobelin stitch. Probably for reasons of economy the bottom left hand corner is formed by a patch with the threads running in a different direction. Christ in Glory with the symbols of the four Evangelists. On the left, the Virgin Mary and St. Peter with, beneath them, Sifridus, Archbishop of Mainz. On the right, Saints Rupert and Hildegarde, the foundress of the Convent of St. Rupert with, beneath them, Agnes, the benefactress of the Convent (1207–13, wife of Ferri II, Duke of Loraine). On the end panel to the left, John the Baptist with St. Mary Magdalene and a kneeling child. On the end panel to the right, St. Martin, as patron saint. In the predella panels a priest named Godefridus, ten nuns with their names inscribed above them and on the right a woman named Adelhedis. Outside the frame a kneeling figure: Cunradus. The altar frontal was made in the time of one of two archbishops of Mainz who bore the name Siegfried: Siegfried II or Siegfried III von Eppstein, who held the See 1201–1230 and 1230–1249 (more probably in the time of Siegfried II). This important work of art passed from Eppstein in the Taunus, by way of the antique trade, to the Brussels Museum in 1896.
Lit.: J. Destrée in Les Musées du Parc du Cinquantenaire . . . à Bruxelles n. d. (1899) 7e livraison – F. Schneider, Gesammelte Aufsätze. Wiesbaden, 1913, I. p. 78 – Creutz, in Zeitschrift für christliche Kunst XXVII, 1914, p. 107 – M. Calberg, in Broderies historiées du Moyen-Age et de la Renaissance – Musées Royaux d'Art et d'Histoire, Bruxelles, p. 7

81–84 ALTAR CLOTH, FRAGMENT
Rhineland (?), c. 1170–1180
Formerly Berlin, Schlossmuseum. Destroyed by fire during the war
113 × 116 cm
Details: Annunciation and Visitation, Nativity and Adoration of the Kings, Ascension. Fine linen ground. Linen thread and a little silk thread. Chain stitch. The vases of ointment, the rosette ornament, the inscriptions and the circles with animals are embroidered throughout in silk, with lozenge and swastika patterns. The cloth is said to have come from the neighbourhood of Fulda.
Lit.: v. Falke in Berliner Museums-Berichte aus den preussischen Kunstsammlungen, XLII, 1921, p. 71 ff.

85 ALTAR CLOTH
Lombardy (?), late 12th century
Rome, Vatican, Museo Sacro
365 × 115 cm. Detail illustrated, 100 × 76 cm
On white linen, embroidery in white linen thread in broad chain and stem stitch. The cover is divided into lozenge-shaped fields. At the intersections of the diagonal lines are circles containing rosettes. Within the lozenges, various motifs, which also occur in woven silks of the 11th and 12th centuries. In early inventories of Italian chur-

ches whitework embroideries of this kind are often designated as "Opus Theotonicum". The illustration is from a photograph taken against the light in order to show the design more clearly.
Lit.: W. F. Volbach, I Tessuti del Museo Sacro Vaticano. Città del Vaticano 1942, p. 59 and Pl. LII–LV

86–90 SO-CALLED IMPERIAL MANTLE OF OTTO IV.
England, c. 1200
Brunswick, Anton-Ulrich-Museum
96 × 308 cm Medallions: 18,5 am. Lion: 10 cm long. Eagle: 14 cm high.
Red Byzantine silk twill with linen lining. Gold and silver-gilt strip wound on silk thread. White and black silk, for eyes and for the inner drawing and outlines, now largely disappeared. The gold and silk threads are worked in underside couching, stem and satin stitch. In the medallions, Christ with a book and the Virgin Mary with a flower. The front is powdered with lions, stars and crescents, the back with eagles. The mantle has been cut up at an unknown period to serve as a cover and reassembled in 1876 and 1930 as nearly as possible in its original form. The name commonly applied to this embroidery cannot be confirmed by documentary evidence. The work came to the Collegium Carolinum in Brunswick in 1814 (probably from Riddagshausen) and was transferred for safe keeping to the Museum in 1858. The lions and eagles in the design suggested the hypothesis of a connection with the Empire and the Guelph family, and more particulary with the Emperor Otto IV, who was crowned in Aachen in 1198. Otto IV, son of Henry the Lion, is known to have bequeathed his "pallium" to the Aegidienkloster in Brunswick.
Lit.: M. Schuette, Gestickte Bildteppiche und Decken des Mittelalters II, 1930, p. 3, Pl. 1 ff. – A. G. I. Christie, English Medieval Embroidery. Oxford, 1938, p. 72, Pl. XXV ff.

91–93 DALMATIC WITH CENTAURS AND STAGS
England, early 13th century
Halberstadt, Cathedral Museum
Length: 141 cm Bottom width: 240 cm
Red silk twill with linen lining. Gold thread (silver-gilt strip wound on yellowish silk thread) in underside couching. Silk threads, white and black, in satin and stem stitch, for eyes and outlines. Poorly preserved; restored. The lion-dalmatic and the centaur-dalmatic from the Treasury of Halberstadt Cathedral seem to be a matching pair, in spite of differences of style.
Lit.: M. Schuette, Gestickte Bildteppiche des Mittelalters, Leipzig 1930, II, p. 68, Pl. 41, 42 – A. G. I. Christie, English Medieval Embroidery, Oxford 1938, p. 75, Pl. XXVIII, XXIX

94 DALMATIC WITH LIONS
England (?), c. 1200
Halberstadt, Cathedral
Height of lion: 10.6 cm
The detail shows a lion in a circle. Red silk twill. Gold thread (silver-gilt strip on yellowish silk thread) and black and white silk, in underside couching, stem and satin stitch.
Lit.: M. Schuette, Gestickte Bildteppiche des Mittelalters, Leipzig 1930, II, p. 68, Pl. 41, 42

95/96 MITRE
England, late 12th century
Munich, Bayerisches Nationalmuseum (T. 17)
Height: 23 cm
The Stoning of St. Stephen and the Martyrdom of St. Thomas Becket, Archbishop of Canterbury (1170).
White silk twill with white linen lining. Gold thread, plied linen thread, and silk in lilac, green and blue. Underside couched gold

thread; the threads running vertically and horizontally. Inner drawing and outlines in split and stem stitch. From the Cistercian nunnery of Seligenthal near Landshut. According to tradition, given to the convent by Ludmilla, Duchess of Bavaria (1170–1240).

Lit.: A. G. I. Christie, English Medieval Embroidery, Oxford 1938, p. 60 – S. Müller-Christensen, Sakrale Gewänder des Mittelalters, Ausstellungs-Katalog Munich 1955, p. 28, No. 51 – A. Geijer, Engelska Broderier av Romansk Typ. Nordenfjeldske Kunstindustrimuseum, Årbok 1956, Trondhjem 1956, p. 46 – D. King, Opus Anglicanum, Exhibition, Victoria and Albert Museum 1963, Cat. p. 19, No. 13

97/98 THE CLARE CHASUBLE
England, late 13th century
London, Victoria and Albert Museum (673–1864)
115 × 66 cm

The Stoning of St. Stephen, Saints Peter and Paul, the Virgin and Child and the Crucifixion. Blue satin with cotton weft. Silver-gilt thread and coloured silks: green, yellow, orange and flesh tones. The metal thread in underside couching; the silk in split stitch and laid and couched work. Re-modelled in baroque shape in the 17th or 18th century. The stole and maniple which originally belonged to the chasuble bore the arms of England, Cornwall, Clare and Lacy, indicative of Edmund Plantagenet, Earl of Cornwall, and his wife Margaret Clare. Their marriage, in 1272, ended in divorce in 1294. The embroidery must have been worked before the latter year.

Lit.: Victoria and Albert Museum, Fifty Masterpieces of Textiles, London 1958, No. 8 – A. G. I. Christie, English Medieval Embroidery, Oxford 1938, p. 78, Pl. XXXI – D. King, Opus Anglicanum, Exhibition, Victoria and Albert Museum 1963, Cat. p. 19, No. 30

99 SIDE PANEL OF THE GRANDSON ALTAR FRONTAL
England, c. 1300
Berne, Bernisches Historisches Museum (No. 18)
88 × 42 cm

Scarlet silk twill; gold embroidery in underside couching. A little silk in split stitch. The origin of the two side panels added to the Grandson altar frontal (Fig. 127) remains uncertain. But Lethaby's observations on the style and technique of *opus anglicanum* (underside couching is the characteristic technique of gold embroidery in opus anglicanum) seem to point in the right direction.

Lit.: M. Lemberg, in Jahrbuch des Bernischen Historischen Museums in Bern, XXXVII, XXXVIII, 1957, 1958, p. 164 ff.

100 CHRIST IN MAJESTY
England, 1300-1320
London, Victoria and Albert Museum (T. 337–1921)
100 × 41 cm

Blue-purple silk twill, with linen lining. Gold, silver, and coloured silks; pearls. Colours: two greens, red, fawn, pink, amber, black and lilac. Underside couching, split stitch. Inscription: Johannis de Thaneto. The name appears in 1316 in an inventory of the sacristy of Canterbury Cathedral.

Lit.: Victoria and Albert Museum, Fifty Masterpieces of Textiles. London 1958, Pl. 9 – A. G. I. Christie, English Medieval Embroidery, Oxford 1938, p. 134, Pl. LXXXVI – D. King, Opus Anglicanum, Exhibition, Victoria and Albert Museum 1963, Cat. p. 22, No. 38

101 COPE
England, c. 1275–1280
Ascoli Piceno, Palazzo Comunale
Length: 163 cm. Diameter: 378.5 cm. Head of Christ: 21 cm high

Linen ground. Mainly gold embroidery in underside couching; silver thread. Silk in salmon pink, light brown, green, indigo, lilac and white. Seed pearls and coloured glass beads. Split stitch. Head of

Christ, Crucifixion, Virgin and Child. On either side, sixteen scenes from the lives of the Popes from Clement I (90–100) to Clement IV (1265–1268). The cope was a gift from Pope Nicholas IV in 1288 to his birthplace, Ascoli.

Lit.: A. G. I. Christie, English Medieval Embroidery, Oxford 1938, p. 89, Pl. XLII ff.

COLOUR PLATE V. CHASUBLE-ORPHREY WITH THE TREE OF JESSE
England, c. 1330
Lyon, Musée Historique des Tissus. (Inventory No. 1189)
145 × 35 cm. Detail illustrated: 70 × 35 cm.

A vine scroll growing from the body of Jesse encloses King David, King Solomon, the Virgin and Child and the Crucifixion. At the sides, the four prophets: Isaiah, Mescias (sic), Jermias and Daniel. Double layer of linen. Gold thread, linen thread, and silk in yellow, red, blue and green, in various shades ranging from light to dark. Outlines in brown silk. All the vine leaves are worked in petit point, with the small tent stitches worked through the upper layer of linen only. Split and satin stitch. The background, in underside couched gold embroidery, is worked with quatrefoils containing lions. – The style of this embroidery is closely related to that of miniatures by the master of the Queen Mary Psalter and his circle.

Lit.: A. G. I. Christie, English Medieval Embroidery, Oxford 1938, p. 114 – E. G. Millar, La miniature anglaise, Paris-Bruxelles 1928, II p. 19, 61 Pl. 39 (Ms. now in Pierpont Morgan Library, New York) – D. King, Opus Anglicanum, Exhibition, Victoria and Albert Museum 1963, Cat. p. 33, No. 57

102 THE SYON COPE
England, 1300-1320
London, Victoria and Albert Museum (83-1864)
Length: 147 cm. Diameter: 294 cm

Double layer of linen, embroidered throughout. Gold, silver, and coloured silk threads in salmon pink, amber colour, light brown, flesh colour, white, violet, purple, deep grass green and light blue. Underside couching, stem stitch, laid and couched work. Orphrey: underside couching, cross and long armed cross stitch. In the centre, Coronation of the Virgin, Crucifixion, St. Michael. Along the upper edge and at the sides, scenes from the lives of Christ and the Virgin, Apostles (incompletely preserved), six-winged seraphim, and two priests. The orphrey, morse, and outer border were added later, presumably when the original chasuble was converted to a cope; the heraldry of these armorial bands dates from the middle of the 13th to the first quarter of the 14th century. The cope owes its name and its preservation to the Bridgettine nunnery of Syon, near London, whose nuns guarded it faithfully for centuries.

Lit.: A. G. I. Christie, English Medieval Embroidery, Oxford 1938, p. 142, pl. XCV ff. – D. King, Opus Anglicanum, Exhibition, Victoria and Albert Museum 1963, Cat. p. 23, No. 40

103 COPE, detail: Nativity
England, 1315-1335
Pienza, Cathedral
Height: 164 cm. Diameter: 350 cm

Double layer of linen. Pearls (stolen in 1882), gold and silver thread, and coloured silk in blue, green shaded with yellow, sepia, fawn, grey, pink, brown and amber. Underside couching, split stitch sometimes alternating with petit point, laid and couched work, and satin stitch. Three zones of Gothic arches containing twenty-seven scenes of the Childhood of Christ, the Life of the Virgin and the lives of Saints Margaret and Catherine. In addition, eight prophets and twelve apostles. A gift from Pope Pius II (1458–1464) to the Cathedral of his birthplace, in the year 1462.

Lit.: A. G. I. Christie, English Medieval Embroidery, Oxford 1938, p. 178, pl. CXXXIX ff. – D. King, Opus Anglicanum, Exhibition, Victoria and Albert Museum 1963, Cat. p. 31. No. 54

104 VATICAN COPE, detail: Coronation of the Virgin
England, c. 1280
Rome, Museo Cristiano
Diameter: 310 cm. Length: 132 cm. Stars: 46 cm high
Slightly faded rose-coloured silk twill on linen lining. Gold and silver thread, and coloured silks in four shades of blue, green shading to yellow, pink, light brown, sepia, white, black. Underside couching, split stitch and laid and couched work. Black outlines. Coronation of the Virgin, Crucifixion, Virgin and Child. To either side, ten apostles and Saints Stephen, Lawrence, Catherine and Margaret.
Lit.: A. G. I. Christie, English Medieval Embroidery, Oxford, 1938, p. 94 ff., pl. XLVI–XLIX – D. King, Opus Anglicanum, Exhibition, Victoria and Albert Museum 1963, Cat. p. 20, No. 32

105 COPE OF CARDINAL GIL DE ALBORNOZ (d. 1367).
Detail: the Apostle Andrew
England, early 14th century
Toledo, Cathedral
Linen ground. Gold and silver thread, and coloured silks in salmon pink, orange, yellow, green, various shades of blue, pink, brown. Underside couching and split stitch. The cope, which is particularly well preserved, is traditionally associated with Cardinal Albornoz. Life of the Virgin, Apostles and Saints, including six saints who are specifically English.
Lit.: A. G. I. Christie, English Medieval Embroidery, Oxford 1938, p. 156, pl. CIX

106–109 Colour Plate VI, CHASUBLE
South-West Germany, late 12th century
Benedictine monastery of St Paul in Lavanttal, Carinthia
Height in front: 145 cm, at the back: 167 cm
Semi-circular chasuble sewn together in front, divided into thirty-eight fields, with scenes from the Old and New Testaments and saints. In the border, medallions with half-length figures of Prophets, Evangelists, Apostles and Princes. Linen embroidered throughout with silk, chiefly in shades of mustard yellow and pale grey, with some light green, pale lilac, light blue and brown. Long-armed cross stitch, with outlines and inner drawing in chain stitch. Originally in the Benedictine monastery of St. Blasien in the Black Forest. Colour Plate VI: Creation of Eve. Fig. 106: Front of the chasuble. Fig. 107: Nativity and Adoration of the Kings; the Prophets Isaiah and Jeremiah, David and Solomon. Fig. 108: the Prophet Balaam; Joseph thrown into the Well; the Prophet Joshua. Fig. 109: the Martyrs Regula and Felix; the Visit of the three Angels to Abraham.
Lit.: E. Heinemeyer, Süddeutsche Stickereien des 13. und 14. Jahrhunderts. Diss. Munich 1958, p. 33 and 107

110 WALL HANGING, fragment: Resurrection, the Three Maries at the Sepulchre, Pentecost
Lower Saxony, 1180–1200
Berlin, Schloss Charlottenburg, Kunstgewerbemuseum (88.470)
113 × 116 cm
Coarse linen. Coloured silks in yellowish white, dull green, light and dark brown, light blue, purple. Much faded. Chain stitch. Two associated borders were destroyed by fire in 1945. From the region of Halberstadt, possibly, according to Lessing, from the Mauritiuskirche (formerly Saints Boniface and Mauritius).
Lit.: B. Kurth, Die deutschen Bildteppiche des Mittelalters. Vienna 1926, I, p. 60 – R. Kroos, Niedersächsische figürliche Leinen- und Seidenstickereien des 12. bis 14. Jahrhunderts, Diss., Göttingen 1957, p. 13, No. 1

111/112 CHASUBLE, details: Adoration of the Magi and Baptism from the orphrey of the green chasuble
Lower Saxony; first half to middle of the 13th century.
Halberstadt, Cathedral Museum
Width: 19 cm
Linen ground. Gold thread (silver-gilt strip on silk thread), and silk in strong tones of blue, red (the back-grounds are red and blue), black and white. Couched work and split stitch.
Lit.: Schuette, Gestickte Bildteppiche des Mittelalters. Leipzig 1927, I, p. 71, pl. 44, 45

113/119 THE GÖSS VESTMENTS. Complete set for a chapel, comprising altar frontal, chasuble, cope, dalmatic (and tunicle, not illustrated).
Benedictine nunnery of Göss, Styria, second to third quarter of the 13th century
Vienna, Österreichisches Museum für angewandte Kunst (T. 6902–6906)
The embroideries are uniform in materials, technique and style. Stout linen embroidered throughout. Wide, glossy, almost untwisted silk thread in red, various shades of blue, violet, white, green, yellow, black. Satin, brick, long-armed cross and stem stitch. The colours are astonishingly well preserved but, on the other hand, the silk is worn in various places, and parts of the vestments have been cut away in order to patch the damaged sections. All the pieces, except the tunicle, bear inscriptions.
According to the inscriptions they were made under the Abbess Kunigund, who ruled the Convent about 1239–1269; her name appears five times – on the chasuble, the frontal, the cope and twice on the dalmatic. One of these latter inscriptions (in contrast to the official Latin text) is in a Middle High German, early Bavarian dialect and is a direct expression of the deep piety with which the Abbess and her nuns created this great and costly work. The portrait of the Abbess appears in a prominent position, next to that of the foundress of the Convent, the Bavarian Countess Adala, who, with her son Aribo, later Bishop of Mainz, founded the nunnery about 1000. The unique importance of the Göss vestments lies in their superbly monumental style and in the completeness and uniformity of this early group. Until their acquisition by the Austrian State in 1908, the vestments remained in their original home, in the conventual church at Göss.

113 CHASUBLE
123 × 73 cm
Back: Christ in Majesty, Angel Choir, Symbols of the Evangelists Mark and Luke (the other symbols are missing). Geometrical ornament. On the front (not illustrated) Christ Crucified, with the Virgin and St John; eight apostles beneath semi-circular arches. Principal colours: blue and red. The original bell shape of the chasuble has been reduced to Baroque form and parts (four apostles from the front and Kunigund, beneath semi-circular arches) used to patch the cope.

114–116 ALTAR FRONTAL
140 × 300 cm
Annunciation, the Virgin Enthroned, the Three Kings. Details: the Abbess Kunigund; the Three Kings and the foundress Adala. The Virgin in the central medallion is worn away in places to the linen ground and has been patched with a fragment of geometrical ornament. The silk has fallen away in many places.

117/118 DALMATIC
122 × 140 cm
Dalmatic with a design of squares of various colours, containing quadrupeds, eagles and mythical beasts, within borders of angular ornament. The Annunciation in a circle at the neck is half cut away and has lost all its silk. Of the symbols of the Evangelists, the eagle

and calf are completely, the lion partially, preserved. The symbol of St Matthew is missing. Sleeves cut and patched.

119 COPE
143 × 272 cm

Virgin nursing the Child and the symbols of the Four Evangelists, in circles, on a background patterned with squares containing quadrupeds, birds and mythical beasts, within borders of angular ornament. The ground colours of the squares are alternately blue, red, green, yellow and violet. The upper parts and the centre are much damaged and patched with pieces of the other vestments.
Lit.: M. Dreger in Kunst und Handwerk XI (1908), p. 613 – E. Heinemeyer, Süddeutsche Stickereien des 13. und 14. Jahrhunderts. Diss. Munich 1958, p. 8, 99

120–122 CHASUBLE WITH THE LEGEND OF SAINT NICHOLAS
Upper Rhine, later 13th century. Vienna, Österreichisches Museum für angewandte Kunst (9125)
151 × 310 cm. Squares: about 35 × 40 cm

Details: St. Nicholas saves a ship in distress. Burial of the saint and miraculous healings at his grave. Loosely woven linen. Gold strip wound on reddish silk. Silk thread in red and green (in alternation for the backgrounds of the squares), violet, blue, white (fallen out from the faces) and black. Gold thread in couched work, silk chiefly in long-armed cross stitch (for backgrounds and larger surfaces); brick, couching and chain stitches. The chasuble comes from the Benedictine Abbey of St. Blasien in the Black Forest. When this house was suppressed in 1805 the monks took the vestment to St. Paul in Lavanttal, in Carinthia, and in 1940 it was acquired by the Austrian State. It was commissioned for the monastery, as appears from the very detailed Latin inscriptions. The subjects include the Lamb of God, the Four Evangelists, the four major Prophets, the Story of the Gospel in ten scenes and the Legend of St. Nicholas in twenty-eight scenes. In the last scene the Abbot offers the vestment to the saint and asks for his protection.
Lit.: Heider, in Jahrbuch d. K. K. Central Commission Wien, IV, 1860, p. 111 – E. Heinemeyer, Süddeutsche Stickereien aus dem 13. und 14. Jahrhundert, Diss. Munich, 1958, p. 32 ff., 122 ff.

123–125 ALTAR FRONTAL
Rome, c. 1300
Anagni, Museo del Duomo
95 × 195 cm

Subjects in two zones. Above, beneath arches, the Virgin and Child with two angels and six apostles; below, the Crucifixion and scenes from the lives of Saints Peter and Paul (Fig. 125). At the sides and below, borders with griffins and parrots in circles. Above, an older border has been attached, with seven half-length figures of Apostles in circles, between foliage scrolls; in addition, a fragment with a half-length figure of Christ between the Virgin and a bearded saint. Linen; gold and silk threads. Couched gold thread for backgrounds and haloes. Silk in split stitch; the silk is worn away in places revealing the preliminary drawing. A gift from Pope Boniface VIII (cf. Fig. 72). Described in a 14th-century inventory as "dossale pro altari laboratum cum acu ad aurum battutum cum ymaginibus crusifixi et beate Virginis, et plurium aliorum scorum, et in circuitu cum rotis ad grifos et pappagallos".
Lit.: B. de Montault: Annales Archéologiques, XVII, XVIII, Paris 1857 and 1858, p. 349 and p. 28 – A. Santangelo, Tessuti d'arte italiani. Milan 1959, p. 19

126/127, and Colour Plate VII. THE GRANDSON ALTAR FRONTAL
Southern Italy, Sicily, Venice (?)
Late 12th to early 13th century.

Berne, Historisches Museum (No. 18). Cf. Fig. 99
88 × 244 cm

The Virgin enthroned between the archangels Gabriel and Michael, with a kneeling donor. Perhaps by a Greek artist working in Western Europe? Purple silk, originally waxed. Gold embroidery in couched work, worked through the silk material and the linen ground, as is also the silk embroidery. The latter is in split, satin, couching, Gobelin and stem stitch. Restricted range of colours; red, deep blue, green, brown, dark olive and white. The black silk has, to a great extent, fallen out. Neither the place nor the date of origin has been established. The altar frontal comes from the Cathedral of Lausanne. The coat-of-arms of the kneeling knight indicates that the donor was a member of the ancient family of Grandson, of Canton Waadt; the figure and the coat-of-arms were embroidered at the same time as the main figures. Members of this family held office repeatedly in the Cathedral Chapter at Lausanne. – The names of the figures appear in three different languages; Greek for the monogram of Christ, Latin for the Madonna (MAT DNI), and French for the Angels (Saint Gabiel, Saint Michiel). The embroidery is Greek, like the monogram of the Child. The other inscriptions point to Western Europe. This suggests the possibility that the work may have been produced by a Greek artist active in the West.
Colour Plate VII: the Angel Gabriel.
Lit.: J. Stammler, Der Paramentenschatz im Historischen Museum zu Bern. 1895, p. 49 – M. Lemberg in Jahrbuch des Bernischen Historischen Museums, XXXVII and XXXVIII (1957 and 1958), p. 143.

128 EUCHARIST CLOTH
Byzantium, late 13th century
Italy, Castell'Arquato (Prov. Piacenza), Collegiate Church
72 × 69 cm

The Eucharist (distribution of bread). Purple silk twill. Faces, hands and feet embroidered in split stitch, in white silk, with green outlines; hair, brown and black. Gold and silver threads used in pairs for garments and architecture, couched with white silk so as to form patterns. A second matching veil shows the distribution of wine. The Greek inscription contains the words of the Communion Service. Gift of the Patriarch of Aquileia, Ottobone Robario de'Feliciani (d. 1314). Possibly the work of a Greek emigrant artist.
Lit.: G. Millet, Broderies religieuses de style byzantin. Paris 1947, p. 72

129/130 STRIP OF LINEN WITH PRELIMINARY TRACINGS AND UNFINISHED EMBROIDERY
Italy (Umbria), middle of the 14th century
Orvieto, Museo dell'Opera
142 × 32 cm

Strip of white linen with pen drawings, showing standing apostles beneath pointed arches (with foliage in the spandrels) and half-length figures of the Virgin, Christ and St. John the Baptist beneath round-headed arches. Some of the drawings have been partially embroidered with thick floss silk in green, red, violet and yellow; split stitch. The embroideries were intended for use on an ecclesiastical vestment.
Lit.: A Santangelo, Tessuti d'arte italiani, Milan, 1959, p. 19

131, 133, 134 ALTAR CURTAIN: "Il Lenzuolo della Beata Benvenuta Bojani"
Friuli, late 13th century
Cividale, Museum
148 × 433 cm. Detail, Fig. 131: 148 × 225 cm. Detail, Fig. 133: 84 × 60 cm. Detail, Fig. 134: 130 × 84 cm

Within a frame of medallions containing busts of St. Ursula and her companions, the main field of the hanging shows the Annunciation and Crucifixion between a double row of saints and apostles. White linen. Embroidery in white linen thread. Satin stitch, sometimes worked in straight or diagonal lines over counted threads; stem, chain and herringbone stitch. (Fig. 131 was photographed against the light in order to show the design more clearly).

Lit.: Itta de Claricini Dornpacher, Il superfrontale detto della Beata Benvenuta Bojani custodito nel Museo di Cividale. 1948

132 CHASUBLE WITH SYMBOLS OF THE EVANGELISTS (detail)

Venice?, early 13th century

Lyon, Musée historique des tissus (Inv. No. 27.042)

Height: 153 cm. Detail: 95 × 145 cm

Linen ground; gold and silk thread. Eagle of St. John in gold, lion of St. Mark in light blue silk; symbols of St. Luke and St. Matthew in light blue, yellow, red and green. Geometrical filling pattern in red, yellow and green. Gold thread in couched work; otherwise satin stitch over counted threads

135–139 ALTAR FRONTAL

Florence, Jacopo Cambi, 1336

Florence, Palazzo Pitti, Museo degli Argenti

105 × 425 cm. Altar band: 18 cm high

On each side of the Coronation of the Virgin are seven figures of apostles and saints. Above, a band with scenes from the Life of the Virgin in eleven rectangles, with figures of saints between. Linen ground; embroidery in gold, silver and silk threads. Split stitch and for outlines – chain stitch. Main colours white, yellow-green, light-blue in the large figures; in the band, most of the garments contain red. The architectural details and the various ornaments and foliage scrolls of the patterned background are worked in gold and silver threads in couched work and raised work. Beneath the Coronation group is the signature of Jacopo Cambi with the date 1336. The composition of the Coronation scene is related to works by Bernardo Daddi and his school (cf. R. Offner, A Critical and Historical Corpus of Florentine Painting, Vol. IV, 1934, Addenda Pl. VI.)

Lit.: M. Salmi, Il Paliotto di Manresa e l'"Opus Florentinum", Bolletino d'Arte 1931, p. 389 – A. Santangelo, Tessuti d'arte italiani, Milan 1958, p. 19, Fig. 35/36 – R. Grönwoldt, Florentiner Stickereien in den Inventaren des Herzogs von Berry: Mitteilungen des Kunsthistorischen Institutes in Florenz, Bd. 10. Florence 1961, p. 33

140/141 SO-CALLED DALMATIC OF CHARLEMAGNE

Byzantium, 14th century

Rome, St Peter's, Treasury

Height: 162 cm. Width at the shoulder: 144 cm. Detail: 50 × 38 cm

On the front, Christ in Judgment between the Virgin and St. John the Baptist, the symbols of the Four Evangelists, angels and the procession of the saved. In the lower corners, the bosom of Abraham and the Good Thief. On the back, the Transfiguration with Christ between Elijah and Moses; below, two appearances of Christ after the Crucifixion. On the shoulders, Christ offering the chalice to St. Paul and the bread to St. Peter. Blue silk twill. Gold embroidery in couched work with the gold threads running in pairs and fastened over a foundation of light-coloured silk embroidery, at right angles to it; the couching threads are arranged in parts in a zig-zag pattern; some gold embroidery over couched cords. Faces, hands and feet worked in silk in split and stem stitch, as is also the inner drawing, which is left in reserve in the gold embroidery.

Lit.: G. Millet, Broderies religieuses de style byzantin. Paris 1947, p. 67 – D. T. Rice, The Art of Byzantium, London 1959, p. 88 and 338, Fig. 195

142/143 LINEN HANGING, two scenes from the life of St. Mary Magdalene.

Lower Saxony, second quarter of the 13th century

Wernigerode, Feudalmuseum

94 × 143 cm

Fairly fine linen ground. Embroidered with white linen thread and black (partially fallen out) and yellow silk thread. Brick, satin, stem, plait and couching stitches. Drawn thread work in yellow silk over counted threads. Inscriptions. Mentioned for the first time in 1863 as a gift to the Chapel of the former Lepers' Hospital of St. George in Wernigerode.

Lit.: M. Schuette, Gestickte Bildteppiche des Mittelalters, Leipzig 1927, II, p. 53, Pl. 34, 35

144/145 ALTAR FRONTAL: CHRIST IN A MANDORLA

Lower Saxony, Convent of Heiningen, 1250

Helmstedt, Kloster St Marienberg

106 × 236 cm

On either side of central figure, Saints Augustine (large section missing), Peter, the Virgin, John the Baptist, Paul, Nicholas. Inscriptions. Detail: the Virgin. – Unbleached linen ground, embroidered with bleached and unbleached linen thread, and coloured silk in reddish brown, golden yellow, white, black (partly fallen out, e. g. the hair of Christ). Satin, brick, couching, stem, and cross stitch. Drawn thread work with counted threads. Old damage on the left and along the bottom. Altered several times in the Middle Ages. The frontal comes from the convent of Heiningen. The inscription names the foundresses, Hildeswit and Walburgis, who are known to have established the convent in the time of Otto III,

Lit.: A. Fink, in Jahrbuch der Berliner Museen, I (1959), p. 168

146 LENTEN CLOTH WITH SCENES FROM THE PASSION OF CHRIST

Detail: Pilate

Kloster Lüne, 2nd half of 13th century

Kloster Lüne

Pilate: 46 cm high

Linen ground in drawn thread work with darned patterns. Damaged places have been backed. White linen thread. Chain stitch of three kinds, herringbone, stem and loop stitches.

Lit.: M. Schuette, Gestickte Bildteppiche des Mittelalters, Leipzig 1927, I, p. 30, Pl. 32

147–150 ALTAR FRONTAL, CRUCIFIXION AND THIRTY-SIX HALF-LENGTH FIGURES OF SAINTS. The details show the Crucifixion, the Eagle of St. John and the upper border

Lower Saxony, late 13th–14th century

Halberstadt, Cathedral Museum

Whole: 109 × 368 cm. Squares: 21.7 cm. Height of band: 18 cm

Linen ground. Fine linen thread and faded silk thread in green, yellow, purple, blue, black (extraordinarily well preserved). Brick, satin, chain, plait, couching, and stem stitch with drawn thread work over counted threads.

Lit.: M. Schuette, Gestickte Bildteppiche des Mittelalters, Leipzig 1930, II, p. 75, Pl. 46, 48

151–153 TABLE CLOTH WITH GROTESQUES, MYTHICAL BEASTS AND ANIMALS

Kloster Feldberg (Thurgau), Switzerland, 14th century

Basel, Historisches Museum (1883/100)

105 × 308 cm

Loosely woven linen. White linen thread with a little coloured silk. Satin, brick, eyelet and plait stitches.

Lit.: V. Trudel, Schweizerische Leinenstickereien des Mittelalters und der Renaissance, Bern, 1952/54, I, Pl. II, III – II, No. 3

154–157 ALTAR CLOTH

Germany, Convent of Altenberg on the Lahn (Hesse), c. 1300

Cleveland, Museum of Art (purchased from the J. H. Wade Fund. 48,352)

159 × 381 cm

The cloth is divided into rectangular fields with quatrefoils at the corners. Scenes from the Passion of Christ, a number of saints (St. Michael, Fig. 155), fantastic animals and dancing couples (Figs. 156, 157), accompanied by explanatory inscriptions. White linen embroidered with linen thread in varieties of satin, chain, herringbone and buttonhole stitch. The altar cloth was originally in the Praemonstratensian nunnery of Altenberg on the Lahn and was doubtless embroidered there. A daughter of St. Elisabeth, Gertrud, was Abbess 1248–1297. The nuns were especially devoted to the cult of St. Elisabeth. (Fig. 154 was taken against the light in order to show the design more clearly).

Lit.: D. Shepherd, A Romanesque Lenten cloth from Germany. Bulletin of the Cleveland Museum of Art. 1953, p. 9 – L. v. Wilckens, Hessische Leinenstickereien des 13. und 14. Jahrhunderts. Anzeiger des Germanischen Nationalmuseums 1954–59. Nuremberg 1959, p. 14

158 SIDE OF AN ALTAR CLOTH: FIGURES OF KINGS AND ADDORSED ANIMALS
Kloster Isenhagen, c. 1300
Quatrefoils: 28 cm high. Figures: 24.5 cm high
146 × 113 cm
Coarse linen ground. Embroidered with linen thread and black silk. Brick, stem and satin stitches worked in patterns. This convent-embroidery is unusual, in that it suggests an iconographical source for this type of work. With its crowned and enthroned figures, seen frontally, and addorsed animals in six-lobed compartments, it is certainly derived, according to Falke, "from a Regensburg brocade of the 13th century."

Lit.: M. Schuette, Gestickte Bildteppiche des Mittelalters, Leipzig 1930, II, p. 41, Pl. 25 – von Falke in Pantheon VIII, (1931), p. 371

159 LINEN CLOTH with Lower Saxon coats-of-arms, and mythical beasts in hexagonal frames formed of roses and fleur-de-lys.
Kloster Isenhagen, second quarter of the 14th century
121 × 165 cm. Hexagon: 41.5 cm
Linen. White and black linen thread; strongly twisted woollen thread in red, green, yellow and blue. Brick, couching and stem stitches; satin stitch forming patterns.

Lit.: M. Schuette, Gestickte Bildteppiche des Mittelalters, Leipzig 1930, II, p. 41, Pl. 26

160–164 ALTAR CLOTH
Hesse, c. 1350
New York, Metropolitan Museum of Art (Fletcher Fund, 1929. Inv. No. 29, 87)
100 × 395 cm
Centre, Christ enthroned in a mandorla. On his right, Saints Augustine, Nicholas (Fig. 164) and Peter. On his left, Nero (Fig. 163), Herod and Pilate. At the two ends, which hung down over the edge of the altar, on one side St. Anne with the Virgin and Child between Saints Catherine and Elizabeth, and a kneeling donor (Fig. 162), on the other side, Adoration of the Kings and kneeling donatrix. Between the figures, foliage scrolls. A Latin inscription names the embroideresses Hadewigis, Sophia and Lucardis. White linen; linen thread. The coloured threads of the outlines are now lost. Stem, chain and satin stitches, the latter forming a great variety of filling patterns. Faces and hands worked with very fine thread in chain stitch. From the Praemonstratensian nunnery of Altenberg on the Lahn (cf. 154–157). Figs. 160 and 161 were taken against the light in order to show the design more clearly.

Lit.: Rorimer, A Fourteenth-Century German Altar Cloth. Bulletin of the Metropolitan Museum, 1930, p. 10 – L. v. Wilckens, Hessische Leinenstickereien des 13. und 14. Jahrhunderts. Anzeiger des Germanischen National-Museums 1954–59, Nuremberg 1959, p. 10

165–167 LECTERN COVER WITH THE STORY OF REYNARD THE FOX
Lower Germany, probably Lübeck, early 14th century.
Lübeck, St.-Annen-Museum (95/1)
300 × 115 cm
Three details showing the two halves and the scene of Reynard preaching to the Geese. Linen ground. White linen thread; woollen thread for the outlines (now almost entirely fallen out) in red, blue, yellow and green. Satin stitch and brick stitch form pattern effects. The coats-of-arms, except for that of Count Schaumburg, are not identified. "probably" from a church in Lübeck.

Lit.: A. Gräbke in Pantheon VII (1934), p. 242

168 ALTAR CLOTH, originally a Lectern Cover
Münster, Westphalia, from a Cistercian Nunnery?, end of the 14th century
Soest, St. Maria zur Wiese
Dimensions of the whole: 135 × 428 cm
Detail: Annunciation with Saints Dorothy and Catherine. Brownish linen ground, white linen thread. Plait and chain stitches.

Lit.: H. Schwartz, Soest in seinen Denkmälern III, 1957, p. 133 – A. Gräbke in "Westfalen" 1938, p. 185, Fig. 75, 78

169 THE GUICCIARDINI QUILT (detail)
Sicily, about 1400
Florence, Museo Nazionale (Palazzo Davanzati) and London, Victoria and Albert Museum (1391–1904)
205 × 256 cm and 310 × 270 cm. Dimensions of the detail (Florence): 105 × 75 cm
The quilt, now divided into two parts, shows, in rectangular fields, scenes from the Tristram legend. Two layers of linen. The outlines in back stitch worked in linen thread are now of brownish colour; the ground is covered with dense rows of small white running stitches.

Lit.: L. Morelli, Un trapunto trecentesco: Dedalo, Anno II, 1921/22, p. 70

170/171 ALTAR FRONTAL FROM BAMBERG CATHEDRAL
South Germany, about 1300
Munich, Bayerisches Nationalmuseum (23/31)
83 × 298 cm
The Three Magi, and the Virgin Enthroned with the Child, in a row of four medallions. In spandrels, half-length figures of Saints Paul and James, three prophets, two angels and two donors. At each end, a knightly saint with the arms of Bamberg. Metrical Latin inscription. Linen ground worked throughout with silk in chain stitches running vertically, and couched gold thread in zigzag patterns. Colours: white, greenish blue, beige shading to golden brown. Red used only for a spiral in chain stitch on the white-embroidered cheeks. The chain mail of the Kings is worked in silver thread.

Lit.: S. Müller-Christensen, Über drei Stickereien im Bayerischen Nationalmuseum: Pantheon, Munich 1941, p. 226 – E. Heinemeyer, Süddeutsche Stickereien des 13. und 14. Jahrhunderts. Diss. Munich 1958, p. 41 and 127.

172 ALTAR FRONTAL, Virgin on the throne of Solomon between the two Saints John
Upper Rhine? (Constance, Zürich?), beginning of the 14th century
Berne, Bernisches Historisches Museum (No. 26)
95 × 180 cm. Figures: 80 cm high. Virgin: 86 cm high
Linen ground (modern). Gold and silver thread couched with red, blue and green silk, with pattern effects. White silk for the flesh. The black outlines and inner drawing have been restored. The face of St. John has been painted in preparation for the embroidery.

Lit.: J. Stammler, Der Paramentenschatz im Historischen Museum zu Bern, 1895, p. 53 – Die Kunstdenkmäler des Kantons Aarau, Bd. III: E. Maurer, Das Kloster Königsfelden, p. 310

173 ALTAR FRONTAL WITH THE TREE OF LIFE (right half)
Rhineland, end of the 13th century
Anagni, Museo del Duomo
95 × 235 cm. Detail: 95 × 118 cm

Christ crucified on the Tree of Life. Above, the pelican in piety. To each side, long branches with angels holding inscribed scrolls at the ends. Above, below and at the sides, circles containing prophets, St. Peter, and the Virgin Mary in prayer, with a star-shaped halo; the circular frames contain inscriptions. Above, a wide band of gold with lozenges; below, a band with coats-of-arms. Linen ground. Gold thread, and silk chiefly in red and green. Gold thread in couched work. The silk in satin stitch and couched work. Much damaged. A gift from Pope Boniface VIII (1294-1303) to the cathedral of his birthplace. (cf. figs. 72 and 123–125). Described in an inventory of the 14th century as: "Dossale ad aurum cum arbore vite cum mantili de opere Theotonico".

Lit.: B. de Montault: Annales Archéologiques, XVII, XVIII, Paris 1857 and 1858, p. 349 and p. 28 – I. Errera in Rassegna d'Arte 1912, p.171

174/175 COPE
Engelberg Nunnery, 1318
Engelberg, Benedictine Abbey
Height: 146 cm. Diam.: 300 cm. Lozenges: 22.5 × 18 cm (internal measurements. Bands: 4 cm

Fine white linen ground; black linen lining. White linen thread and slightly twisted silk thread. Slate blue, old rose, celadon green, yellow, light blue, white. Brick and stem stitch; minute tent stitch at the edge. The outlines are worked in stem stitch in various colours. Detail: the hood, which was not originally associated with the cope and was worked by another hand. It is very large (62 × 48 cm) and made up from several pieces. The lower part consists of two sections of Cologne borders sewn together. Embroidery: gold strip wound on white silk thread; silk threads in red, a little green and white; gold and red predominate. The subjects are the Nativity, the Annunciation, the Adoration of the Magi, the Last Supper (Christ holds the Host in his raised right hand, the chalice in his left hand), the Crucifixion, the Harrowing of Hell, the Resurrection, Christ appearing to St. Mary Magdalene, the Ascension (two angels and Christ in a mandorla). The incomplete inscriptions in the borders of cope and hood refer to Abbot Walther, Magistra Maria, Adilheid. Abbot Walther is Abbot Walther III of Engelberg, 1317 to 1331. In 1318 the Nunnery, which later removed to Sarnen, was in Engelberg, where this embroidery was probably executed by the nuns. The tradition that the cope was embroidered by the hand of the Hungarian Queen Agnes, the great benefactress of the Convent, appears first in the Annals of the chronicler Straumeyer in 1732 (Annals II, p. 17). This information cannot be found in the mutilated inscription.

Lit.: R. Durrer, Die Kunstdenkmäler des Kantons Unterwalden, Zürich 1899/1928, p. 161

176 HANGING, FRAGMENT WITH SCENES FROM THE STORY OF ST NICHOLAS
Lower Saxony (Göttingen), second half of the 14th century
Berlin, Schloss Charlottenburg, Kunstgewerbemuseum (86 : 13)
Whole: 96 × 115 cm. Detail: 52 × 80 cm

Detail: St. Nicholas appears to the royal couple in a dream. St. Nicholas saves a boy in danger of drowning. Loosely woven linen. White linen thread and coloured silk in red, blue-green, green, yellow, light blue, brown, beige, lilac. Brick, stem, satin and convent stitch. On the two symmetrical fragments, the stories of St. Nicholas and St. Augustine are depicted in six scenes.

177 HANGING WITH THE STORY OF ST. MARGARET
Lower Saxony, Kloster St. Marienberg, about 1290
Helmstedt, Kloster St. Marienberg
Dimensions of the whole: 52.5 (55) × 74 cm. Squares: 23.5 (25) × 24 (25.5) cm

Detail: Origen meets Margaret keeping her sheep; her imprisonment; her trial. Arms: Warberg, Everstein, Reinstein. Nettle cloth with lightly embroidered panels of silk applied. White linen thread; coloured silk in two shades of blue, yellow, brownish purple, dark green. Laid gold thread; brick, satin and stem stitch. The black has partially fallen out. Two fragments with twenty-three scenes from the story of St. Margaret and eight coats-of-arms. Hedwig von Wernigerode (arms on one of the scenes not illustrated), was a nun at St. Marienberg from 1281 onwards; Mechthild von Warberg was Prioress from 1296 onwards.

Lit.: R. Kroos, Niedersächsische figürliche Leinen- und Seidenstickereien des 12. bis 14. Jahrhunderts. Diss. Göttingen 1957, p. 99 (unpublished)

178 CUSHION
Westphalia, 14th to 15th century
Berlin, Schloss Charlottenburg, Kunstgewerbemuseum (88.663)
28 × 40 cm

Grey linen canvas. Embroidered with untwisted floss silk in brick stitch. Colours: green, yellow, red, white. On the underside, striped Spanish silk. From the Treasury of Enger. Acquired from the Dionysianisches Kapitel der Johanniskirche in Herford.

179 CORPORAL BOX WITH EMBROIDERED COVER
Westphalia, 14th to 15th century
Berlin, Schloss Charlottenburg, Kunstgewerbemuseum (88.651)
Height: 4.6 cm. Width: 22.4 cm. Length: 22.4 cm

Wood, originally with four (now only three) ornamental metal feet of spherical shape. Covered inside and outside with linen. The six outer sides embroidered with floss silk in green, red, blue, white, pink. The underside and side walls have similar patterns in long-armed cross stitch. The cover, illustrated, is in brick stitch. From the Treasury of Enger. Acquired from the Dionysianisches Kapitel der Johanniskirche in Herford.

180 CHRIST IN GLORY, detail of the Altar Frontal from Marienwerder
Lower Saxony, 14th century
Hanover, Kestnermuseum (W.M. XXII, 5)
102 × 180 cm. Detail: Mandorla, 38 cm high

Chinese red silk damask, 14th century; seed pearls, coral beads, semi-precious stones in metal settings, stamped parcel-gilt silver plaques, stars and rosettes. Black, turquoise coloured and gold glass beads. Applied work and bead embroidery. The figures are worked on parchment. The silver plaques on the outer border of the altar frontal (not shown here) bear the arms of the Hamersen family.

Lit.: Norddeutsche Goldschmiedearbeiten und Stickereien des Mittelalters. Ausstellung, Museum für Kunst und Gewerbe, Hamburg 1948, No. 92 – Sonderausstellung, Kestnermuseum, Hannover 1956/57, No. 54

Colour Plate VIII. ALTAR FRONTAL OF THE HIGH ALTAR OF HALBERSTADT CATHEDRAL
Lower Saxony, second half of the 13th century
Halberstadt, Cathedral Museum, No. 203
Throne: about 58 cm high

Detail. Red satin faded to old rose. Bead embroidery on parchment and linen. Coral and glass beads of cylindrical and spherical form, opaque and transparent. Predominant colours: coral red, two shades of green, dark blue shading, to light blue, turquoise, aubergine, gold, black. All the seed pearls and most of the violet glass beads and the gilded plaques are now missing. The outer edge and inner fields of the throne had metal plaques with Romanesque foliage and palmettes (their imprints remain on the material). The effect of the whole is impaired by the white patches left where the seed pearls and gold plaques have disappeared.

Lit.: M. Schuette, Gestickte Bildteppiche des Mittelalters, Leipzig 1930. II, p. 74, Pl. 46 and 47

181 REMAINS OF A HANGING WITH SIX FIGURES OF PROPHETS
Lower Saxony, about 1300
Kloster Wienhausen
230 × 158/143 cm. Detail: about 160 cm high
Detail: the prophets Hosea and Jonah. Linen ground. Coloured wool in dark blue, red, yellow, green, ochre, white, black. The colours are in part much faded. Convent stitch.
Lit.: M. Schuette, Gestickte Bildteppiche des Mittelalters, Leipzig 1927, I, p. 14, Pl. 12 and 13

182–184 RATIONALE (EPISCOPAL COLLAR)
South Germany, Regensburg, about 1320–1340
Regensburg, Cathedral Treasury
Height: 62 cm. Width: 67 cm
The front shows scenes from the Song of Songs, with Christ as King Solomon, the figure of Ecclesia, two martyrs and St. John the Evangelist (Fig. 183); below, Saints Martha and Mary; right and left, Saints Peter and Paul, and border with apostles beneath arches (Fig. 182). Back: (Fig. 184); Christ in Judgment with the Lamb of God below, surrounded with the symbols of the Evangelists and with angels. Borders with apostles. The circular shoulder pieces show allegories of Charity and Truth, Justice and Peace. The iconography is based on that of a rationale of about 1020 in Bamberg Cathedral Treasury. Gold and silk embroidery on linen. Faces, hair and hands in chain and stem stitch, inner drawing with red and brown silk. Garments, scrolls and architecture, like the ground, worked in couched gold thread; the ground is couched in zigzag patterns. The inner drawing and inscriptions were left in reserve in the gold embroidery and worked with coloured silk.
Lit.: S. Müller-Christensen, Sakrale Gewänder des Mittelalters, Ausstellungs-Katalog 1955, No. 61, p. 31 – E. Heinemeyer, Süddeutsche Stickereien des 13. und 14. Jahrhunderts. Diss. Munich 1958, p. 62

185/186 Colour Plate IX. THE MALTERER HANGING
Freiburg (Breisgau), about 1310 to 1320
Freiburg (Breisgau), Augustinermuseum (11.508)
68 × 490 cm
Two details and colour plate: Iwein and Laudine (1 : 1), Phyllis and Aristotle; Virgil and the Emperor's daughter. Linen ground. Coloured wool in blue, yellow, green, rust light brown, white. Convent stitch, stem stitch. The hanging illustrates the evil consequences of earthly love. In eight quatrefoils arranged in pairs: Samson and Delilah, Aristotle and Phyllis, Virgil and the daughter of the Emperor Augustus, Iwein and Laudine. Finally, as a symbol of Christian love and chastity: the Virgin with a Unicorn. At both ends, the arms of the Malterer family, who gave the hanging to the Convent of St. Catherine at Freiburg i. Breisgau, where Anna Malterer was a nun.
Lit.: F. Maurer, in Vierteljahrsschrift für Literaturwissenschaft und Geistesgeschichte, Jg. 27, (1953), Heft 2, p. 182 – Schweitzer in Schauinsland XXXI (1904), p. 50

187 BACKCLOTH, HERALDIC HANGING
Upper Rhine, about 1330
Freiburg (Breisgau), Augustinermuseum (11.506)
53 × 183.5 cm
Linen ground. Embroidered with coloured wool, slightly twisted, in red, two shades of blue, yellow, green, two shades of brown, white.

Convent and stem stitch (for the faces). Subjects: Samson, Phyllis and Aristotle. In between, the arms of the noble Breisgau family of Reich von Reichenstein (boar spear). The following item belongs to the same series.

188 BOAR HUNT WITH THE ARMS OF SCHNEWELIN
Basle, Historisches Museum (1901–134)
50 × 122.5 cm
A third piece from this series, not illustrated, in Freiburg, Augustinermuseum (11.507), shows Alexander, Queen Kandace and a servant girl, with the arms of the families of Munzingen and Falkenstein.

189 WALL HANGING
Iceland, 14th century
Copenhagen, Nationalmuseum (inv. CLII)
Height: about 60 cm. Length: about 75 and 210 cm
Detail: 60 × 180 cm
Black woollen cloth, with the design in reserve on a background embroidered in white. Laid and couched work with the outlines in a thicker couched thread. The Icelandic and Norwegian name of this type of laid and couched work, which we have already encountered in the Bayeux Tapestry of 1066/77 (cf. figs. 31–33), is "Refilsaum". – From the church of Hvam (Northern Iceland).

190 PART OF A CANOPY
Sweden, 15th century
Stockholm, Statens historiska Museum (6932)
58 × 59 cm
Patchwork and applied work of red, blue and white woollen material; outlines and inner drawing in leather strips fixed by couching stitches. From the church of Hög (Hälsingland).
Lit.: A. Branting and A. Lindblom, Medieval Embroideries and Textiles in Sweden, Stockholm 1932, I, p. 31, II, Pl. 25 – A. Geijer, Medeltida Textilier av svensk tillverkning, Stockholm 1932, p. 4, Fig. 1

191 WALL HANGING
Iceland, 16th century
Copenhagen, Nationalmuseum (Inv. CCCLXXI)
Height: 0.95 cm. Length: 10 m. Length of detail: 2.60 m
Black woollen material. Long armed cross stitch in white, beige, light brown, brown (originally red?) and blue. From Hof in northern Iceland. A characteristic example of the persistence of medieval motifs.

192 ALTAR HANGING: SCENES FROM THE LIFE OF THE VIRGIN (detail)
Iceland, 14th century
Copenhagen, Nationalmuseum (CLV)
100 × 85 cm. Diameter of the medallions: 25 cm
Three rows of three medallions with scenes from the Life of the Virgin. Linen. Red, light and dark blue, brown, green and yellow plied woollen thread; white linen thread. Faces and hands in chain and stem stitch. The remainder in "Refilsaum" (cf. Fig. 189). Outlines in couched threads. The hanging was, until 1819, in the church of Reikjalid (northern Iceland).
Lit.: G. Wandel, To broderede Billedtæpper og deres islandske Oprindelse. Fra Nationalmuseets Arbejdsmark, Copenhagen 1941, p. 71

193–195 TRISTRAM HANGING
Lower Saxony, about 1300
Kloster Wienhausen
233 (originally about 300) × 404 cm. Figures: 15 cm high
The whole and two details: Tristram in the boat and Tristram being bathed by Iseult (1:1). Linen ground. Loosely spun woollen yarn:

dark blue, red, green, yellow, white, black. Convent stitch. Cut at the edges and patched. Twenty-three scenes from the Tristram Legend following a version of the original story which was popularly current in Lower Saxony.

Lit.: M. Schuette, Gestickte Bildteppiche des Mittelalters, Leipzig 1927, I, p. 3, Pl. 1–5 – J. Ricklefs in Cellesche Zeitung, Der Sachsenspiegel, 30. Juni 1950 und 16. Mai 1953

196/197, 201/202 Colour Plate X. ALTAR FRONTAL WITH SEVEN SCENES FROM THE PASSION OF CHRIST
The band shows the Coronation of the Virgin and Angels
Austria, region of Vienna, about 1340–1350
Berne, Bernisches Historisches Museum (27 and 51)
90 × 318 cm and 18 × 292 cm (the band has been shortened)
The whole and four details: Ascension, Christ and an Angel from the band, and, in the colour plate, Christ before Pilate. Linen ground. Gold and silver threads and cords. Coloured silks in light, cool colours: blue, green, grey, brown, yellow, black. The gold is couched in various patterns. Split stitch, applied work (the piers) and raised work. Scenes: the Agony in the Garden, Christ before Pilate, Christ carrying the Cross, the Crucifixion, the Ascension, the Coronation of the Virgin, Christ in Glory. In places where the embroidery has fallen out, the careful preliminary drawing is visible; Maurer considers that the artist is close to the Master of the Hohenfurt altar and the Kaufmann Crucifixion. The altar frontal comes from the Convent of Königsfelden and is mentioned in the inventory, which was drawn up in 1357 by Queen Agnes herself, as "from our dear brother Duke Albrecht" (II of Austria, d. 1358).

Lit.: J. Stammler, Der Paramentenschatz im Historischen Museum zu Bern, 1895, p. 65 – Die Kunstdenkmäler des Kantons Aarau, Vol. III, Basel 1954: E. Maurer, Das Kloster Königsfelden, p. 279

198–200 KOENIGSFELDEN ALTAR FRONTAL: Crucifixion and Six Saints
Upper Rhine and Königsfelden, second third of the 14th century
Berne, Bernisches Historisches Museum (No. 19)
90 × 318 cm. Figures: about 59/60 cm high
Whole and two details: Crucifixion and St Catherine. Carmine velvet ground. The figures embroidered on linen over a parchment foundation and applied. Gold and silver strip wound on silk thread, gold cord, silk, copper foil, seed pearls. Needle painting, split and satin stitches, raised work and laid gold thread. Soft shaded colours: light blue, yellow-green, ochre, carmine, salmon pink, white. The shafts of the columns are formed from tablet-woven bands; the bases and capitals are of copper foil, as are also the raised lines forming the pointed arches. The outlines have been reinforced with brown wool in modern times. During the restoration of 1889 the parchment foundation was found to include part of a letter of 1334–1335 from the Emperor Ludwig the Bavarian to Queen Agnes of Hungary, who was living at Königsfelden from 1316 onwards and died there in 1364. Stylistic differences among the figures indicate three separate hands. One of these executed the Crucifixion group and Saints Catherine and John the Baptist, which are artistically important examples of the High Gothic style; two others were responsible for Saints Agnes and Andrew and Saints Peter and Paul, which are artistically and technically much inferior. This has suggested the hypothesis that the finer figures were perhaps executed in the region of the Upper Rhine (possibly in the neighbourhood of Strassburg or Freiburg), while the two principal apostles and the two favourite saints of Queen Agnes were added subsequently in Königsfelden to make a wider altar frontal.

Lit.: J. Stammler, Der Paramentenschatz im Historischen Museum zu Bern, 1895, p. 59 – Die Kunstdenkmäler des Kantons Aarau, Vol. III, Basel 1954: E. Maurer, Das Kloster Königsfelden, p. 297

203/204 ALTAR FRONTAL OF GIOVANNI DI NICOSIA
Italy, Pisa, 1325
Pisa, Museo Nazionale
98 × 303 cm
Coronation of the Virgin, flanked above by Saints Peter and Paul, and below by Saints John the Baptist and John the Evangelist with a priestly donor and a donatrix (Giovanni di Nicosia and his mother?). On either side, in two bands to the left, the Annunciation, Nativity, Adoration of the Magi, Presentation in the Temple, and to the right, Resurrection, Ascension, Death of the Virgin and Pentecost. Along the upper edge, shields of arms (lion and eagle) in a flowering scroll; below, a Latin inscription stating that the paliotto was given to the cathedral of Pisa by Archbishop Giovanni di Nicosia, in 1325, for the soul of his mother, Jacoba. Giovanni di Nicosia was Bishop of Pisa 1299–1312. White silk twill (much worn) on a linen lining. Silk and gold embroidery; robes of the Virgin and Christ in white silk with folds in blue and red; other garments chiefly in gold and silver threads, which are lightly twisted with red or green silk threads, so as to produce a shimmer of colour. The inner drawing is left in reserve in the gold and embroidered with coloured stem stitches. Silk embroidery in split and a little chain stitch; architectural parts in polychrome silk in satin and split stitch. The date beneath the throne was added at a later restoration.

Lit.: A. Santangelo, Tessuti d'arte italiani. Milano 1958, p. 18

205–207 THE SALZBURG ALTAR FRONTAL
Austria, 3rd to 4th decade of the 14th century
Vienna, Österreichisches Museum für angewandte Kunst (T 8543)
96 × 390 cm. Quatrefoils: about 46 to 48 cm. Standing figures: about 37 cm high
Three details: the two halves and the Lamentation over the Dead Christ. Gold thread (tarnished) in underside and surface couching. Coloured silks, shaded, and much faded: blue, yellow, cinnabar red, grey, white, black, ochre. The silk is worn. Metal plaques: the crowns of the old king, of the Virgin and of Pilate are of gold foil, the three cups held by the kings are of silver-gilt foil with an inscription: "Praesul Fridricus Leibnicensi Sanguine natus hoc opus aptavit altari quod decoravit Seidlit de Petovia me paravit." The Life of Christ is illustrated with unusual completeness in eighteen scenes, from the Annunciation to the Ascension; sixteen half-length figures of prophets. Left: a bishop with a halo (perhaps the titular saint of the altar for which the frontal was made). Right: a second bishop without a halo, probably Bishop Friedrich, the donor. Judging from the inscription, the donor was doubtless Friedrich von Leibnitz, Archbishop of Salzburg 1315–1338, and the embroiderer was Seidlit, from Pettau (Styria). Until 1906 in the Cathedral of Salzburg.

Lit.: Österreichische Kunsttopographie, Bd. IX, H. Tietze, Die kirchlichen Denkmale der Stadt Salzburg. Vienna 1912, p. 66, Pl. XVIII–XXI – E. Heinemeyer, Süddeutsche Stickereien des 13. und 14. Jahrhunderts, Diss. Munich 1958, p. 53

208–210 DALMATIC, SO-CALLED "EAGLE DALMATIC". One of the insignia of the Holy Roman Empire
Austria, third to fourth decade of the 14th century;
Chinese silk material of about 1300 or earlier
Vienna, Weltliche Schatzkammer
Length in front from the neck opening: 152 cm, from the shoulder: 160 cm. Orphreys: 13 cm wide; on the shoulders: 9.5 cm. Medallions: 7.5 cm in diameter
The whole, and two details showing orphreys and eagles. Purple silk damask with applied circular medallions showing eagles embroidered in black on a gold ground. At the hem, neck opening, shoulders and cuffs, embroidered orphreys showing thirty-nine crowned kings holding, except for the six at the neck opening, orb and sceptre.

Linen. Gold and coloured silks: shaded blue. red shading to pink, green shading to yellow, brown, black. The eyes of the eagles are of black glass. Needle painting; chiefly split stitch. The gold partly in raised work. Couched work. The garment was recorded for the first time in 1350.

Lit.: H. Fillitz, Die Insignien und Kleinodien des Heiligen Römischen Reiches, Vienna-Munich 1954, p. 61, Fig. 38–40 – E. Heinemeyer, Süddeutsche Stickereien des 13. und 14. Jahrhunderts. Diss. Munich 1958, p. 4

211 CHASUBLE EMBROIDERED WITH EAGLES
Lower Saxony (?), second half of the 13th century
Halberstadt, Cathedral Museum, No. 210
Length in front: 113 cm, at the back: 159 cm
Silk twill and linen lining, both dark blue. Silver-gilt strip wound on yellow and white silk. Gold cord effects without a linen foundation. The gold is couched with coarse white linen threads; outlines in red silk in stem stitch. – Curtailed at the bottom.
Lit.: M. Schuette, Gestickte Bildteppiche des Mittelalters, Leipzig 1930, II, p. 82, Pl. 52

212/213 TWO FRAGMENTS OF AN EMBROIDERED COAT OF ARMS
Lower Rhine or Southern Netherlands, middle of the 14th century
Paris, Musée de Cluny
52 × 120 cm
On each panel, heraldically stylised leopards. The background is covered with a dense pattern of foliage scrolls among which are small male and female figures. Red silk velvet. Embroidery in two kinds of gold thread and in red, white and blue silk. Pearls and gems. Glass eyes. Gold embroidery in couched work, the gold threads following the direction of the outlines. The inner drawing is emphasised by the use of thicker gold threads. The eyes, tongues and claws of the leopards are worked in coloured silk, in chain, stem and satin stitch. The foliage scrolls and figures are worked in white silk in running and satin stitch, outlined with gold thread. Were the embroideries perhaps originally emblems for a tent roof or for a horse trapper? Subsequently, they were sewn together and used as a chasuble. They were formerly in the sacristy of the Praemonstratensian Nunnery of Altenberg, near Wetzlar on the Lahn, which was suppressed in 1802, and later at Schloss Braunfels. The miniature-like powdering of tiny figures recurs in the funerary shield of Landgraf Heinrich I (d. 1308) from the Elisabethkirche at Marburg on the Lahn, now in the University Museum, Marburg. At the same time, the linear stylisation recalls English heraldry of the first half of the 14th century. (Translator's note: English-speaking readers will recognise the golden leopards on a red ground as the Royal Arms of England. These fragments have generally been thought to be English embroideries.)
Lit.: M. Symonds and L. Preece, Needlework through the Ages, London 1928. p. 201 – D. King, Opus Anglicanum, Exhibition, Victoria and Albert Museum 1963, Cat. p. 38, No. 76

214/215 FRONT AND BACK OF A PURSE
France (Paris?), second half of the 14th century
Lyon, Musée Historique des Tissus (30.020/1 and 2)
21 × 20 cm
A lady being crowned by a falconer; huntsman with hawk and hood. Gold and silk embroidery on linen, worked on a thin foundation and applied to red velvet, now somewhat worn, embroidered with flowers. Gold thread, white, red and brown silk. Satin, stem and split stitch. Couched work. Sequins.

216 Colour Plate XI. PURSE WITH LOVERS (AUMONIÈRE)
France (Paris), about 1340

Hamburg, Museum für Kunst und Gewerbe (Inv. 56, 137)
16 × 14 cm
Linen, with embroidery in gold and silk. Split, chain, stem and knot stitches. Background covered with gold thread, couched with red silk in zig-zag patterns.
Lit.: Stiftung zur Förderung der Hamburger Kunstsammlungen, Erwerbungen 1956, p. 28

217/218 PURSE WITH LOVERS (AUMONIÈRE)
France, middle of the 14th century
Sens, Cathedral, Treasury
21 × 18 cm
On one side, a seated lady with a garland of flowers in her hand receives a ring from her lover. On the other side, the return of the lover from the hunt. (Subjects from the poem of the Châtelaine de Vergy). Linen ground. Silk embroidery in split stitch; the ground covered with gold and silk threads in couched work.
Lit.: Chartraire, Le trésor de la cathédrale de Sens: Les Arts, November 1913, p. 14 – Reallexikon zur Deutschen Kunstgeschichte I, Stuttgart 1937. p. 394

219/220 MITRE OF JEAN DE MARIGNY
Northern France, middle of the 14th century
Evreux (Eure), Museum
Height: 25 cm
On the front, St. Peter enthroned between kneeling figures of Cornelius and Dorcas (Acts 9/10). On the back, Saint Eloi, with crozier and goldsmith's hammer, between two donors, probably Enguerrand de Marigny and his wife Alips de Mons. Green silk taffeta. Coloured silk embroidery, with flesh parts in chain stitch, garments partly in split stitch, partly in couched gold threads. Jean de Marigny was Bishop of Beauvais 1312–47 and died in 1351 as Archbishop of Rouen. He was buried in the Collegiate Church at Ecouis which was founded by his brother Enguerrand in 1310. The mitre is recorded in an inventory of this church in 1565.
Lit.: E. Gresy, Mitra de Jean de Marigny: Annales archéologiques, XIII, Paris 1853, p. 68–74 – De Farcy, La Broderie, Angers 1890, p. 126. Pl. 33

221 PURSE (AUMONIÈRE)
France (Paris?), middle of the 14th century
Xanten, Cathedral Treasury
35 × 31 cm
Three musicians. The figures are embroidered with polychrome silk threads in chain stitch and couched work on linen, applied to a background covered with couched gold threads.
Lit.: Reallexikon zur deutschen Kunstgeschichte I, Stuttgart 1937, p. 394

222 PURSE (AUMONIÈRE)
France (Paris?), middle of the 14th century
Paris, Musée de Cluny
Height: 35 cm. Width at the bottom: 31 cm
On the cover, a grotesque monster playing a tambourine; below, a harpy, half woman, half bird, and a bearded man. These figures probably symbolise the sins of Vanity, Frivolity and Avarice. The background material was originally red silk and green velvet with a linen foundation. The figures are worked on linen and applied to the ground. Faces and hands are worked in silk in very fine chain stitch, garments with gold threads in couched work.

223 and 225 MITRE FROM THE SAINTE CHAPELLE, PARIS
Paris, about 1380–1390
Paris, Musée de Cluny
Height: about 40 cm

On the front, the Nativity, Crucifixion, John the Baptist and a Bishop Saint. On the back, the Adoration of the Magi, Annunciation, Saints Denis and Catherine. On the lappets, the Virgin and Child with a kneeling bishop as donor. White silk taffeta, with linen lining. Gold thread; silk in pink, white and green. Seed pearls. The figures are worked in relief over a linen foundation, and applied. Gold embroidery in couched work, with black chain stitches indicating the folds. Faces, hands and parts of the draperies in very fine chain stitch; hair partly in knot stitch. The embroidery representing the ground beneath the figures is worked in or nué; architectural parts worked in metal thread in relief.

224 MITRE
Paris, about 1380
Paris, Musée de Cluny
Height: about 30 cm
On the front, Coronation of the Virgin, and Saints. On the back, Annunciation. Linen. Gold thread; silk, chiefly in light red and light blue. Figures in chain stitch; hair partly in knot stitches. The background is worked in couched gold thread, with geometrical patterns.

226/227 TRIPTYCH: PIETA
Paris, about 1410
Chartres, Musée des Beaux-Arts
Christ of Pity between the Virgin and St John the Evangelist. On the wings, Saints John the Baptist and Catherine. Silk and gold embroidery, partly in relief. The flesh and parts of the draperies are embroidered in silk with very fine split stitches which follow the direction of the outlines. Noses, mouths, hair and haloes are raised in slight relief. Mary's robe is blue with gold stars, her dress is of gold thread couched with white and red silk in patterns, like the cloth beneath the figure of Christ. John the Evangelist wears a red mantle and John the Baptist a red mantle over a camel skin. The blue mantle of St. Catherine is lined with ermine and the edges of her dress are emphasised with a band of chain stitch. The lamb is in knot stitch. Architecture and background in couched gold thread. This work shows embroidery attaining a degree of perfection which is comparable with that of contemporary goldsmiths' work.
Lit.: De Farcy, La Broderie, Angers 1890, Pl. 50 – Europäische Kunst um 1400, Ausstellung Wien 1962, No. 531

228 ST. JOHN THE BAPTIST
France, about 1400
Lyon, Musée historique des Tissus (Inv. No. 24054)
Height: 73 cm. Width: 28 cm
Linen. Gold and silver thread; silk, chiefly white shading to blue, red shading to dark lilac and yellow shading to brown, worked with delicate shaded effects in split stitch. The lamb is worked with silver thread in spirals. A few gold and silver threads are used in the representation of the camel skin. The background is worked with two kinds of gold thread, couched with red silk. The halo is couched with white silk. Architectural parts are of gold cords, formed of plied gold threads. In the style of Jacquemart de Hesdin, from Picardy, one of the Court artists of the Duc de Berry. Probably a fragment of an altar frontal or triptych.
Lit.: Europäische Kunst um 1400, Ausstellungs-Katalog Wien 1962, p. 477, Nr. 532

229 Colour Plate XII. WALL HANGING: PAIRS OF LOVERS (details)
Bavaria, about 1370–1380
Regensburg, Museum der Stadt
335 × 275 cm. Diam. of the medallions: 47 cm
Six rows of four medallions with scenes of love, partially derived from poetry and legend. The inscriptions relate to love, faithfulness

and unfaithfulness. Coarse linen. Plied woollen thread. Convent stitch.
Lit.: F. v. d. Leyen, Die altdeutschen Wandteppiche: Das Rathaus zu Regensburg, Regensburg 1910, p. 74

230 WALL HANGING: TRISTRAM AND ISEULT
North Germany, second half of the 14th century
London, Victoria and Albert Museum (T. 1370–1864, Bock)
Detail: about 42 × 40 cm
Detail: King Mark in the Tree. From a North German convent, locality unknown. Background of dark blue cloth. Square fields, alternately blue and red with applied figures in red, blue, green, brown. Gilt leather strip. Metal plaques. Spiral cords (Iseult's hair). Coloured silk threads. Couching and split stitches. Very poor state of preservation. Remains of twenty-two scenes from the Tristram legend.
Lit.: J. Ricklefs in Cellesche Zeitung, Der Sachsenspiegel, 16. Mai 1953

231 EMBROIDERED PICTURE (Detail)
Bohemia, about 1370
Munich, Bayerisches Nationalmuseum (T. 4086)
56 × 78 cm. Detail: 28 × 62 cm
Two princely couples, among foliage scrolls; in the four corners, quatrefoils, each containing a fashionably dressed figure. Embroidery in pale-coloured silks on white silk material, lined with red painted linen, which, owing to the damage to the silk material, is visible in many places. Split and stem stitch; knot stitch for the hair. There were originally pearls on the crowns and girdles.

232–235 THE PIRNA ALTAR FRONTAL
Bohemia, about 1360
Meissen, Staatliche Kunstsammlungen
95 × 335 cm
Whole and three details: the two halves and a Bishop Saint. Linen ground. A little gold: couched work and raised work. Coloured silks in split stitch and couched work. The preliminary drawing is visible at many points where the embroidery is worn away. The Coronation of the Virgin with five saints on either side: Wenceslaus, a Bishop Saint, Andrew, Peter, John the Evangelist. John the Baptist, Paul, an Apostle, Adalbert, Stephen. The altar frontal comes from the Marienkirche in Pirna.
Lit.: Z. Drobná, Les trésors de la broderie religieuse en Tchécoslovaquie, Prague 1950, p. 16, Fig. 17, 18

236 ALTAR HANGING (Detail)
Southern Bohemia, about 1370–1380
Prague, Nationalmuseum
70 × 123 cm. Detail: 70 × 40 cm
Three rectangles, each with three bands showing half-length figures of personages from the Old and New Testaments and, in the centres, the Virgin and Child, the Lamb of God, the pelican, Christ as the Man of Pity and shields of the Rosenberg family. Double layer of linen with gold and silk embroidery. Beneath the silk embroidery is a further layer of fine coloured material of silk or linen. Figures in polychrome silks, richly shaded, chiefly in split stitch. The Lamb of God, in slight relief, is worked in knot stitch. The ground is covered with gold threads running in pairs and couched in lozenge and zig-zag patterns. The hanging was given by Hans von Rosenberg (d. 1389) and his wife Elizabeth von Hals (married 1370, d. 1385), to the Convent Church of St. Aegidius in Wittingau (Trebon).
Lit.: Z. Drobná, Les trésors de la broderie religieuse, Prague 1950, p. 18, Fig. 26–28 – V. Denkstein und F. Matous, Südböhmische Gotik, Prag 1955, p. 252

237 HANGING: CHRIST IN THE WINE PRESS AND THE THRONE OF
MERCY
Franconia, about 1380
Nuremberg, Germanisches Nationalmuseum (Gew. 2464)
75 × 125 cm
Linen cloth with silk embroidery in stem, split and chain stitch. The
eyes and noses are in slight relief. The hair of the angels is of wire
wrapped with silk. Light, bright colours. The robe of Christ, yellow-
ish-white shading to red; the mantle of God the Father, light
yellow, salmon, pink, violet. Hair, light blue; bench, white and light
blue. The female donors wear a blue mantle over a plum coloured dress with some beige and light grey. Some later additions, e. g.
monogram of an owner.

238/239 CHASUBLE ORPHREY
Bohemia, late 14th century
Brno, Moravian Museum of Decorative Arts
Height: 112.5 cm
Chasuble orphrey with the Crucified Christ, the Virgin supported by
St. John and the second Mary, and the mourning figure of Mary Mag-
dalene. Double layer of linen. Silk in split stitch, shading from
greenish blue to dark blue, yellow to dark green, red and brown.
Background and haloes in couched gold thread. From the Church of
Saints Peter and Paul in Brno.
*Lit.: Z. Drobná, Les trésors de la broderie religieuse en Tchécoslovaquie,
Prague 1950, p. 21, Fig. 31*

240 CHASUBLE ORPHREY
Bohemia, about 1380–1390
Rokycany (Rokitzan, near Pilsen), Collegiate-church
Height: 104 cm
Two sections joined together; above, the Virgin playing with the
Child, attended by three angels; below, the Annunciation. Linen
ground, polychrome silk and gold embroidery. Split and stem
stitch; couched work in a weaving effect and in a pattern of circular
suns. One of the most beautiful examples of Bohemian art, both in
composition and in drawing. The silk material of the chasuble dates
from the second half of the 18th century.
*Lit.: Z. Drobná, Les trésors de la broderie religieuse en Tchécoslovaquie,
Prague 1950, p. 22, Fig. 21*

241 CHASUBLE ORPHREY
Southern Bohemia, early 15th century
Paris, Musée du Louvre (Inv. No. OA 9943)
110 × 65 cm
In the vertical band, the Annunciation and the Visitation; in the
horizontal band, the Adoration of the Magi. Linen ground. The
figures are worked in coloured silks in very fine chain stitch. Spiral
gold threads and pearls for crowns and jewellery. The background is
worked with gold threads couched in lozenge patterns.
*Lit.: Europäische Kunst um 1400. Ausstellungs-Katalog, Wien 1962,
p. 469, No. 528*

Colour Plate XIII. SAINT JOHN THE EVANGELIST, detail from a
chasuble orphrey
East Germany or Bohemia, about 1410
Lübeck, formerly Danzig, Marienkirche
Length of the orphrey: 128 cm. Detail: 38 × 15 cm
Linen ground. Gold and silver thread in couched work, partially
with patterns of circular suns. Silk in split stitch, laid and couched
work and satin stitch. On a chasuble of Italian brocaded silk dating
from the late 14th century.
*Lit.: W. Mannowsky, Danziger Paramentenschatz, Berlin 1931–38, Bd.
II, 1, Nr. 84 – Ausstellung: "Aus dem Danziger Paramentenschatz."*

*Nürnberg, Germanisches Nationalmuseum, Nürnberg 1958, Kat. Nr.
44*

242 HOOD OF A COPE: VIRGIN AND CHILD
Bohemia, early 15th century
Lübeck, formerly Danzig, Marienkirche
34 × 39 cm
Linen. Gold thread and coloured silks in couched work and split stitch.
*Lit.: W. Mannowsky, Danziger Paramentenschatz, Berlin 1931–38,
Bd. I, Nr. 24, Pl. 33, 34, 35*

243–248 APPARELS OF A SET OF VESTMENTS of Georg von Liech-
tenstein, Bishop of Trento 1390–1419
Austria or Bohemia, about 1410
Trento, Cathedral Sacristy
*Chasuble cross: 107 cm high. Dimensions of the details: 44 × 22 cm,
32 × 22 cm, 23 × 22 cm, 22 × 20 cm. Apparel of the dalmatic:
40 × 50 cm*
Chasuble cross with the Virgin and Child standing on a full moon
(Fig. 243), St. Vigilius, as a Bishop giving a blessing (Fig. 244), and a
kneeling Bishop with acolytes holding mitre and crozier (Fig. 245).
At the sides, half-length figures of St. John the Evangelist (Fig. 246)
and St. Peter. Linen ground. Gold thread, polychrome silk, coral and
pearls. Chiefly in chain stitch, with some stem stitch for the delicate
drawing of the faces. Noses sewn over linen threads to give slight
relief. The background in gold threads couched in lozenge patterns.
The apparels of the dalmatic show scenes from the life of St. Vigilius,
Bishop of Trento: St. Vigilius celebrating Mass; St. Vigilius overturn-
ing a figure of Saturn (Fig. 247), the Emperor Honorius winning a
battle with the help of the saint (Fig. 248). Linen ground. Gold
thread and polychrome silk. Chiefly chain stitch, with some knot
stitch (hair, beard and trees), laid and couched work, herringbone
stitch, some loop stitches. The figure of Saturn is worked over linen
threads to give slight relief. The background is of gold threads
couched in lozenge patterns. Two further pieces survive. Georg von
Liechtenstein belonged to a South Bohemian family and, before he
was appointed Bishop, was Provost of St. Stephan in Vienna. The
design for the embroideries was probably by Master Wenceslaus,
who signed the frescoes of the Cemetery Chapel at Riffiano, near
Merano, in 1450 and was perhaps the Court painter of the Bishop.
*Lit.: A. Morassi, Storia della Pittura nella Venezia Tridentina. Rome
1935, p. 353 – N. Rasmo, Venceslao da Trento e Venceslao da Merano:
Kultur des Etschlandes, 1957, p. 27*

249 LID OF A PYX: The Lamb of God
South Germany, about 1450–1470
Munich, Bayerisches Nationalmuseum (NN 1100)
Diameter: 8 cm
Red velvet with gold sequins. Relief embroidery. Linen ground with
pearls. Halo and banner in gold and silk embroidery in couched
work, satin and chain stitch. On the other side of the lid is the Vera-
con, in silk embroidery.

250 EMBROIDERED VELVET CLOTH
Danzig, second half of the 15th century
Lübeck, formerly Danzig, Marienkirche
56 × 231 cm
Detail: Virgin and two kneeling priests with an inscribed scroll. Red
silk velvet with flowers and trees worked on the velvet ground, while
the figures are worked on linen and applied. Gold and silver thread,
coloured silks, pearls. Stem stitch and couched work, but chiefly split
stitch.
*Lit.: W. Mannowsky, Danziger Paramentenschatz, Berlin 1931–38,
Bd. II, 2, IV, p. 44, Pl. 178, Nr. 368*

The three Maries at the sepulchre. Linen. Silk and gold thread in or nué, stem, chain, and satin stitch; laid and couched work and couched gold cords.

Lit.: A. Beltran, Valencia, Barcelona 1953, p. 47

288–291 ALTAR FRONTAL, "FRONTALE RICO" (Details)
Spain, Castile, 1483–1495
Guadalupe, Monastery
Dimensions: 108 × 372 cm. Fig. 288: about 85 × 60 cm
The centre of the altar frontal is occupied by the scene of the Assumption of the Virgin. To the left, the Nativity and Adoration of the Magi; to the right, the Resurrection and Ascension. The terminal panels at the two ends show the Virgin and the Angel Gabriel (Annunciation). Linen ground. Embroidery in silk, in stem, chain, and satin stitch and laid and couched work. Gold threads in couched work. Much restored in the 16th century and again in 1679 and 1689. At the last restoration, adorned with pearls and gems. According to tradition, the original work was done by a monk, Brother Diego from Toledo.

Lit.: A. C. Floriano, El Bordado, Barcelona 1942, p. 95

292 CHASUBLE ORPHREY, Detail
Spain, about 1470
Lyon, Musée historique des Tissus (Inv. No. 28.272)
125 × 18 cm. Detail: 85 × 18 cm
Linen; gold thread and polychrome silks in couched work and split stitch.

293 ANGEL FROM A COPE ORPHREY
Spain, 15th century
London, Victoria and Albert Museum (T. 763–1919)
Height: 29 cm (including the halo)
Linen ground. Gold threads in couched work. Coloured silks, chiefly blue, in split, stem, Gobelin, satin and couching stitches. The embroidery is applied to green velvet.

294 ST. GEORGE BENEATH AN ARCHITECTURAL CANOPY
Sweden, Stockholm, middle of 15th century
Vassunda Church, Sweden
Height: 63 cm
Embroidery from a banner or wall hanging. Linen. Gold and silver threads in couched work. Armour of the Saint in silver threads couched with blue silk; the dragon in gold, couched with green silk. Face and parts of the architecture embroidered in silk, in chain and satin stitch. The embroidery was applied to silk material.

Lit.: A. Geijer, Albertus Pictor, Exhibiton Stockholm 1949, Cat. p. 41 – A. Branting and A. Lindblom, Medieval Embroideries and Textiles in Sweden, Stockholm 1932, I, p. 70, II, Pl. 97 – W. Paatz, Bernt Notke und sein Kreis, Berlin 1939, p. 102, Pl. 101

295 EMBROIDERY OF A CHASUBLE: THE VIRGIN AND CHILD ENTHRONED
Sweden, Stockholm, late 15th century, workshop of Albertus Pictor
Uppsala Cathedral
Chasuble: 134 cm high. Detail: 90 cm high
Virgin and Child surrounded with representations of the Seven Joys of the Virgin in quatrefoils. Linen ground. Gold thread, gold spirals, coloured silk and pearls. Some parts are worked separately in relief and applied. The Christ Child, and the faces and hands in Gobelin stitch. Gold thread in couched work. The circles on the Virgin's robe imitate the effect of blue velvet with gold loops.

Lit.: A. Branting and A. Lindblom, Medieval Embroideries and Textiles in Sweden, Stockholm 1932, I, p. 68 – A. Geijer, Albertus Pictor, Exhibition, Stockholm 1949, Cat. p. 42

296/297 WALL HANGING WITH THE LEGEND OF ST. THOMAS, SO-CALLED THOMAS TAPESTRY
Lower Saxony, end of the 14th century
Kloster Wienhausen
Dimensions of the whole: 205 × 445 cm
Detail: 205 × about 145 cm, and about 68 cm high.
Two details: Christ and St. Thomas; St. Thomas commanded to go to India; the King gives St. Thomas his treasure to pay for the building of a palace; the King's brother dies and is resurrected; St. Thomas distributes the king's treasure to the poor. Heavy linen. Slightly twisted wool in dark and light blue, white, ochre, yellow, red, reseda green faded from sap green, light reddish lilac faded to grey, black. (The details of the faces have fallen out). Outlines and inner drawing in red. Convent stitch. The hanging depicts the legend of St. Thomas in seventeen scenes derived from the Golden Legend and popular traditions.

Lit.: M. Schuette, Gestickte Bildteppiche und Decken des Mittelalters, Leipzig 1927, I, p. 41, Pl. 26

298 WALL HANGING : LOVERS AND A MUSICIAN, Fragment
Franconia (?), about 1470
Nuremberg, Germanisches Nationalmuseum (Gew. 2446)
67 × 48 cm
Linen ground. Loosely plied, thick, coloured wool. Blackish green ground, rust red, wine red, olive, blue, light blue, beige, golden yellow, black. Convent stitch.

Colour Plate XVII. HANGING WITH THE STORY OF ST. ELIZABETH
Kloster Wienhausen, last quarter of the 15th century
Kloster Wienhausen
Whole: 460 × 705 cm. Bands: about 97 cm high. Figures: about 46 cm high
Detail: Elizabeth's nightly flagellation. Stout linen ground. Coloured woollen yarn. Basic colour, dull yellow-green; two blues, lilac, red, brown, yellow, ochre, black. The black has fallen out from the faces. Faded. Convent stitch. The life of St. Elizabeth is depicted in thirty-three scenes. This is the only one of the Wienhausen hangings which is known, from the presence of the patron saints, Mary and Alexander, to have been made for the convent.

Lit.: M. Schuette, Gestickte Bildteppiche und Decken des Mittelalters, Leipzig 1927, I, p. 24, Pl. 25

299/300 LECTERN COVER
Germany, Upper Rhine, 1500–1510
Baden-Baden, Cistercian Nunnery of Lichtenthal
225 × 72 cm
Two strips of white linen, now sewn together. On the left, Judith slaying Holofernes; on the right, St. George and the Dragon. Embroidery in white linen threads with blue linen threads for the outlines. Convent, chain, stem, herringbone and buttonhole stitch in various forms.

301 Colour Plate XVIII. WALL HANGING
Franconia, about 1480
Kalchreuth, Central Franconia, Parish Church
84 × 407 cm
Old Testament subjects, wild men and women, and mythical beasts, among foliage scrolls. Black woollen stuff (sewn together from several pieces). Wool, silk, and some linen, in white. Stem, satin, chain, knot and couching stitches.

Colour plate XIX see p. 317

302 WALL HANGING: ST. SEBASTIAN
Franconia, late 15th century
Munich, Bayerisches Nationalmuseum (T. 1675)
93 × 75 cm

Black woollen cloth. Plied woollen thread in white, pale pink and red, yellow, yellow-green, blue and brown. Couched work.

303 LONG CUSHION COVER
Southern Germany or Switzerland, 3rd quarter of the 16th century
Munich, Bayerisches Nationalmuseum (T. 1707)
45 × 75 cm
Black cloth. Plied wool in faded red, brown, blue and blue-green tones. In the shields of arms, a little silk. Couched work.

304 FUNERAL PALL
Upper Rhine, Kloster Adelhausen near Freiburg (Breisgau) (?),
second half of the 15th century
Freiburg (Breisgau), Augustinermuseum (11.510)
294 × 158 cm. Squares: 50 × 58 cm
Fifteen (three rows of five) squares of black cloth, sewn together. Applied work. The pattern is cut from white woollen twill and outlined with leather strips which were originally gilt and silvered. The arrangement of the squares is probably to be explained by the position of the cover on the tomb, around which a procession took place. – From Kloster Adelhausen.

Colour Plate XIX. HANGING: ADORATION OF THE MAGI
Swabia or Franconia, about 1450
Munich. Bayerisches Nationalmuseum (T. 3798)
100 × 135 cm
Linen, Coloured wool, white linen thread, a little silk and membrane gold (in the crowns and jewellery). Couched work and laid work.

305 WALL HANGING: ADAM AND EVE
South East Germany, early 16th century
Vienna, Österreichisches Museum für angewandte Kunst (T 9126)
110 × 90 cm
Linen. Embroidery in coloured wool; red, green, brown, blue, white, in shaded tones. Chiefly red and green. Convent stitch, sometimes with threads couched in pairs, with a relief effect. Four scenes after three woodcuts by Michael Wohlgemut and Wilhelm Pleydenwurff in Schedel's Weltchronik, Nuremberg, Koburger, 1494.
Lit.: B. Kurth in Ciba Rundschau 1941, No. 48

306–309 EMBROIDERED LINEN WALL HANGING
Upper Germany, last quarter of the 15th century
Formerly Berlin, Schlossmuseum and Figdor Collection, Vienna
Destroyed by fire during the war
44 × 278 cm
The whole and three details: a pair of lovers amid foliage scrolls, birds and uninscribed scrolls. White linen ground embroidered with white linen thread and some faded silk (fallen out). Couching, herringbone and chain stitch. Style of the Housebook Master.
Lit.: V. Trudel, Schweizerische Leinenstickerei, I, Pl. V, II, Nr. 10, p. 137

310–313 CHASUBLE OF THE PALATINE COUNT PETER KMITA (Details)
Cracow, about 1504
Cracow, Treasury of the Cathedral on the Wawel
Height: 137 cm. Each field: about 23.5 × 23.5 cm
The chasuble cross consists of eight rectangles of relief embroidery with scenes from the Life of St. Stanislaus. The figures are almost in the round. Linen and silk material. Embroidery in various types of gold thread, coloured silks and pearls. Details of the faces in fine stem stitch; garments and architecture in couched gold thread.
Lit.: B. Kurth, Eine Hochreliefstickerei des 16. Jahrhunderts im Wiener Diözesan-Museum: Jahrbuch der Kunsthistorischen Sammlungen in Wien, Neue Folge, Bd. IX, Vienna 1939, p. 93 – T. Mankowski, Polskie Tkaniny i Hafty XVI–XVIII wieku, Wroclaw 1954, p. 8, Pl. II and 9

314/315 TWO WINGS OF A RELIQUARY ALTAR
South Germany, Franconia, 1519
Munich, Bayerisches Nationalmuseum (42/23, 42/24)
46.5 × 18.5 cm
Saints Sebastian and Ursula. In high relief. Faces in white satin with details in fine stem stitch. Hair and beard of spiral wire wound round with silk. The garments in couched work of gold threads, sequins and pearls. The figures are applied to a satin ground, embroidered with gold thread and silk, in laid work and couched work. Strips of parchment with inscriptions refer to the attached relics. The central panel with the Crucifixion (private collection) is dated 1519. It shows the arms, attached in 1680, of Johann Eustachius von Westernach, Bishop of Augsburg 1681–1707.

316 CHASUBLE, DETAIL: VIRGIN AND CHILD
Austria, about 1470
Pilgrimage Church of Mariazell, Styria, Treasury
Height: 129 cm. Height of the detail: 43 cm
Cross orphrey with the Virgin, Saints Barbara and Dorothy and, at the sides, Saints Catherine and Ursula. Relief embroidery with gold brocade, pearls, gold thread and silk. The Child, and the faces and hands, in silk, in satin and stem stitch. Background of couched gold threads.

317 CORNER SQUARE OF THE BANNER OF JULIUS II: THE ANNUNCIATION (Copy for use)
Upper Rhine, 1513
Basle, Historisches Museum (1882–1892)
37.5 cm × 37.5 cm
Italian white silk damask. Relief embroidery, or nué, needle painting. Abundant use of pearls, silver-gilt sequins, gold thread. Faces covered with silk and embroidered. The preserved portions are the two identical sides of the corner square. The banner was an honorific gift from Pope Julius II to his faithful allies of Basle as a sign of his gratitude for their assistance in the capture of Pavia. On 2nd July, 1512, the Council of Basle commissioned the banner in Milan and a year later ordered a copy for use from a foreign embroiderer and from the Basle goldsmith Jörg Schweiger. His design for the silver-gilt sceptre of the angel was preserved in the Amerbach Collection and is now in the Historisches Museum at Basle.
Lit.: W. Schneewind, Die Waffensammlung, Schriften des Historischen Museums III, Basle 1958, p. 74 – A. B. Bruckner, Schweizer Fahnenbuch, p. 171–175, Pl. 38

318 PALIOTTO, detail
Sicily, about 1520–1540
Palermo, Cathedral Treasury
Detail: 21 × 34 cm
Velvet with applied work of pearls and gold embroidery; gold ornaments of the 13th century. Figures and foliage scrolls in couched work with applied pearls; gold threads laid in pairs, gold cords for the outlines. Faces embroidered with silk. The paliotto was a gift from Archbishop Jean Carandelet (1520–1544).
Lit.: E. Steingräber, Antique Jewelry, London 1957, p. 40

319 ALTAR FRONTAL, DETAIL: VISITATION
Florence, between 1322 and 1357, by Geri di Lapo
Catalonia, Manresa, Cathedral
Detail: about 30 × 42 cm
In the centre, the Crucifixion. On each side, three rows each with three scenes from the Life of Christ, beginning with the Betrothal of the Virgin and concluding with the Harrowing of Hell. Linen ground, polychrome silks, gold and silver threads. Split and satin stitch, couched work. The altar frontal is signed: "Geri Lapi racha-

matore me fecit in Florentia". The fittings of the altar of the Cathedral were a gift from Raimondo de Area of Catalonia.
Lit.: M. Salmi, Il Paliotto di Manresa e l'opus florentinum: Bolletino d'Arte 24, 1930/31, p. 385 – A. Santangelo, Tessuti d'arte italiani. Milan 1958, p. 19 – (on the export of Florentine embroideries: R. Grönwoldt, Florentiner Stickereien in den Inventaren des Herzogs von Berry und der Herzöge von Burgund: Mitteilungen des Kunsthistorischen Institutes in Florenz, X, 1961, p. 33)

320 EMBROIDERY FOR A CHASUBLE: MARRIAGE OF THE VIRGIN
Florence, about the middle of the 15th century
Vienna, Museum für angewandte Kunst (T. 705)
24.5 × 18.5 cm
Linen ground. Gold, silver and silk threads. Chain, split and satin stitches. Garments partly in couched gold thread, with patterns in coloured silks. Architecture in silver with ornaments in gold. Part of a chasuble orphrey.
Lit.: Cf. A. Cavallo, A newly discovered Trecento Orphrey from Florence: The Burlington Magazine, Vol. CII, London 1960, p. 505

321/322 ALTAR FRONTAL, Details of band
Florence, middle of the 15th century
Florence, S. Egidio
18 × 434 cm, each field: 18 × 26 cm
Thirteen rectangles with scenes from the life of the Virgin; at both ends an additional rectangle with three male saints. Fig. 321: Meeting of Joachim and Anne at the Golden Gate. Fig. 322: Birth of the Virgin. Linen. Polychrome silk in split stitch, finely shaded from white to dark blue, yellow to green and pink to brown. The faces are embroidered with very small split stitches. The background and architectural details are worked with gold and silver thread, couched with coloured silk in various patterns.
Lit.: L'antico Tessuto d'Arte Italiana nella Mostra del tessile nazionale, Rome 1938, p. 36

323 HOOD AND ORPHREY OF A COPE
Florence, about 1420–1430
Florence, S. Margherita a Montici
Hood: about 35 cm high. Orphrey: 20 cm wide
On the hood, the Ascension; on the orphrey, the Man of Sorrows between the Virgin and St. John the Evangelist, and scenes from the Life of the Virgin. Linen ground; polychrome silk embroidery in split stitch; background in couched gold threads.
Lit.: A. Cavallo, A newly discovered Trecento Orphrey from Florence: The Burlington Magazine, Vol. CII, London 1960, p. 505

324 APPAREL OF A DALMATIC
Umbria, late 15th century
Orvieto, Museo del Duomo
140 × 150 cm, Apparel: 29 × 43–48 cm
Dalmatic of rich red brocaded velvet with embroidered apparels. On the front, above, the Adoration of the Magi, below, the Presentation in the Temple; on the back, the Resurrection and Ascension. The embroideries are worked on taffeta over a linen lining. The figures – worked singly or in groups and then applied to the backgrounds – are chiefly in silk thread in strong colours which are very beautifully distributed in the composition, and by the shading evoke a plastic effect. Split and chain stitch. Faces and hands in vertical split stitches with details in fine stem stitches. Backgrounds of gold thread laid vertically, in pairs, and couched with white, red and blue. A chasuble and a second dalmatic belong to the same set of vestments. The design of the embroideries has been ascribed to painters such as Luca Signorelli, Sandro Botticelli or Rafaelino del Garbo.

Lit.: F. Gamba, Ricami da disegni di Sandro Botticelli: La Critica d'Arte, 1956, p. 89

325/326 SALOME WITH THE HEAD OF ST. JOHN, BIRTH OF ST. JOHN
Florence, 1466–1479, after designs by Antonio Pollaiulolo
Florence, Museo di S. Maria del Fiore
30 × 22 and 36 × 21 cm
Linen ground. Gold thread and gold cord. Coloured silks. Or nué. Needle painting. Couched work, satin, Gobelin, stem and chain stitches. From a series of 27 embroideries (originally probably 28 to 31) with scenes from the life of St. John the Baptist, which were designed by Antonio Pollaiuolo for the Merchants' Guild of Florence and embroidered in Florence by nine embroiderers of various nationalities. They were intended for a set of vestments to be used in the Cathedral on the principal feasts (chasuble, cope and dalmatics). Detached from the vestments in 1730. Well preserved on the whole.
Lit.: S. Schwabacher, Die Stickereien nach Entwürfen von Antonio Pollaiuolo in der Opera di S. Maria del Fiore zu Florenz, Strassburg 1911

327 UNFINISHED EMBROIDERY IN SILK ON LINEN
Italy, middle of the 16th century
Florence, Museo Nazionale (Inv. No. 2250c)
33 × 42 cm
White linen. The pattern is worked in running stitches – "punto scritto" – in red silk in the upper band, in green silk in the lower band.

328 SILK EMBROIDERY ON LINEN, detail
Italy, middle of the 16th century
Florence, Museo Nazionale (Inv. No. 2248c)
74 × 55 cm. Detail: 19 × 41 cm
Hanging with four identical bands one above the other. The pattern is in reserve in white linen; inner drawing with running stitches – "punto scritto" – background in long-armed cross stitches in red silk. The pattern is a variant of one which occurs in a printed pattern book.

329 SILK EMBROIDERY ON LINEN, detail
Italy, 2nd half of the 16th century
Florence, Museo Nazionale (Inv. No. 2253c)
73 × 90 cm. Detail: 22 × 62 cm
Subjects from the Old Testament in three bands; in the bottom band, Judith and Holofernes. Design in reserve in white linen; background and inner drawing in green silk, worked in dense long-armed cross stitch.

330 LINEN CLOTH: ORPHEUS AND THE ANIMALS
Italy, about 1500
Hamburg, Museum für Kunst und Gewerbe (Inv. No. 1888, 71)
45 × 60 cm. Detail: 42 × 45 cm
White linen; embroidery in white linen thread in double sided satin stitches.

331 FRAGMENT OF SILK EMBROIDERY: THE LOVES OF JUPITER
Italy (Venice?), about the middle of the 16th century
Frankfurt (Main), Kunstgewerbemuseum
64 × 93 cm
Fine white linen. Gold and a little silver thread. Coloured silks. Double-sided needle painting. Split, stem and satin stitch. Principal colours: carmine, blue, green, gold. One end of a linen cloth; the other end, with the Loves of Neptune, is in the Österreichisches Museum für angewandte Kunst in Vienna. The subjects, according to information which has been kindly communicated by Dr. Meister, are derived from Ovid's Metamorphoses, Book 6, verses 108–128, the description of the web woven by Arachne in competition with

Pallas Athene. They represent the loves of Jupiter: Leda and the Swan, the Daughter of Nycteus and the Satyr, Danae with the Shower of Gold, Europa and the Bull, Asteria and the Eagle. Below: Jupiter as Fire with Aegina, (left) as Amphitryon with the Woman of Tiryns and (right) as a Shepherd with Mnemosyne. In the central oval, Neptune as a Horse beside Ceres, the Goddess of Plenty.
Lit.: M. Dreger, Künstlerische Entwicklung der Weberei und Stickerei. Vienna 1904, p. 234

Colour Plate XX. Detail: Asteria and Jupiter as an Eagle

332/333 ALTAR FRONTAL: THE EUCHARIST, whole and detail
Brabant, first third of the 16th century
Brussels, Musées Royaux d'Art et d'Histoire
93 × 380 cm
The Marriage at Cana, the Meal at the house of Simon, the Last Supper, the Meal at the house of Zacharias, the Supper at Emmaus. Linen ground. Gold embroidery in or nué and raised work. The heads worked in needle painting and applied, except for the head of the bride. Certain figures are reminiscent of the style of Quentin Massys. Formerly in the Chapel of the Hôtel de Nassau in Brussels and the Abbey of Grimberghe, the arms of which, together with those of the Abbot, Christoph Outers (1643–1647), are additions of the 17th century.
Lit.: M. Calberg in Bulletin des Musées Royaux d'Art et d'Histoire, Bruxelles XII (1940), p. 98: XV (1943) – M. Calberg, Broderies historiées du Moyen Age et de la Renaissance. Musées Royaux d'Art et d'Histoire, Bruxelles, p. 12

334 CHASUBLE ORPHREY, detail
Florence, third quarter of the 16th century
Florence, Opera del Duomo
Back of the chasuble: 140 × 85 cm. Detail: 42 × 22 cm
Dark violet silk twill. Foliage scrolls in couched work, with pairs of silver and gold threads and gold cords; among these are applied figures of painted white silk twill with a fine silver weft (cf. Fig. 335). The orphrey is in couched work and raised work of gold threads, gold cords and gold wire. In the cartouche, arms and imprese of Cardinal Alessandro Farnese (d. 1589). Part of a set of vestments, with an altar frontal.

335 PALIOTTO
Florence, third quarter of the 16th century
Florence, Opera del Duomo
93 × 235 cm
Dark violet silk twill. Among foliage scrolls in couched work, with pairs of silver and gold threads, gold cords and gold wire, applied angels and putti, painted on white silk twill with a fine silver weft. In the centre, arms of Cardinal Alessandro Farnese. The altar band is in relief embroidery (cf. Fig. 334).
Lit.: E. Ricci, Ricami italiani, Florence 1925, Pl. XXXVIII

336 LINEN CLOTH WITH THE STORY OF TOBIAS, detail
Switzerland, 1563
Basle, Historisches Museum (1874/41)
138 × 161 cm
Reddish-white linen mixture cloth. Embroidered with white, blue and dark brown linen, metal threads and animal hair. Couching, loop, herringbone, satin, cross, knot, chain, and oriental plait stitch. Inscription. The design is derived from a woodcut by Hans Holbein the Younger in the "Gantze Bibel", Zürich, Froschauer, 1540, Tobit, f. 52 recto.
Lit.: V. Trudel, Schweizerische Leinenstickerei, Berne 1954, I, p. 39, Taf. X, XI, – II Nr. 45, p. 80

337–339 LINEN CLOTH WITH ZODIAC AND HEAVENLY BODIES
South German, middle of the 16th century
Munich, Bayerisches Nationalmuseum (T. 1746)
140 × 172 cm. Details: each 62 × 82 cm
Light blue linen. Embroidery in white, blue and brown linen thread. Imaginative use of convent, satin, stem, herringbone, buttonhole and knot stitch. The stars in the figures are left in reserve, but were perhaps originally embroidered with silk. In the style of the followers of Hans Holbein the Younger.
Lit.: V. Trudel, Schweizerische Leinenstickereien, Berne 1954, I, Taf. XXVI, II, p. 183

340 WALL HANGING: WOMEN BREAKING FLAX
South Germany, 1544
Munich, Bayerisches Nationalmuseum (T. 1676)
72 × 106 cm
Black woollen material; several pieces sewn together. Plied woollen thread in light blue, white shading to pink, and faded green tones. White linen thread; a little membrane gold. The ground was originally worked with parallel lines of couched black thread. Couching and buttonhole stitch. Inscription: "Manche ratschen vor der tür – wer besser sei spint im hus dar für 1544."

341 WALL HANGING: THE WILES OF WOMEN, DETAIL: DAVID AND BATHSHEBA
Switzerland, probably Zürich, 1522
Zürich, Schweizerisches Landesmuseum (L. M. 1969)
247 × 233 cm
Black linen. Coloured wool. Convent stitch.
Lit.: J. Schneider, Schweizerische Bildstickereien des 16. und 17. Jahrhunderts. Aus dem Schweizerischen Landesmuseum, 14 (1960), p. 10, Fig. 2

342 WOOLLEN EMBROIDERY: THE WEEKLY WASH
Switzerland, 1556
Zürich, Schweizerisches Landesmuseum (AG 2369)
52 × 47 cm
Linen. Coloured wool and gold thread (for head coverings, sleeves and architecture). Colours: blue, tones of brown and beige, black, yellow, in a few places faded red. Chiefly blue and brown. Convent stitch. Coat-of-arms on the right: Unmut of Überlingen (?).

343 THE "BISCHOFSZELL HANGING"
Eastern Switzerland, first third of the 16th century
Basle, Historisches Museum (1873.6)
175 × 290 cm
Dark blue-green woollen stuff. Twisted coloured wool; green, light and dark brown, red, blue, white. Convent and running stitch. The upper part (the sky) has been restored. An animated landscape. Above, the town of Bischofszell in an astonishingly realistic rendering. On the castle, the arms of Bishop Otto VI of Constance (1474–1491), Lord High Steward of Waldenburg and Count of Sonnenberg. In the foreground, the streams of Thur and Sitter with two stone bridges.
Lit.: Die Kunstdenkmäler des Kantons Thurgau, Bd. III. A. Knoepfli, Der Bezirk Bischofszell, Basle 1962, p. 35, Fig. 34
I am grateful to Herr Konservator Knoepfli for the information which he kindly gave me.

344 EMBROIDERED SONG BOOK (one of four)
Augsburg, 1530
Schloss Ambras, near Innsbruck
14 × 19 cm
Fine linen, each sheet of the books consisting of a double layer.

Titles and frames of couched gold thread and black silk in cross stitch. The notes and texts of the songs are in satin and running stitch. The bag to contain the books is knitted in green silk. The illustration shows the title-page of the counter tenor part of the song for four voices "Aus guetem Grund". Commissioned in Augsburg for the marriage of the Emperor Charles V in Bologna in 1530. The double eagle and the Imperial insignia, in applied work, on the opening pages of the song books, indicate the exalted patron.

345 LINEN CLOTH, detail
Italy or Spain, 16th century
Hamburg, Museum für Kunst und Gewerbe (1888, 68)
49.5 × 44 cm. Detail: 16 × 23 cm
White linen embroidered in red silk. Cross and long-armed cross stitch. The edge is knotted with the threads of the cloth and embroidered. The Hebrew inscription on the cloth includes texts from the Psalms and the Book of Genesis. "Karla daughter of Salomo iben Pschat" signs the cloth "as the work of my hands".

Colour Plate XXI. SAMPLER
Bavaria, 1706
An old Bavarian family collection
70 × 42 cm. Original length: 50 cm
The bottom section, of the same linen material, was attached for the patterns in satin stitch. Loosely woven unbleached linen. The edges hemmed. The slightly twisted silk thread retains the original freshness of colour. Three reds, three blues, dark brown, grey shading to lilac, dark blue-green, moss green shading to yellow-green, white, yellowish white, gold and silver threads. The black thread (inscription and date) has fallen out. Cross, long-armed cross, satin, couching, stem and Gobelin stitch. Fine tent stitch over single threads. Needle painting.

346/347 HANDKERCHIEF
Moravia (?), 1560
Brno, Moravian Museum
About 45 × 40 cm
Linen. Red silk embroidery. Cross, back and loop stitches. A married couple. The woman holds a flower, the man a double cup; at the sides, a dove on a heart transfixed by an arrow, and clasped hands.

348 WALL HANGING, FAMILY TREE OF THE COUNTS VON KYBURG AND VON DILLINGEN, IN HONOUR OF ST ULRICH
Switzerland, Zürich, 1568
Zürich, Schweizerisches Landesmuseum (L. M. 4694)
191 × 165 cm
Detail (from the 40 medallions): Grandparents, parents, the elder brothers of St. Ulrich, and the Saint himself. Unbleached linen. Coloured wool, silk, cotton and human hair (for the plaits of the Saint's mother), metal threads, sequins. Convent stitch. Chiefly dull green, on a blue ground with damask patterns, in the manner of a woven stuff. Arms of Bernhard von Cham, Burgomaster of Zürich (1560/76), Landvogt of Schloss Kyburg 1542–1548.
Lit.: J. Schneider, Schweizerische Bildstickereien des 16. und 17. Jahrhunderts. Aus dem Schweizerischen Landesmuseum, 14. (1960), p. 11, Figs. 5, 6

349 FRIEZE, WITH THE ARMS OF THE ARCHDUKE FERDINAND, COUNT OF TYROL AND THE VORLANDEN (1529-1595)
Probably South German, Austria, second half of the 16th century
Vienna, Österreichisches Museum für angewandte Kunst (2406)
38.5 × 167 cm
Red satin. Applied work of silver and gold tissue. Outlines in gold cord. Gold and silver threads. Coloured silk threads: a little green,

red, blue, white, chamois. A fragment in the Kunstgewerbemuseum in Berlin.
Lit.: M. Dreger, Künstlerische Entwicklung der Weberei und Stickerei. Vienna 1904, p. 237, Pl. 244

350 BAND WITH THE HOLY FAMILY. Detail: the Virgin, Joseph and the Christ Child.
Switzerland or South Germany, 1591
Constance, Rosgartenmuseum (No. 2)
44 × 248 cm
Linen ground. White and blue linen thread. Faded silk in dull blue, yellow, celadon-green, brown, pink. Gold thread tarnished to black (for all the haloes). Convent, herringbone, loop, satin, cross, couching, chain, back, stem, knot and other stitches. Inscriptions. Coats-of-Arms.
Lit.: V. Trudel, Schweizerische Leinenstickerei, II, No. 129, p. 110

351 WALL HANGING: CHILDREN AT PLAY
South Germany, 1551
Munich, Bayerisches Nationalmuseum (T. 1666)
102 × 220 cm
Linen ground, densely embroidered with plied green woollen thread in parallel vertical lines of running stitches. The design is embroidered with couching and satin stitches in wool. Colours: yellow shading to red, white shading to blue, and yellow-green.

352/353 CHIMNEY HANGING
Leipzig (?), 1572
Leipzig, Museum des Kunsthandwerks (V 466)
40 × 285 cm
Two details: the Frenchman and the German. Nine fields of silk, alternately yellow, white and black, each containing a male costume-figure with explanatory inscription. The figures are modelled in relief from paste-board; the flesh parts are covered with yellowish satin and embroidered. The costumes of the nine different nations represented are tailored and embroidered. The figures include "the white Moor", the "Hungarian", "an Italian", a "black Moor", the "Frenchman", "a Swiss", the "Turk", and the "High German", represented naked, with a bale of cloth on his arm and the words «the dress of all nations pleases me. I know not what to do for they all please me equally . . .". This satire on German want of dignity probably derives from the Shrovetide revels, but no definite source has yet been found. Old municipal collection. Provenance unknown.
Lit.: M. Schuette, Mitteilungen des Städtischen Kunstgewerbe-Museums zu Leipzig, Nr. 3, April 1913, p. 32

354/355 SHIELDS OF CRAFT GUILDS IN RELIEF EMBROIDERY
Passau, 1574–1575, by Wolf Popp
Munich, Bayerisches Nationalmuseum (T. 6870/61)
Height: 29 cm
Blue and gold coat-of-arms with the date 1574 and scroll inscribed "Barbara Behamin". Couched gold cords on red satin. Boat hook and oar in couched gold thread. Signed on the back by Wolfgang Popp, from Rothenburg ob der Tauber, who is recorded from 1563 to 1574 as a silk embroiderer in the painters' guild of Passau. Barbara Beham was the wife of the boatman Hans Beham in Passau.
By the bank of the Ilzstadt in Passau, a skiff with three men. The little figures are of wire and wadding, covered with pieces of cloth and embroidered with gold and silk. The details of the faces are worked in stem stitch. Hair, beard and hands are of wire, wrapped with silk. The background is very thinly painted over gold and silk threads laid horizontally; details are embroidered in satin and stem stitch. Boat hook and rudder of silver gilt.

Lit.: S. Müller-Christensen, *Passauer Reliefstickerei des 16. Jahrhunderts: Pantheon, Munich 1942, p. 145*

356 LINEN CLOTH: VIRGIL'S TRAP FOR ADULTERERS
Switzerland, 1575
Zürich, Schweizerisches Landesmuseum (A. G. 2390)
156 × 117 cm
White linen. Linen thread in white, brown and blue. Couching, herringbone, chain and fishbone stitch.
Lit.: V. Trudel, *Schweizerische Leinenstickerei, Berne 1954, I, Taf. XXII, p. 47/48, II, Nr. 78, p. 93*

357 TABLE CARPET, detail
England, about the middle of the 16th century
London, Victoria and Albert Museum (T. 41–1928)
287 × 147 cm
Heavy linen cloth. Coloured woollen threads in cross and long-armed cross stitch. Colours: four blues, two greens, yellow, two reds and black.
Lit.: J. L. Nevinson, *Catalogue of English Domestic Embroidery, London, 1950, p. 8, Pl. IV*

358 CARPET WITH THE ARMS OF STOKAR AND TSCHACHTLAN
Switzerland, Schaffhausen, 1533
Zürich, Schweizerisches Landesmuseum (6097)
183 × 138 cm
Linen. Coloured wool: chiefly red, greenish blue and beige-grey tones. Cross and long-armed cross stitch.
Lit.: J. Schneider, *Schweizerische Bildstickereien des 16. und 17. Jahrhunderts. Aus dem Schweizerischen Landesmuseum. Nr. 1, Fig. 1*

359 WALL HANGING WITH TWENTY-ONE SCENES FROM THE TRISTRAM LEGEND
Alsace, 1539
Leipzig, Museum des Kunsthandwerks (23.51)
76 × 18 cm. Figures: 16.5 to 18 cm high
Detail with four scenes, from the discovery of Tristram by Iseult and Brangane to their departure. Coarse linen. Coloured wool, silk (for the inscription, much faded), and white linen thread. Couching (convent) and satin stitches, but chiefly long-armed cross stitch. Colours: the background of the ornament is now celadon green (faded from dull blue and green) while the ornament itself is in natural coloured wool, two yellows, black, a little blue and shaded red (rose). The figure-band has a ground of mid-blue and green with the figures in purple, strawberry red, light blue, celadon green, honey yellow, shaded brown; black lettering on natural wool; white linen thread for the underlinen. Arms of the Gäller family and of the Alsatian families of Landsperg, Ratsamshausen, Trauner and Adlstetten. This rendering of the Tristram legend is based on the chap-book of 1498, containing the story in the version of Eilhard von Oberg, itself deriving from the chap-book of 1484.
Lit.: Bau- und Kunstdenkmäler des Königreichs Sachsen: A.-H. Schwarzenberg, Dresden 1887, p. 62, Fig. 23, Beilage XV-XVII – J. Ricklef in Cellesche Zeitung, Der Sachsenspiegel, 16. Mai 1953

360 Colour Plate XXII. DRESS COAT, SAFAVID TUNIC
Persia, 17th century
Vienna, Österreichisches Museum für angewandte Kunst (T 4734)
Length: 120 to 110 cm
Open cotton cloth. Heavy, plied coloured silk. Colours excellently preserved: black, red and white are the dominant colours, with some light blue, green, salmon and yellow. Running stitch over five warp threads of the ground. The details of the faces have fallen out. Colour plate: detail.

361 COVER
North-west Persia, Caucasus, 16th–17th century
London, Victoria and Albert Museum (70–1909)
Repeat: 90 × 66 cm
Cotton ground. Silk thread. Double sided darning stitch. Dark blue, dark brown, old rose, yellow, white and red.
Lit.: Victoria and Albert Museum, *Brief Guide to Persian Embroideries 1950, Pl. 2, p. 10*

362 CLOTH, detail
Turkey, 17th to 18th century
London, Victoria and Albert Museum (121–1899)
Repeat: 41.5 × 33.5 cm
Linen ground. Coloured silk threads. Red, blue, green. Weaving stitch.

363 CLOTH, detail
North-west Persia, 17th century
London, Victoria and Albert Museum (65–1877)
Repeat: 15 × 13 cm
Cotton ground. Coloured silk threads. Old rose, dark green, olive; light blue. Double sided darning stitch.
Lit.: Victoria and Albert Museum, *Brief Guide to Persian Embroideries 1950, Pl. 6, p. 10*

364 LARGE WALL HANGING, detail
Turkey, 18th century
London, Victoria and Albert Museum (588–1890)
Red satin. Gold thread and coloured silks. Yellow, white, blue. Couching stitches.

365 FRAGMENT OF A HANGING WITH GROTESQUES
France, second half of the 16th century
Paris, Musée des Arts Décoratifs (A. 6452)
44 × 28.5 cm
Blue satin. Applied work of yellow satin attached with couching stitches. Inner drawing in back and chain stitches; some satin stitch in white and blue silk. Probably based on a contemporary French or Flemish ornamental engraving.

366, 368 PART OF A BED VALANCE
France, about 1560
Lyon, Musée historique des Tissus (29.055)
Detail: 26 × 68 cm
Scenes from Ovid in framed compartments with costume-figures between, surrounded by grotesques, garlands and lambrequins. Yellow satin. Silk threads in light colours (red, blue, green and yellow). Stem, split and chain stitch. Edged with blue-green braid above and below. Matching pieces in the Metropolitan Museum of Art, New York.
Lit.: E. A. Standen, *A Picture for every Story. Metropolitan Museum of Art. Bulletin Vol. XV, 1957, p. 165*

367 WALL HANGING: JEANNE D'ALBRET AS VENUS, WITH CUPID
Paris, about 1600
Paris, Musée de Cluny (1209 a-d)
300 × 340 cm
Beige satin with linen lining. Wool and silk threads and a little metal thread. The figures worked in satin, stem, chain and Gobelin stitch and applied. The foliage scrolls are worked directly on the satin. One of a set of four hangings with representations of King Henri IV and Marie de Médicis, and the King's parents, Antoine de Bourbon and Jeanne d'Albret, in the characters of the gods of antiquity. Originally in Sully's apartments in the present Palais de l'Arsenal.

369 BIRTH OF ST. JOHN THE BAPTIST, WITH THE FOUR FATHERS
OF THE CHURCH
Spain, second half of the 16th century
London, Victoria and Albert Museum (529–1877)
Circle: about 39 cm
Detail of a lectern cover with figure subjects. Linen, embroidered
and applied. Rich gold embroidery. Silver-gilt and silver threads;
gold cords. Coloured silks in shaded tones. Chiefly blue and red;
green, black. Needle painting. Split, satin, Gobelin and couching
stitches. Arms of the Dominican Order. From the Convent of La
Madre de Dios in Seville.

370 DANCE OF DEATH: CARDINAL AND DUKE
Netherlands, middle of the 16th century
Osnabrück, Cathedral
Width: 24 cm
Details of a cope-orphrey. Red velvet ground. Embroidery worked
on linen and applied. Gold and silver threads and coloured silks;
yellow, blue, green. Or nué. Flesh parts in needle painting. Canopies
in couched work, applied. Much worn and restored. The other sub-
jects show Pope, Nobleman, Priest and Emperor.
*Lit.: Zeitschrift für christliche Kunst 1902, p. 238. – Die Kunstdenk-
mäler der Provinz Hannover IV, Stadt Osnabrück.*
Hanover 1907, p. 71, Fig. 78

371 LITURGICAL EMBROIDERY: ST. JOHN THE BAPTIST
Italy, 1557
Basle, formerly Historisches Museum
Red velvet ground. Gold thread and coloured silks. Couched work.
Or nué and satin stitch.

372 CHALICE VEIL
France, before 1668
Brussels, Musées Royaux d'Art et d'Histoire (2745)
About 61 × 63 cm
Red satin. Very rich embroidery in gold, pearls and raised work.
Gold strip, gold cord and couched gold thread. A little red and black
silk. A gift from Queen Henrietta Maria of France, widow of
Charles I of England, to the Carmelites of Amiens, in the year 1668.
*Lit.: M. Calberg, Une voile de Calice: Bull. des Musées Royaux, Bruxelles
1937, p. 91*

373 ALTAR FRONTAL: ANNUNCIATION
Munich, about 1620
Munich, Residenzmuseum
94 × 177 cm
Fine canvas ground; flesh parts in applied white silk taffeta. Gold
and silver threads and polychrome silk. Very minute tent stitch; the
applied faces, hands and feet in satin and chain stitch. Embroidered
for the Reiche Kapelle of the Residenz in Munich, probably after
a design by the Court painter, Peter Candid.
*Lit.: L. Hager, Die Paramentenkammern: Die Residenz zu München.
Sonderausgabe der Zeitschrift Bayerland, München, n. d., p. 36*

374 CHASUBLE OF BISHOP C. MADRUZZO OF TRENTO
Italy, between 1600 and 1629
Trento, Cathedral Sacristy
107 × 67 cm
Blue silk twill. Gold and silver embroidery in couched work.

375 CHASUBLE OF THE ELECTOR CASIMIR ANSELM OF MAINZ
Germany, second quarter of the 17th century
Munich, Bayerisches Nationalmuseum (T. 218)
98 × 69 cm

Wine-red satin. Flowers in natural colours within an interlace-
pattern of gold bands and foliage. Gold thread, gold strip, wire and
cords in couched work; silk embroidery in shaded satin stitch. The
arms of the Elector Casimir Anselm (1629–1647) are applied below.

376 THE BRADFORD TABLE CARPET, detail
England, late 16th century
London, Victoria and Albert Museum (T. 134–1928)
About 400 × 175 cm
Heavy linen. Silk threads. Brilliant colours in a great variety of tones,
with blue-green shades predominating. Tent stitch.
*Lit.: J. L. Nevinson, Catalogue of Emglish Domestic Embroidery, London
1950, p. 7, Pl. III.*

377 HANGING: BANQUET OF LUCRETIA
England, end of the 16th century
London, Victoria and Albert Museum (T. 125–1913)
297 × 167 cm
Stout linen. Wool and silk. Tent stitch. Wool in three blues, three
creams, three greens, two reds, brown, light sepia, lilac, black. Silk
in light blue, green, white, yellow. The central scene is partially
based on an engraving by P. Galle.
*Lit.: J. L. Nevinson, Catalogue of English Domestic Embroidery, London
1950, p. 7, Pl. XXV*

378–380 BED VALANCE, three details: Tight Rope Walker, Prome-
nade, Vintage.
England, late 16th century
Leipzig, Museum für Kunsthandwerk (14.51)
Whole: 19 × 391 cm. Figures: 15–17 cm
Coarse linen canvas. Embroidered chiefly in wool. Predominant
tone, blue-green. Coloured silk for the shading: yellow shading to
old gold, old rose, blue, black. Fine tent stitch.
*Lit.: Mitteilungen des Städt. Kunstgewerbemuseums zu Leipzig, Nr. 5,
(März 1914), p. 51, Fig. 43, 44*

381 LONG CUSHION
England, first quarter of the 17th century
London, Victoria and Albert Museum (816–1893)
51 × 97 cm
Stout linen. Silver gilt thread and coloured silk and wool. Chiefly in
tent stitch with a little plait and long-armed cross stitch. Silk in
three blues, grass-green, yellow, chamois, cream, two reds, black.
Wool in light blue, dark green, yellow, chamois, two reds, black,
white. Signed: Mary Hulton. Royal arms of England with initials IR
for James I.
*Lit.: J. L. Nevinson, Catalogue of English Domestic Embroidery, London
1950, p. 12, Pl. VIII*

382 CUSHION OF THE MAYOR OF HEREFORD
England, 1604
London, Victoria and Albert Museum (T. 147–1941)
55 × 106 cm
Linen canvas. Coloured wool in lilac, two blues, two greens, cream,
light yellow, chamois, pale orange, light brown, three pinks, scarlet,
black. A little silk, for the arms of the town of Hereford, in light
blue, white and faded pink. Tent stitch. Inscription, including date.
*Lit.: J. L. Nevinson, Catalogue of English Domestic Embroidery, London
1950, p. 11, Pl. VII*

383 LADY'S JACKET
England, late 16th century
London, Victoria and Albert Museum (919–1873)
Length of back: 65 cm

Linen. Silver-gilt and silver thread; coloured silks in two blues, two yellows, two reds, olive-brown. Chain and buttonhole stitch.
Lit.: J. L. Nevinson, Catalogue of English Domestic Embroidery, London 1950, p. 79, Pl. LIV

384 DOUBLET
Denmark (?), about 1640
Copenhagen, Rosenborg Castle
64 cm high
Salmon pink satin. Gold and silver threads and cords, and silver sequins. Couched work, with small leaves and other details in satin stitch. The object is listed in the inventory of the wardrobe of the Danish King Frederick III (1609–1670) as the "naccarat" doublet.
Lit.: S. F. Christensen, Kongedragterne paa Rosenborg. Copenhagen 1940, I, p. 93, II, Pl. L

385 PINCUSHION
England, early 17th century
London, Victoria and Albert Museum (T. 317–1898)
26.5 × 15 cm
Linen ground. Silver thread and coloured silks. Tent stitch. Colours: violet, three blues, three greens, cream, yellow, two browns, two reds. The ground is silver.
Lit.: J. L. Nevinson, Catalogue of English Domestic Embroidery. London 1950, p. 14, Pl. LXIX

386 PURSE AND PINCUSHION
England, early 17th century
London, Victoria and Albert Museum (316–1898)
11.25 × 13.75 cm. Pincushion: 6.25 × 6.25 cm
Canvas ground. Silver thread; silk in green-blue, yellow-green, yellow, three reds, black. Tent and chain stitch.
Lit.: J. L. Nevinson, Catalogue of English Domestic Embroidery, London 1950, p. 98, Pl. LXIX

386 PURSE
England, early 17th century
London, Victoria and Albert Museum (T. 87–1936)
11 × 11 cm
Canvas ground. Silver and silver-gilt thread; silk to two blues, two greens, yellow, brown, two reds, black, white. Tent, Gobelin and plaited braid stitch.
Lit.: J. L. Nevinson, Catalogue of English Domestic Embroidery, London, 1950, p. 98, Pl. LXIX

386 PURSE IN THE SHAPE OF A BUNCH OF GRAPES
England, early 17th century
London, Victoria and Albert Museum (T. 172–1921)
7.5 × about 5 cm
Silk. Metal threads and coloured silk in two blues, two greens, pink. Buttonhole stitch.
Lit.: J. L. Nevinson, Catalogue of English Domestic Embroidery. London, 1950, p. 99, Pl. LXIX

Colour Plate XXIII. GLOVES, PIN-CUSHION AND PRAYER BOOK
Netherlands, about 1630
Munich, Bayerisches Nationalmuseum (Inv. No. 62/21)
Gloves: 33 cm long. Pincushion: 5.5 × 5 cm. Bookbinding: 7 × 4.5 cm
Leather gloves; the gauntlets, the pin cushion and the binding of violet satin, embroidered with flowers in polychrome silk, framed by ornaments in raised work of gold, sequins and pearls. In the centre of the gauntlets, a flaming heart pierced by arrows, with the initial E above. Silk embroidery in split and satin stitch and, on the bands, in double-sided satin stitch; gold embroidery in couched work. This set of objects originally belonged to Elizabeth Stuart (1596–1662), wife of the Winter King, Frederick V. Elizabeth, grand-daughter of Mary, Queen of Scots, and daughter of James I of England, married the Elector Frederick V in 1613. The flaming heart is probably an allusion to her nickname "Queen of Hearts". The book of Psalms, printed in Sedan in 1629, contains some prayers and canticles of the Elector's ancestors.
Lit.: M. Braun-Rönsdorf, Die Handschuhe der Elisabeth Stuart: Waffen- und Kostümkunde, Bd. V. München 1963, p. 1

387 PAIR OF LADY'S MITTENS
England, late 16th to early 17th century
London, Victoria and Albert Museum (1507–1882)
40 × about 20 cm
Red velvet with gauntlets of white satin. Silver-gilt and silver thread; silk in two greens, two blues, violet, yellow, cream, yellow-brown. Satin stitch and couched work. Traditionally said to have been given by Queen Elizabeth to Margaret Edgcumbe, wife of Sir Edward Denny.
Lit.: J. L. Nevinson, Catalogue of English Domestic Embroidery, London, 1950, p. 91, Pl. LXVI

388 LADY'S GLOVE
England, second quarter of the 17th century.
London, Victoria and Albert Museum (4665–1858)
32.5 × about 14 cm
Red satin gauntlet. Silver, gilt and silver threads. Couched work, partially raised over padding of pink and yellow silk. Gold bobbin lace. The seams of the fingers are covered with gold braid. Blue silk lining.
Lit.: J. L. Nevinson, Catalogue of English Domestic Embroidery, London 1950, p. 94

388 GAUNTLET OF A LADY'S GLOVE
England, about 1600
London, Victoria and Albert Museum (320–1876)
10 × 15 cm
White satin. Silver-gilt thread; silk in bright green, yellow-green, pink, orange, yellow, two blues, brown, cream. Satin stitch and couched work. Gold bobbin lace.
Lit.: J. L. Nevinson, Catalogue of English Domestic Embroidery, London 1950, p. 92

388 LADY'S GLOVE
England, second quarter of the 17th century
London, Victoria and Albert Museum (711–1875)
27.5 × 13.5 cm
Satin. Gold thread and a little pink silk; seed pearls. Entirely in couched work. The seams of the fingers are covered with gold braid.
Lit.: J. L. Nevinson, Catalogue of English Domestic Embroidery, London 1950, p. 93

389 LADY'S COIF
England, late 16th century
London, Victoria and Albert Museum (252–1889)
25 × 22.5 cm
Linen. Silver-gilt thread and black silk. Chain stitch and speckling, with plaited gold thread.
Lit.: J.L. Nevinson, Catalogue of English Domestic Embroidery, London 1950, p. 84, Pl. LX

389 LADY'S COIF AND FOREHEAD CLOTH
England, late 16th century
London, Victoria and Albert Museum (868–1924)
21.25 × 21.25 cm. Forehead cloth: 16,5 × 35 cm

Linen. Silver-gilt thread; silk in faded tones of dull yellow, cream, two greens, four reds, three blues. Chiefly buttonhole and plaited braid stitch.
Lit.: J. L. Nevinson, Catalogue of English Domestic Embroidery, London 1950, p. 83, Pl. LX

390 LADY'S BODICE
England, late 16th century
London, Victoria and Albert Museum (1359–1900)
Length: 42 cm
Fine linen. Silver-gilt thread; silk in two blues, two greens, yellow, orange, two pinks, cream, dark red, black. Sequins. Chain, buttonhole and plaited braid stitch. Altered at a later date.
Lit.: J. L. Nevinson, Catalogue of English Domestic Embroidery, London 1950, p. 78 – Victoria and Albert Museum, Fifty Masterpieces of Textiles, London, 1958, Pl. 25

391 LADY'S HOOD
England, end of the 16th century
London, Victoria and Albert Museum (135–1924)
51.25 cm × 52.5 cm
Linen. Black silk thread. Stem and coral stitches and speckling. Bobbin lace.
Lit.: J. L. Nevinson, Catalogue of English Domestic Embroidery, London 1950, p. 83, Pl. LVII

392 LADY'S COIF, not made up
England, about 1600
London, Victoria and Albert Museum (T. 32–1936)
22.5 × 41 cm
Linen. Red silk thread and silver-gilt sequins. Buttonhole, speckling, and herringbone stitch.
Lit.: J. L. Nevinson, Catalogue of English Domestic Embroidery, London 1950, p. 85, Pl. LXIII

393 CUSHION COVER
England, 16th to 17th century
London, Victoria and Albert Museum (T. 80–1946)
52.5 × 109 cm
Black velvet. The motifs applied. Silver and silver-gilt thread and coloured silk embroidery, worked on linen, in bright colours. Tent, cross, long-armed cross, stem stitch; laid work.
Lit.: Victoria and Albert Museum, English Embroidery by Barbara Morris, London 1954, Pl. 9

394 SQUARE PILLOW COVER
England, late 16th century
London, Victoria and Albert Museum (T. 31–1914)
50.8 × 48.25 cm
Heavy linen. Wool and silk threads. Wool in deep blue-green (for the background), light green, two reds, yellow. Silk in dull blue, cream, dull yellow, dull brown.
Lit.: J. L. Nevinson, Catalogue of English Domestic Embroidery, London 1950, p. 13, Pl. X

395 PILLOW COVER WITH BLACKWORK EMBROIDERY
England, second half of the 16th century
London, Victoria and Albert Museum (T. 81–1924)
47.5 × 85 cm
Lit.: J. L. Nevinson, Catalogue of English Domestic Embroidery, London 1950, p. 17, Pl. XII

396 EMBROIDERED PICTURE: DAVID AND BATHSHEBA
England, 1656

London, Victoria and Albert Museum (T. 52–1934)
43 × 54.5 cm
White satin. Embroidery in metal thread and coloured silk. Bathsheba and her serving maid, Uriah and Nathan, in split stitch; the remaining figures in raised work, some of them worked in buttonhole stitches (resembling needlepoint lace), padded, and applied to the satin ground. A little couched work; seed pearls for necklaces and for the signature and date. Based directly or indirectly on the engravings in Gerard de Jode's Thesaurus Veteris Testamenti, Antwerp, 1585.
Lit.: J. L. Nevinson, Catalogue of English Domestic Embroidery, London 1950, p. 42, pl. XXX b

397 WEDDING ROBE OF DUKE WILHELM V OF BAVARIA
Munich, 1568
Munich, Bayerisches Nationalmuseum (T. 4061)
Length in front: 95 cm. Width of border: 11 cm
Violet silk velvet. Raised embroidery in various kinds of gold and silver strip, wire and cord. The mantle was worn by Duke Wilhelm V for his marriage to Renate of Lorraine in Munich in 1568.
Lit.: S. F. Christensen, Die männliche Kleidung in der süddeutschen Renaissance, Berlin 1934, Fig. 13, 14

398 TABLE COVER OF APPLIED WORK, detail
Sweden, 1630
Stockholm, Nordiska Museet (192.040)
187 × 155 cm. Detail: 61 × 45 cm
Blue taffeta (lined with linen). Rich pattern of foliage scrolls. In the centre, in a garland of laurel, coats-of-arms commemorating the marriage of Count Gustav Horn and Christine Oxenstierna, together with their initials G. H. and C. O. and the date 1630. Applied work in black velvet edged with yellow silk thread.
Lit.: A. M. Nylén, Broderier från Herremans och Borgarhem 1500–1850, Stockholm 1950, p. 12, Fig. 1

399 LADY'S BODICE
England, second half of the 17th century
Stockholm, Nordiska Museet (43.556)
Length in front: 50 cm
White cotton lined with wool. Quilted background pattern in chain stitch in blue silk; floral sprays in coloured wools, in chain, stem and satin stitch. Based in Indian models.
Lit.: A. M. Nylén, Broderier från Herremans och Borgarhem 1500–1850, Stockholm 1950, p. 74 och Fig. 29 – G. Hazelius-Berg, Modedräkter från 1600–1900, Stockholm 1952, Fig. 8

400 EMBROIDERED DRESS, detail
England, early 18th century
Stockholm, Nordiska Museet (214.268)
Detail: 35 × 69 cm
"Adrienne", a negligée robe of white cotton twill, embroidered with flowers and fruit, with birds, squirrels and butterflies between; coloured wools, in chain stitch.
Lit.: A. M. Nylén, Broderier från Herremans och Borgarhem 1500–1850, Stockholm 1950, p. 76, Fig. 32 – G. Hazelius-Berg, Modedräkter från 1600–1900, Stockholm 1952, Fig. 9

401 BED COVER IN WHITEWORK EMBROIDERY, Detail
Sweden, beginning of the 18th century
Stockholm, Nordiska Museet (18.355)
216 × 240 cm. Detail: 22 × 17 cm
Two layers of white linen. The ground is guilted in spiral patterns with running stitches, with slight relief effects produced by cotton cords. Flowers and leaves outlined and filled with innumerable

filling patterns, embroidered with white linen thread in satin and knot stitches; couched threads of various types.

Lit.: A. M. Nylén, Broderier från Herremans och Borgarhem 1500–1850, Stockholm 1950, p. 47, Fig. 22

402, 405 CORONATION DRESS OF KING GUSTAV II ADOLPH OF SWEDEN
Stockholm, 1617
Stockholm, Livrustkammaren (3374)
Length of doublet in front: 66 cm
White satin. Embroidery in silver threads, cords and sequins. Satin stitch and couched work. The embroidery was perhaps worked by the German bead-embroiderer, Carl Plagemann.

Lit.: G. Ekstrand, 1600-talets vita kröningdräkter i Livrustkammaren: Livrustkammaren, Vol. VIII, Stockholm 1960, p. 227

403 COURT DRESS OF SAXONY
Dresden, early 17th century
Dresden, Historisches Museum
Doublet, sword-hanger and hat of sea-green satin, embroidered with medallions, linked by loops and flowering scrolls. These medallions contain landscapes and town views (Dresden and the Elbe). The medallion-frames and loops are worked in applied gold thread; the flowers and landscapes in polychrome silk, in satin stitch and couched work.

Lit.: E. Haenel, Hofkleider Johann Georgs I. Mitteilungen aus den Sächsischen Kunstsammlungen II, 1911, p. 50

404 SUIT OF KING GUSTAV II ADOLPH OF SWEDEN
Hamburg, 1620
Stockholm, Livrustkammaren (Inv. No. 3347)
Violet cloth for cassock and breeches, violet satin for the doublet. Embroidery of gold thread, cords and sequins. Couched work

Lit.: K. E. Steneberg, En dräkt med kasack från 1620: Livrustkammaren, Vol. I, Stockholm 1939, p. 197

405 See 402

406 COVER WITH SCATTERED FLOWERS, fragment, detail
England, early 17th century
London, Victoria and Albert Museum (T. 63–1933)
67.5 × 75 cm
Linen. Coloured silks. Lilac, two blues, three greens, cream, yellow, orange, two reds. Long and short, stem, herringbone and couching stitches. The other half of the cloth is in the Museum of Fine Arts, Boston.

Lit.: J. L. Nevinson, Catalogue of English Domestic Embroidery, London 1950, p. 25, Pl. XIX

Colour Plate XXIV. SASH, detail
England, 1630–1640
Copenhagen, Rosenborg Castle
212 × 65 cm. Detail: 30 × 20 cm
Light pink taffeta. In zig-zag bands, naturalistic birds, insects and caterpillars, among flowers. Gold thread and polychrome silks in satin and stem stitch.

Lit.: S. F. Christensen, Kongedragterne paa Rosenborg. Copenhagen 1940, I, p. 61, II, Pl. XXIII, XXIV

Colour Plate XXV. SLEEVE OF A LADY'S BODICE
France or England, about 1640–1650
Copenhagen, Rosenborg Castle
Detail: 36 cm long
Lady's jacket with round neck, short waist and long sleeves. White silk rep with silver weft. Gold threads, cords and wire, in couched

work. Polychrome silk. Long and short stitch. The jacket probably belonged to the Danish Queen, Sophie Amalie.

Lit.: S. F. Christensen, Kongedragterne paa Rosenborg, Copenhagen 1940, I, p. 97, II, Pl. LIV, LV

407 SET OF BED HANGINGS
England, second half of the 17th century
London, Victoria and Albert Museum (T. 13–1929)
Curtains: 190 cm long × 220 and 100 cm wide
Cotton and linen twill. Woollen embroidery. Colours: indigo, blue-green, three greens, yellow shading to dark brown, carmine. Satin, split, stem, Gobelin, herringbone, cross, and couching stitches. Signed Abigail Pett.

Lit.: J. L. Nevinson, Catalogue of English Domestic Embroidery, London 1950, p. 61, Pl. XLIII

408 LADY'S BAG
Regensburg, 1604
Munich, Bayerisches Nationalmuseum (T. 4097)
24 × 17 cm
Chamois leather. Green plied silk. Satin, stem, knot, chain and herringbone stitch.

409 HUNTING-POUCH OF THE ELECTOR MAXIMILIAN I OF BAVARIA
Munich, about 1620–1630
Munich, Bayerisches Nationalmuseum (T. 4063)
50 × 52 cm
Green silk velvet, embroidered with gold and silver threads, cords, wire and strips; laid and couched work. Perhaps embroidered by Georg Frichtl or Hans Mensinger

410 TOILET BAG (COMB CASE)
Netherlands, middle of the 17th century
Copenhagen, Rosenborg Castle
68 × 66 cm
Pink satin, richly embroidered with cartouches in slight relief, with a variety of gold and silver threads, strips, wire and cords, in couched work. Sequins and small gold and silver balls. Birds embroidered on white satin with chenille thread in naturalistic colours; long and short and stem stitch. Recorded in the Wardrobe Inventory of Rosenborg in 1718

411/412 PARTS OF A SET OF BED HANGINGS
Italy, late 17th century
Copenhagen, Rosenborg Castle
Valance, detail: 32 × 80 cm. Medallion: 82 cm wide
Valance: Diana, with Cupid and Nymphs, hunting. Medallion: the Punishment of Cupid. Silk rep with polychrome silk embroidery in satin, stem and split stitch, with delicate effects of shading. The scenes are reminiscent of Italian classicising landscape painting, especially the works of the Bolognese, Francesco Albani. The embroideries were probably acquired by King Frederick IV while travelling in Italy, 1692–93 or 1709.

413/414 WALL HANGING
England, about 1675
Berne, Institut für angewandte Kunst, Abegg-Stiftung, Riggisberg
175 × 346 cm. Each rectangle: 25 × 19 cm
Rectangles containing bunches of flowers alternate with rectangles containing trees and animals, in part with symbolic or emblematic significance. Blue woollen twill embroidered with wool in red, green, yellow, blue and brown tones. Long and short stitch. The designs are derived from embroidery pattern books, and works on natural history and emblems.

415 WALL HANGING, ONE OF SIX HANGINGS FROM HATTON GARDEN
England, second half of the 17th century
London, Victoria and Albert Museum (517 to 522–1896)
About 228 × 145 cm
Stout linen. Woollen embroidery. Four blues, four greens, orange, cream, brown in numerous shades, and some red. Gobelin, cross, rococo, knot, tent and couching stitches.
Lit.: J. L. Nevinson, Catalogue of English Domestic Embroidery, London 1950, p. 71, Pl. LIII

Colour Plate XXVI. EMBROIDERED COVER FOR A SMALL SETTEE
England, 1700–1720
New York, Irwin Untermyer Collection
Height: 127 cm. Width: 122 cm. Depth: 57.5 cm
Canvas, embroidered with wool and silk, in tent stitch.
Lit.: Y. Hackenbroch, English and other Needlework in the Irwin Untermyer Collection. London 1960, p. 44, Pl. 96

416 EMBROIDERED COVER FOR THE BACK OF A CHAIR
Germany, first half of the 18th century
Munich, Bayerisches Nationalmuseum (R 8892)
80 × 65 cm
Canvas: coloured wools and silks. Tent stitch; the stitches for the figures are half as big as those for the background pattern.

417 BACK OF AN ARMCHAIR, detail
England, about 1700
London, Victoria and Albert Museum (W. 25–1922)
Height: about 90 cm
Embroidered cover. Cross and tent stitch. Wool and silk. Colours: chiefly shades of blue and red. Subjects derived from illustrations, by W. Hollar and Pierre Lambert, in John Ogilby's edition of the Iliad, 1658
Lit.: P. Macquoid and R. Edwards, Dictionary of English Furniture, London 1954, III, p. 5, 6

418 ARMCHAIR WORKED IN PETIT POINT
South Germany, first half of the 18th century
Munich, Bayerisches Nationalmuseum (R 8893)
Cover for the back: 76 × 64 cm
The embroidery shows an Oriental lady dancing to an orchestra. Canvas; coloured wool; silk in beige and light blue. Tent stitch; the stitches for the figures are half as big as those for the "bizarre" background pattern.

419 WING CHAIR
England; cushion dated 1744
London, Victoria and Albert Museum (W. 62a–1926)
Height: 122 cm
Cover embroidered with coloured silk and wool in cross stitch.

420 COAT
India, Mughal, first half of the 17th century
London, Victoria and Albert Museum (IS 18–1947)
100 × 91.5 cm
Satin. Silk embroidery in chain stitch. On a cream background, delicate tones of blue, yellow, green, gold, brown.
Lit.: Victoria and Albert Museum, Indian Embroidery, London 1951, p. 7, Nr. 1 – The Art of India and Pakistan, 1950, p. 66

421 KNUCKLE PAD FROM A SHIELD GRIP: Scene in a palace garden
India (Jaipur, Rajputana), about 1700
London, Victoria and Albert Museum (IM 107–1924)
13.6 × 13.6 cm
Coarse unbleached cotton. Silver and coloured silk threads. Chiefly chain stitch. Delicate greenish-blue tones.
Lit.: Victoria and Albert Museum, Indian Embroidery, London 1951, p. 7, Nr. 7

422 PRAYER MAT
India, Mughal, about 1700
London, Victoria and Albert Museum (I. S. 168–1950)
116 × 71 cm
White cotton ground. Coloured silk threads in shaded red, blue, yellow (faded), green. Chain stitch.
Lit.: Victoria and Albert Museum, Indian Embroidery, London 1951, p. 7, Fig. 6

423 BED CURTAIN
England, middle of the 17th century
London, Victoria and Albert Museum (T. 38–1909)
About 200 × 109 cm
Linen and cotton twill. Embroidery in coloured wool in three shades of green varying from a blackish green to emerald green. Stem, braid, long and short, chain and satin stitch.
Lit.: J. L. Nevinson, Catalogue of English Domestic Embroidery, London 1950, p. 66, Pl. XLIX

424 BED CURTAIN
England, late 17th century
London, Victoria and Albert Museum (72–1897)
Length: about 223 cm
Linen and cotton twill. Embroidered in coloured wools in five blues, four greens, cream, three yellows, sepia, four reds, magenta. Satin, long and short, stem, couching and knot stitches.
Lit.: J. L. Nevinson, Catalogue of English Domestic Embroidery, London 1950, p. 67, Pl. LI

425 DOGE'S CAP
Venice, about 1700
Venice, Museo Correr
White linen lined with cotton. Quilting in white linen thread. Back and knot stitch. The cap is exhibited beneath the ceremonial cap of the Doge Barbarigo (1485–1502)

426 CHRISTENING CAP FOR A BOY AND A GIRL
Munich, 1717
Munich, Bayerisches Nationalmuseum (Loan 56/105 and 106)
a) Height: 10 cm, diameter: 12 cm, b) Height: 10 cm, width: 11 cm
White satin. a) Couched work with gold thread, gold strip and wire, b) Embroidery in gold thread, gold strip wire, and polychrome silks. Part of a complete set for a christening, a gift from the Bavarian Elector Max Emanuel (1662–1726) to Max Joseph, Baron von Perfall auf Greifenberg (1686–1752), who married Maria Anna, Baroness von Neuhaus, in 1716; their son Emanuel Maximilian was born in 1717.

427 CHRISTENING ROBE
North Germany, about 1700
Hamburg, Museum für Kunst und Gewerbe (Inv. No. 1900, 526)
Height: about 52 cm
White cotton twill. Guilted whitework embroidery with linen threads. Satin and knot stitches and drawn thread work in a great variety of patterns.

428 LINEN CLOTH WITH WHITEWORK EMBROIDERY, detail
Holland, 1694
St. Gall, Industrie- und Gewerbe-Museum (100)
Height of the border: 4–17 cm

Fine white linen. White linen thread in satin and chain stitch. Around the border, delicate embroidery with scenes of country life. Inscription in Dutch.
Lit.: Industrie- und Gewerbe-Museum, St. Gallen, Textilsammlung Iklé. Katalog 1908, p. 28, Nr. 100

429, Colour Plate XXVII. THREE OF A SET OF TWELVE WALL PANELS with figures from the Italian Comedy
Colour Plate, detail: *figure in the manner of Callot*
Dresden, between 1711 and 1719
Nuremberg, Germanisches Nationalmuseum (4020–4022, 4033–4035)
Height: 285–290 cm. Width: 83–85 cm
Canvas ground in a light tobacco colour. Coloured silk threads. On the parchment-coloured ground, broken tones; two browns, two blues, yellow-green, dark green, cream, flesh tone. Cross and tent stitch. The figures are copied in part from anonymous 17th century engravings of comedy-figures and from an ornamental engraving by Jean Bérain (1638–1711). The figures in the manner of Callot are taken from the "Callotto Resuscitato" in the first (Augsburg) edition.
Lit.: L. v. Wilckens: Pantheon XX, 1962, p. 69

430 COVER: FLORAL DESIGN
Switzerland, probably Schaffhausen, 1700
Zürich, Schweizerisches Landesmuseum (L. M. 26058)
192 × 160 cm
Dark brown woollen material, embroidered with coloured wools and silks. Long and short stitch. Four symbolic flowers with inscriptions. Below, on the left, the arms of Stokar.
Lit.: J. Schneider, Schweizer Bildstickerei des 16. und 17. Jahrhunderts. Aus dem Schweizerischen Landesmuseum, p. 15, Fig. 16

431/432 TWO EMBROIDERED PICTURES from a set representing the Eight Taoist Immortals
China, Ming period, probably 14th century
London, Victoria and Albert Museum (T. 89–1948 and T. 92–1948), from the Vuilleumier Collection
51 × 45 cm and 37 × 35 cm
Natural coloured twill silk for the background. Coloured silk thread. Stem stitch, long and short stitch, partly with long floats of twisted thread. Very delicate colours: broken yellow, pink, deep blue (the strongest tone), a little black; in places (for the shading of the ground) touched with paint. Li T'ieh-Kwai, a lame beggar, Han Stang-Tsen with a flute, and T'sao Kwoh-ts'in with castenets (T. 89–1948). Si Wang Mou, the symbol of feminine longevity (92–1948).

433 CONGRATULATORY HANGING, detail
China, 17th century
Sweden, Gottröra Church
120 × 221 cm. Detail: 48 × 70 cm
Dragons playing ball, animals with good luck symbols, children carrying flowers, and the god of longevity, all expressing good wishes for a birthday. Velvet with couched gold embroidery. The gold thread consists of a strip of gilt paper wound on a pink silk thread. In places, e. g. flesh parts and flowers, worked in polychrome silk in satin stitch. The hanging was converted in 1705 to serve as an altar frontal for the church of Gottröra and at that time a dedicatory inscription was added relating to the donor Count Adam Ludwig Lewenhaupt.
Lit: A. Geijer, Oriental Textiles in Sweden. Copenhagen 1951, p. 76. Pl. 61

434 LADY'S DRESS, detail
China, early 18th century
Stockholm, Nationalmuseet (107 081 : c)
Detail, about 70 × 50 cm

At the lower hem of the white silk skirt, symmetrical ornaments with lattice and scale patterns, partly in gold embroidery; above, polychrome flower scrolls. The gold embroidery is worked over parchment; silk embroidery of plied silk in satin and stem stitch. A typical Chinese export embroidery following a European model.
Lit.: A. Geijer, Oriental Textiles in Sweden. Copenhagen, 1951, p. 121, Pl. 62

435 LADY'S DRESS
Sweden, about 1750–1760
Stockholm, Nordiska Museet (198.965)
Width of the border of the skirt: 25.7 cm
Jacket ("Caraco") and skirt of yellowish silk taffeta with flower scroll borders in polychrome silk, silver strip, silver thread and sequins. Stem, knot and satin stitch, with shaded effects; couched work.
Lit.: A. M. Nylén, Broderier från Herremans och Borgerhem 1500–1850, Stockholm 1950, p. 60, Fig. 33

436 GENTLEMAN'S SUIT
Sweden (or France), about 1770
Stockholm, Nordiska Museet (77.161)
Width of the flower scroll: 7.5 cm
Coat, waistcoat and breeches, of yellow-striped silk velvet, with flower scrolls embroidered in polychrome silk. Stem, knot and satin stitch, with shaded effects.
Lit.: A. M. Nylén, Broderier från Herremans och Borgarhem 1500–1850, Stockholm, 1950, p. 61, Fig. 34 – G. Hazelius-Berg, Modedräkter från 1600–1900. Stockholm 1952, Fig. 29

437 PRAYER CARPET
Persia (Resht), 19th century
London, Victoria and Albert Museum (463–1895)
About 206 × 122 cm
Background of blue and red cloth. Applied work of patches of coloured woollen material, outlined with cords. Chain, satin and couching stitches. Dull yellowish and grey tones.
Lit.: Victoria and Albert Museum, Brief Guide to Persian Embroideries, London 1950, p. 11, Pl. 16

438 FIRE SCREEN
England, 18th century
London, Victoria and Albert Museum (T. 2–1929)
55 × 35 cm
Cream coloured silk ground. Silk embroidery in soft colours: pink, blue, green, yellow, cream. Long and short stitch and French knots.
Lit.: The Embroideress, No. 29, 1929, p. 675

439 CHRISTENING SHAWL, detail
Germany, Franconia, about 1732
Leitheim Castle, near Donauwörth
135 × 160 cm. Detail: 60 × 85 cm
Silk taffeta; flower scrolls and bouquets in fresh natural colours, embroidered with silk in long and short and stem stitch. This christening cloth is thought to have been designed by the Markgräfin Wilhelmine von Bayreuth, sister of Frederick the Great.

440/441 WALL HANGING: CHINOISERIE, whole and detail
Austria, 1720–1730
Vienna, Österreichisches Museum für angewandte Kunst (8425)
371 × 363 cm. Figure in detail: 62 cm high
The ornaments, cut from printed chintz, are applied to a background of whitish cotton and outlined with white and coloured strips. The faces are embroidered with silk and cotton in black,

white and salmon pink. Colours of the hanging: yellow, green, peacock blue, and red (the dominant colour). The hanging belongs to a set of six large and thirteen smaller pieces, from Schlosshof.

442 WALL PANELS
France, about 1720–1730
Schloss Favorite, near Rastatt, Baden
275 × 108 cm, including frames; the pictoral subjects above, 66 × 74 cm, below, 86 × 68 cm
Bedroom of the Markgraf Ludwig Georg von Baden. In each panel are two pictures worked in petit point with subjects from classical myths and allegories, framed with scroll work in relief, covered with silk material. Canvas: tent stitch in wool, chiefly in bright red and blue; the heads of the figures in satin and stem stitch, sometimes with details in slight relief.
Lit.: E. Petrasch, Schloss Favorite, Baden-Baden 1960, p. 20

443 WALL PANELS
Germany, about 1720–1730
Schloss Favorite near Rastatt, Baden
250 × 55 cm
In the small dining room, wall panels with "bizarre" leaves and flowers, worked in petit point in wool, in red, yellow and green on a black background. Animals and fantastic figures, embroidered in petit point (these stitches half the size of the rest) in silk, in lighter colours. Two similar panels in the Museum of Art, Baltimore (from the collection of Irwin Untermyer, New York).
Lit.: E. Petrasch, Schloss Favorite, Baden-Baden 1960, p. 19 – Y. Hackenbroch, English and other Needlework in the Irwin Untermyer Collection. London 1960, Pl. 152–153

Colour Plate XXVIII. STATE BED WITH HANGINGS
France, early 18th century
New York, Metropolitan Museum of Art (Irwin Untermyer Collection)
Height: 181 cm. Width: 80 cm
Mythological subjects and scenes from Aesop's Fables. Hangings of canvas with embroidery of wool and silk in tent, cross and stem stitch. The faces are worked in slight relief.
Lit.: Y. Hackenbroch, English and other Needlework in the Irwin Untermyer Collection, London 1960, p. 59, Pl. 146–148

444 PANEL WITH MARKET SCENES
Southern Netherlands, early 18th century
Benedictine Abbey of Göttweig, Austria
310 × 51 cm. Detail: 132 × 51 cm
In a landscape setting, market stalls selling porcelain, gloves, purses and children's toys. Canvas; tent stitch; wool in red and green, silk in light blue and yellow-green. The faces in tent stitch (one quarter the size of the tent stitch used elsewhere in the hanging); eyes worked with silk in satin stitch. A gift from Prince Eugene of Savoy (d. 1736).

445 WALL HANGING
Paris, 1683–1684
New York, Metropolitan Museum of Art (Rogers Fund, 1946, Inv. No. 46.43.2)
425 × 275 cm
The hanging shows a son of Louis XIV and Madame de Montespan, the young Louis César Bourbon, Comte de Vexin (1672–1683). He was Abbot of the Abbey of St Denis, which appears in the background, but he wears the costume of a general, and is surrounded by numerous symbols of the element "Fire". Canvas ground. Wool and silk, embroidered in tent stitch (49 stitches to the square centimetre),

on a background of silver, gilt thread, couched in a pattern of zigzag twill and sometimes in spirals. The principal colours are red and blue, with some green, yellow and brown. The hangings belonged to a series of the Four Elements, which were embroidered for Madame de Montespan in an institute for poor girls, "Saint Joseph de la Providence", of which she was patron.
Lit.: E. A. Standen, Le Roi Soleil and some of his Children. The Metropolitan Museum of Art, Bulletin, Vol. IX, 1951, p. 133

446 COURT DRESS OF AUGUSTUS THE STRONG OF SAXONY, 1719
Dresden, Historisches Museum (Inv. 28)
Gold brocade with gold embroidery.

447 COAT OF KING CHRISTIAN VI, OF DENMARK: detail
Denmark, Copenhagen, 1743
Copenhagen, Rosenborg Castle
Width of border: 12 cm
On dark violet silk material, woven with a pattern in silver, gold embroidery along the front edge and on the coat pockets. Embroidered with various kinds of gold thread, gold strip and wire. The coat was worn by King Christian VI on the 11th December, 1743. The pattern of the embroidery closely resembles a design by Saint-Aubin in his book "L'art du Brodeur", Paris, 1770, Pl. 9.
Lit.: S. F. Christensen, Kongedragterne paa Rosenborg, Copenhagen 1940, I, p. 162

448 CHASUBLE WITH GOLD EMBROIDERY
France, about 1700
Paris, Musée des Arts Décoratifs (A. 6018)
110 × 80 cm
Red satin. Couched work in gold thread with a great variety of patterns. Outlines in gold cord.

449 CHASUBLE OF DAMIAN HUGO VON SCHÖNBORN (d. 1743)
South Germany (?), second quarter of the 18th century
Bruchsal, Pfarrkirche, St Peter
110 × 76 cm
Silver brocade. Rich gold embroidery employing every technique: couched work, etc. Gold threads. Cords. Arms: below left, Weissenburg-Speyer; centre, Teutonic Knights; right, Schönborn.
Lit.: O. Roegele, Bruchsal wie es war, Karlsruhe 1955, Pl. 152, 153, p. 210 – Die Kunstdenkmäler des Großherzogtums Baden, Bd. IX, Tübingen 1913, p. 41, Fig. 17

450 PALIOTTO, detail
Bologna, middle of the 18th century
Bologna, S. Bartolomeo
90 × 294 cm. Detail: 90 × 129 cm
In the centre, a painting of the Martyrdom of St Bartholomew, within a richly embroidered frame, and surmounted by a canopy. On each side, large shells and ornaments embroidered in gold and silver, and floral scrolls in strong natural colours, embroidered with silk in long and short stitch. Background, white silk. The gold embroidery is in couched work, with various kinds of gold threads.

451 COPE
Bologna, about 1700
Bologna, S. Pietro Metropolitana
Height at the back: 155 cm
Deep red gold-moiré, embroidered with various kinds of gold thread and gold strip in couched work. Very rich, dense pattern with bizarre motifs.

452, Colour Plate XXIX. SILK HANGING
North Italy, about 1740
Munich, Bayerisches Nationalmuseum (55/132)
Height: 8.10 m. Width: 6.80 m. Detail: 5.40 × 3.40 m
Light blue silk. Gold and silver embroidery. Gold thread couched in twill pattern, silver gilt strip, sequins. Silk embroidery in long and short stitch, shading from white to blue, yellow to green, white to pink and violet. Probably originally, the rear wall of a canopy used for ecclesiastical purposes.

453 WALL HANGING
France, about 1800
Vienna, Österreichisches Museum für angewandte Kunst (T. 9410)
Height: 393 cm
Cream coloured silk twill. Chenille embroidery. Soft colouring. Shaded green, olive, dull blue, pink. From a set of five wall hangings.

454 SAMPLE OF EMBROIDERY FOR A GENTLEMAN'S COAT
France, Lyon, about 1780
Hamburg, Museum für Kunst und Gewerbe (Inv. 1882, 52)
30 × 19.5 cm
Silk material striped with black and blue. Silk embroidery, chiefly in white, light blue and green. Satin and stem stitch. Applied work in tulle. From a book of samples from a firm in Lyon.

455 SAMPLE OF EMBROIDERY FOR A GENTLEMAN'S COAT
France, Lyon, about 1780
Hamburg, Museum für Kunst und Gewerbe (Inv. 1882, 59)
37 × 28 cm
Silk velvet – "Velour en Mignatures" – black with turquoise, coloured spots. Silk embroidery in satin and stem stitch, chiefly in white, copper and pink, with sequins and metal plaques. From the same pattern-book as Fig. 454.

456 SAMPLE OF EMBROIDERY FOR A LADY'S DRESS
France, Lyon, late 18th century
Hamburg, Museum für Kunst und Gewerbe (Inv. 1882, 53)
24 × 34 cm
Very fine white muslin with applied work in muslin and silk embroidery in "Pompeian colours": terracotta, yellow and white. Satin and stem stitches.

457 FICHU WITH WHITEWORK, "POINT DE SAXE"
Germany, 1750–1780
Munich, Bayerisches Nationalmuseum (T. 4453)
53 × 124 cm
Triangular fichu of cotton muslin. Embroidered in linen thread. Sixteen different background patterns in various stitches.

458 CHRISTENING ROBE, detail
Scotland, Ayrshire, second third of the 19th century
St Gall, Kunst- und Industrie-Museum (J 3117)
Length from neck opening to hem: 104 cm. Width of the embroidered band in front, at the hem: 52 cm.
The detail shows the lower part of the band. Fine linen. Cotton thread. Drawn thread work, with satin stitch and lace stitches.

Lit.: M. H. Swain, The Flowerers, The Origin and History of Ayrshire Needlework, London und Edinburgh, 1955

459 EMBROIDERED FLOWER PICTURE
Vienna, dated 1824
Vienna, Museum für angewandte Kunst (T. 8457)
48 × 39 cm
Very fine white canvas ground. Coloured silk in a variety of shades (faded). Minute tent stitch. The inscription has fallen out.

460 PANEL "WHIPLASH", designed by Hermann Obrist (1863–1927)
Munich or Florence, 1892–1895
Munich, Stadtmuseum
119.5 × 183.5 cm
Light grey woollen material. The orchid, stylised in the form of a whiplash, is executed in yellowish-brown silk in satin and stem stitch. Signed in the bottom right corner HO.
Lit.: F. Ahlers-Hestermann, Stilwende, Berlin 1941, p. 31 – J. Cassou, E. Langui and N. Pevsner, The Sources of Modern Art, Europe 1880-1914, London 1962, p. 238, fig. 242

461 BED COVER, designed by Hermann Obrist (1863–1927)
Munich, about 1895
Munich, Stadtmuseum
228 × 204 cm. Detail: 55 × 75 cm
Foliage ornament along the two longer sides. Yellowish raw silk. Satin and stem stitch in rust red silk. Signed in one corner HO.
Lit.: Ausstellung: München 1869–1958, Aufbruch zur modernen Kunst, Munich 1958. Kat. Nr. 658

462 WALL HANGING, after a design by William Morris
England, 1875–1880
London, Victoria and Albert Museum (T. 192–1953)
214 × 188 cm
Silk embroidery in Gobelin and satin stitch on canvas.
Lit.: Victoria and Albert Museum, William Morris, London 1958, Pl. 4

463 WALL HANGING: CONCERT, designed by Aristide Maillol
France, 1896–1898
Copenhagen, Kunstindustrimuseum (B 43/1935)
155 × 203.5 cm
Linen ground. Coloured wool, a little silk, gold and silver thread. Satin stitch, couched work, chain stitch. Pink, brown, green and beige.
Lit.: E. Lassen, To syede Tæpper af Maillol. Kunstmuseets Aarsskrift 1944/1945. Copenhagen 1945, p. 65

464 CUSHION COVER, designed by Thorvald Bindesböll (1846–1908)
Copenhagen, about 1900–1908
Copenhagen, Kunstindustrimuseum (B 11–1942)
43 × 59 cm
Beige woollen material. Applied work of greenish-brown silk velvet; embroidery in light brown and yellowish silk in stem and satin stitch. Embroidered in 1908 by Bolette Hartmann, née Puggaard.
Lit.: K. Madsen, Thorvald Bindesböll. Copenhagen 1943, p. 84 – J. Cassou, E. Langui and N. Pevsner, The sources of Modern Art, Europe 1880-1914, London 1962, p. 237

Marie Schuette was responsible for the descriptions of the following pieces: 2, 7–10, 46–51, 65–71, 78–84, 86–94, 97–105, 110–122, 126–127, 142–153, 158–159, 165–168, 172, 174–181, 185–188, 193–202, 205–211, 230, 232–235, 242, 250–273, 293, 296–298, 304–309, 317, 325–326, 331–333, 336, 341–343, 346–350, 352–353, 356–364, 369–372, 376–383, 385–395, 406–407, 415, 417, 419–424, 428–432, 437–438, 440–441, 446, 449, 453, 458–459, 462. Colour Plates VII–X, XIV–XVII, XX–XXII, XXVII.

Sigrid Müller-Christensen was responsible for the following: 1, 3–6, 11–45, 52–64, 72–77, 85, 95–96, 106–109, 123–125, 128–141, 154–157, 160–164, 169–171, 173, 182–184, 189–192, 203–204, 212–229, 231, 236–241, 243–249, 274–292, 294–295, 299–303, 310–316, 318–324, 327–330, 334–335, 337–340, 344–345, 351, 354–355, 365–368, 373–375, 384, 396–405, 408–414, 416, 418, 425–427, 433–436, 439, 442–445, 447–448, 450–452, 454–457, 460–461, 463–464. Colour Plates I–VI, XI–XIII, XVIII–XIX, XXIII–XXVI, XXVIII–XXIX.

Sources of Illustrations

Colour Plates

The following museums and institutions have permitted the use of
colour-blocks in their possession:

Sources of the following Colour Plates

The other Colour Plates were made for the publishers of the German
edition. Plates VIII and XVII are from M. Schuette, Gestickte Bildteppiche und Decken des Mittelalters, Leipzig, 1927–30

Index

References to text matter are in roman numerals. The arabic numerals refer to the pages of the catalogue. Numerals in italics refer to the plates.

INVENTORY 74

INVENTORY 1983